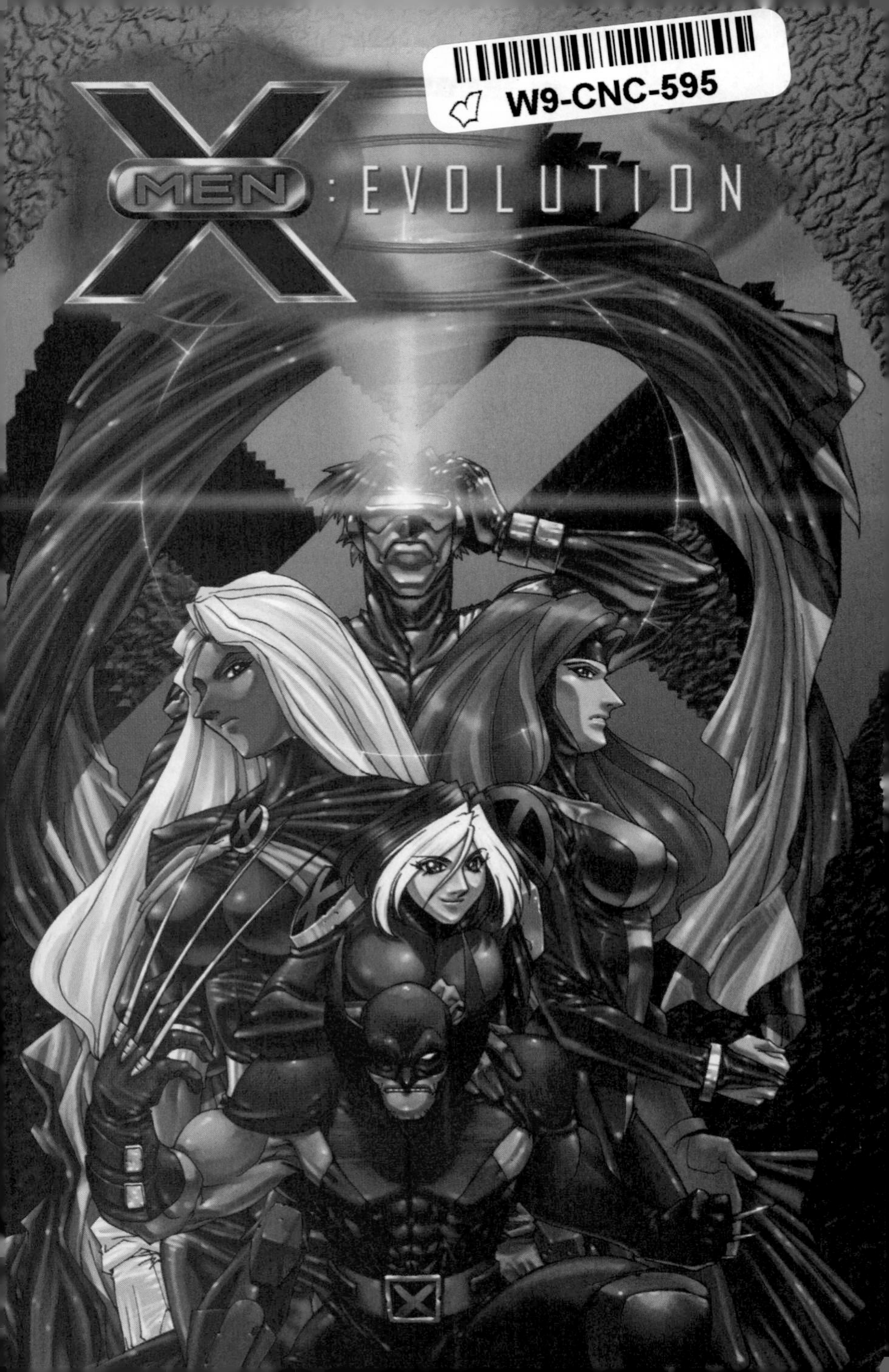
X
MEN
: EVOLUTION

X-MEN : EVOLUTION

CREDITS

WRITER
DEVIN GRAYSON

ARTWORK & COLORS
UDON WITH LONG VO, CHARLES PARK
& SAKA OF STUDIO XD

LETTERS
RANDY GENTILE

EDITOR
RALPH MACCHIO

ASSOCIATE EDITOR
BRIAN SMITH

EDITOR IN CHIEF
JOE QUESADA

PUBLISHER
DAN BUCKLEY

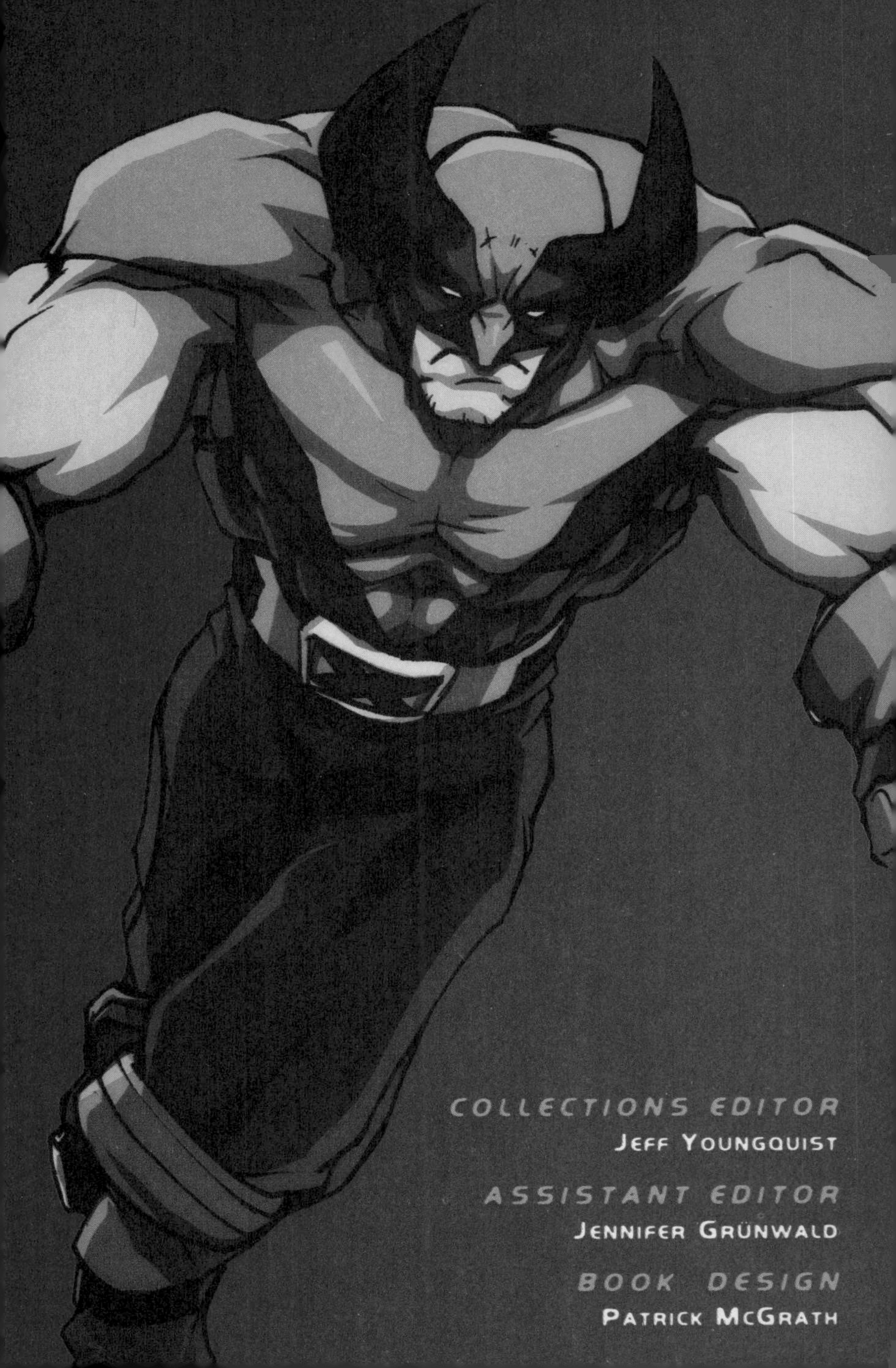

COLLECTIONS EDITOR
JEFF YOUNGQUIST

ASSISTANT EDITOR
JENNIFER GRÜNWALD

BOOK DESIGN
PATRICK McGRATH

X-MEN: EVOLUTION

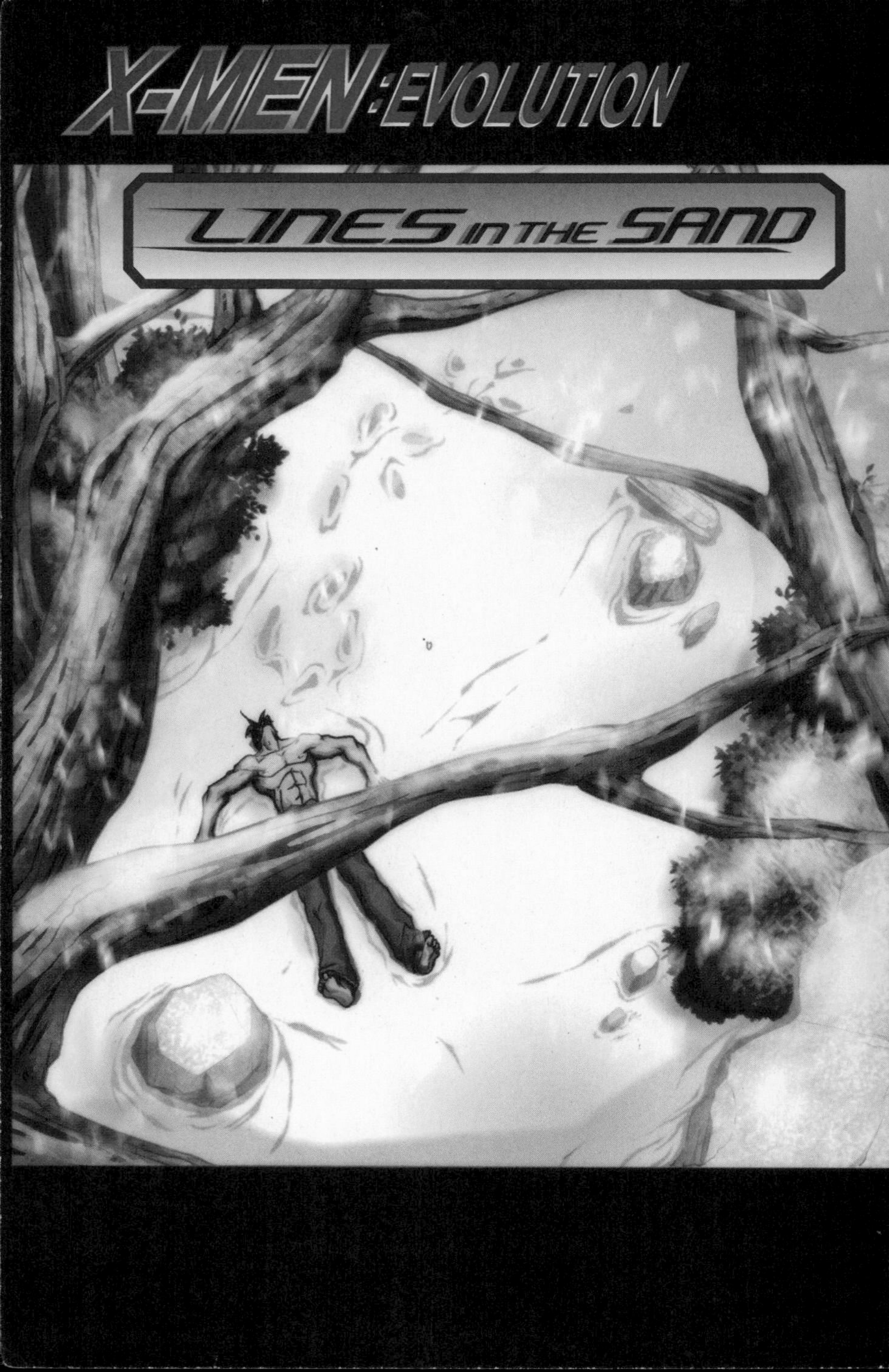
LINES IN THE SAND

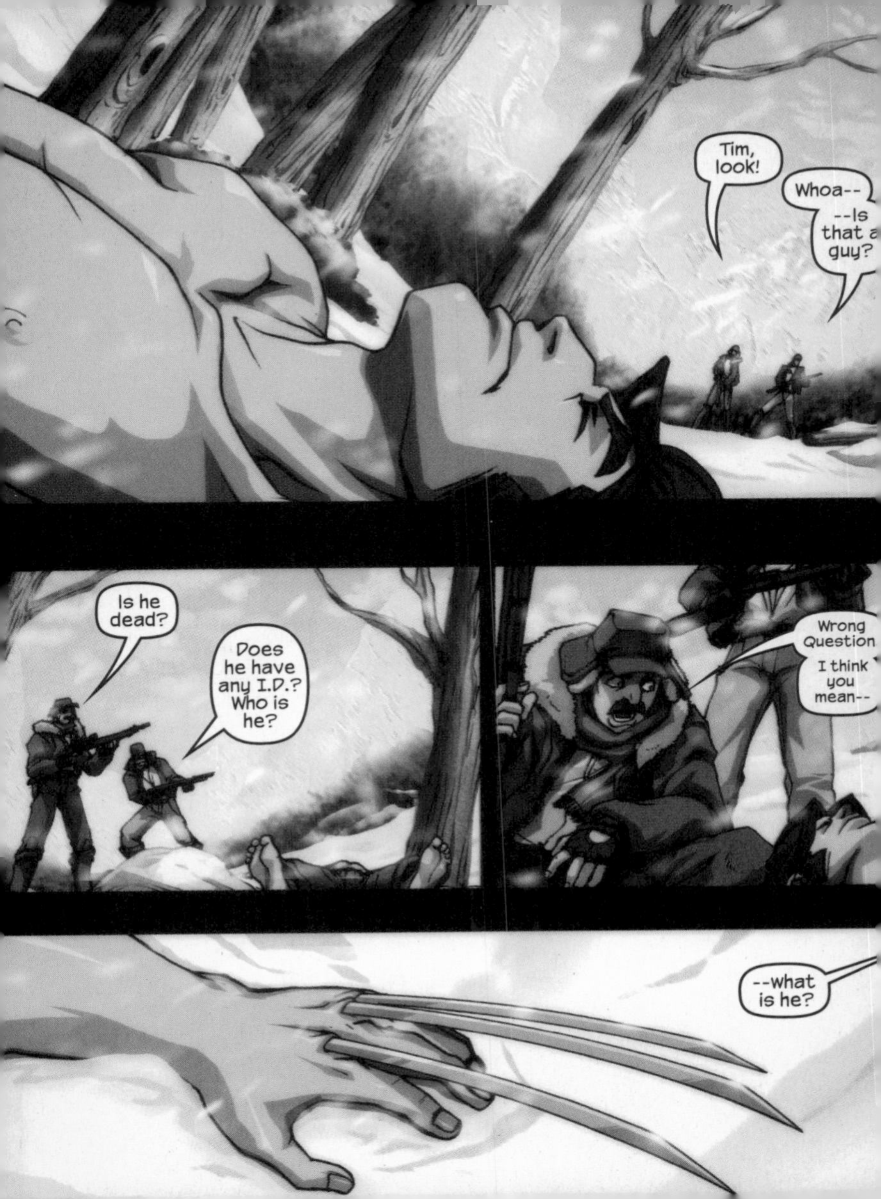
Tim, look!
Whoa--
--Is that a guy?
Is he dead?
Does he have any I.D.? Who is he?
Wrong Question
I think you mean--
--what is he?

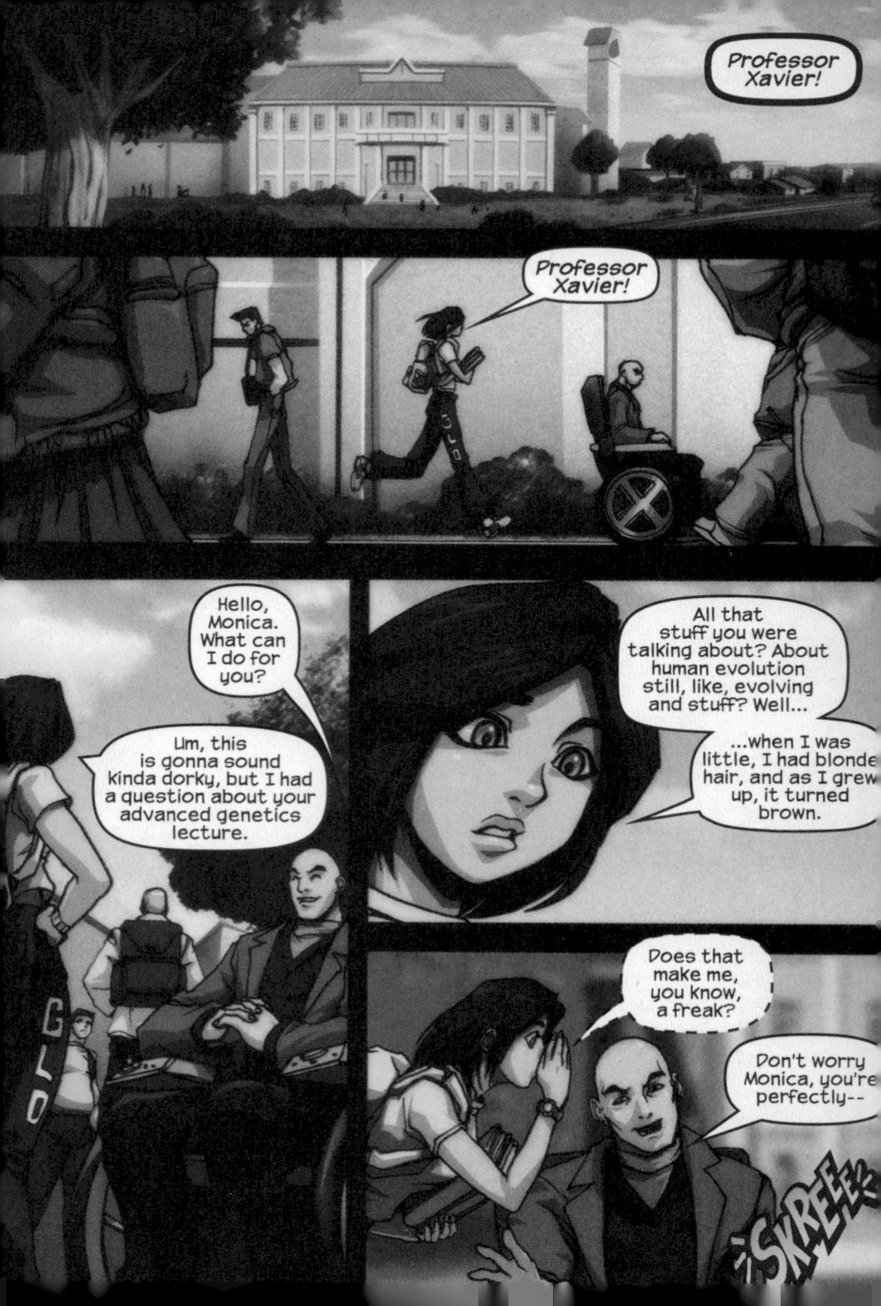
Professor Xavier!
Professor Xavier!
Hello, Monica. What can I do for you?
Um, this is gonna sound kinda dorky, but I had a question about your advanced genetics lecture.
All that stuff you were talking about? About human evolution still, like, evolving and stuff? Well...
...when I was little, I had blonde hair, and as I grew up, it turned brown.
Does that make me, you know, a freak?
Don't worry Monica, you're perfectly--
SKREEE

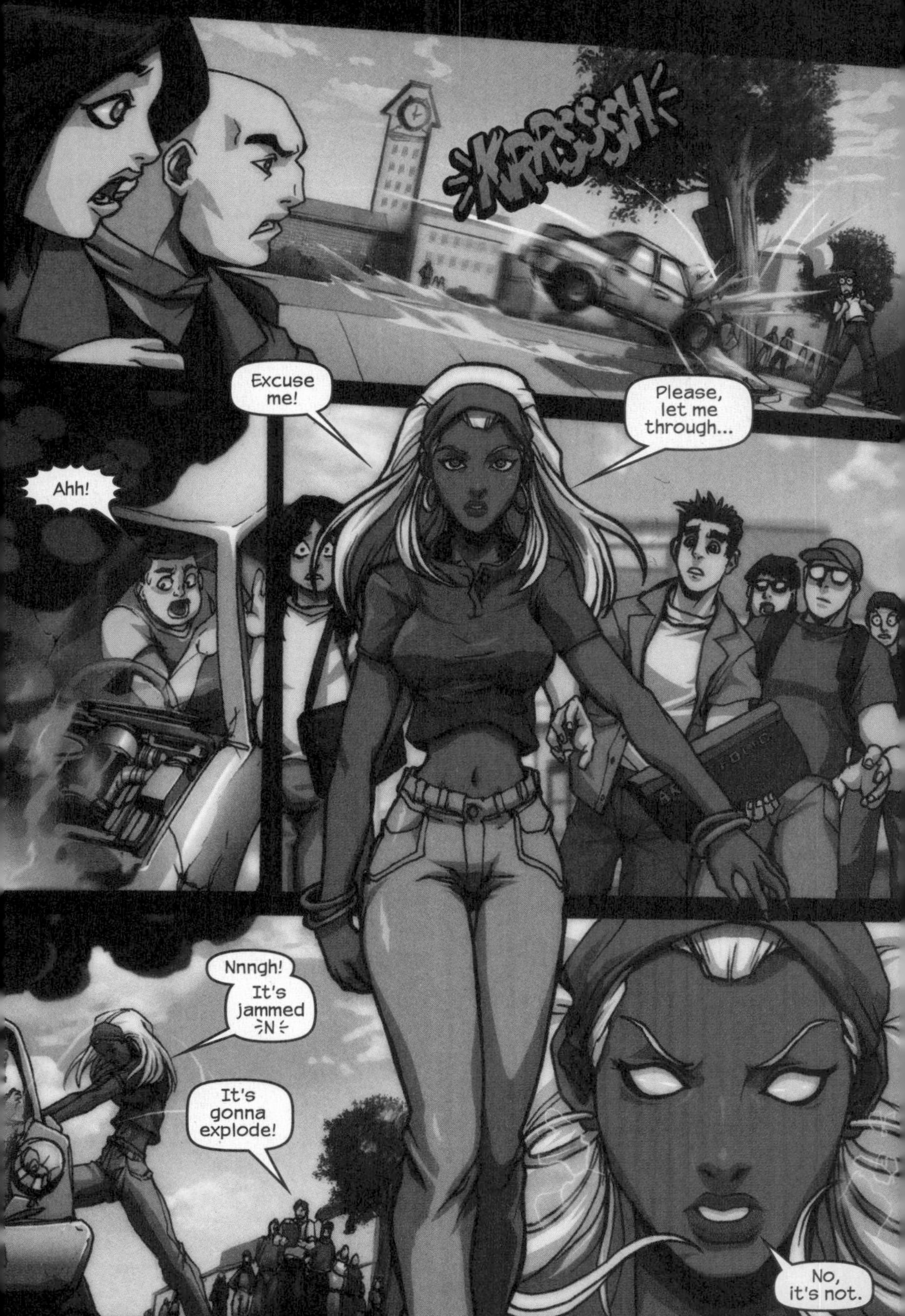
KRRSSSH!
Excuse me!
Please, let me through...
Ahh!
Nnngh! It's jammed
N
It's gonna explode!
No, it's not.

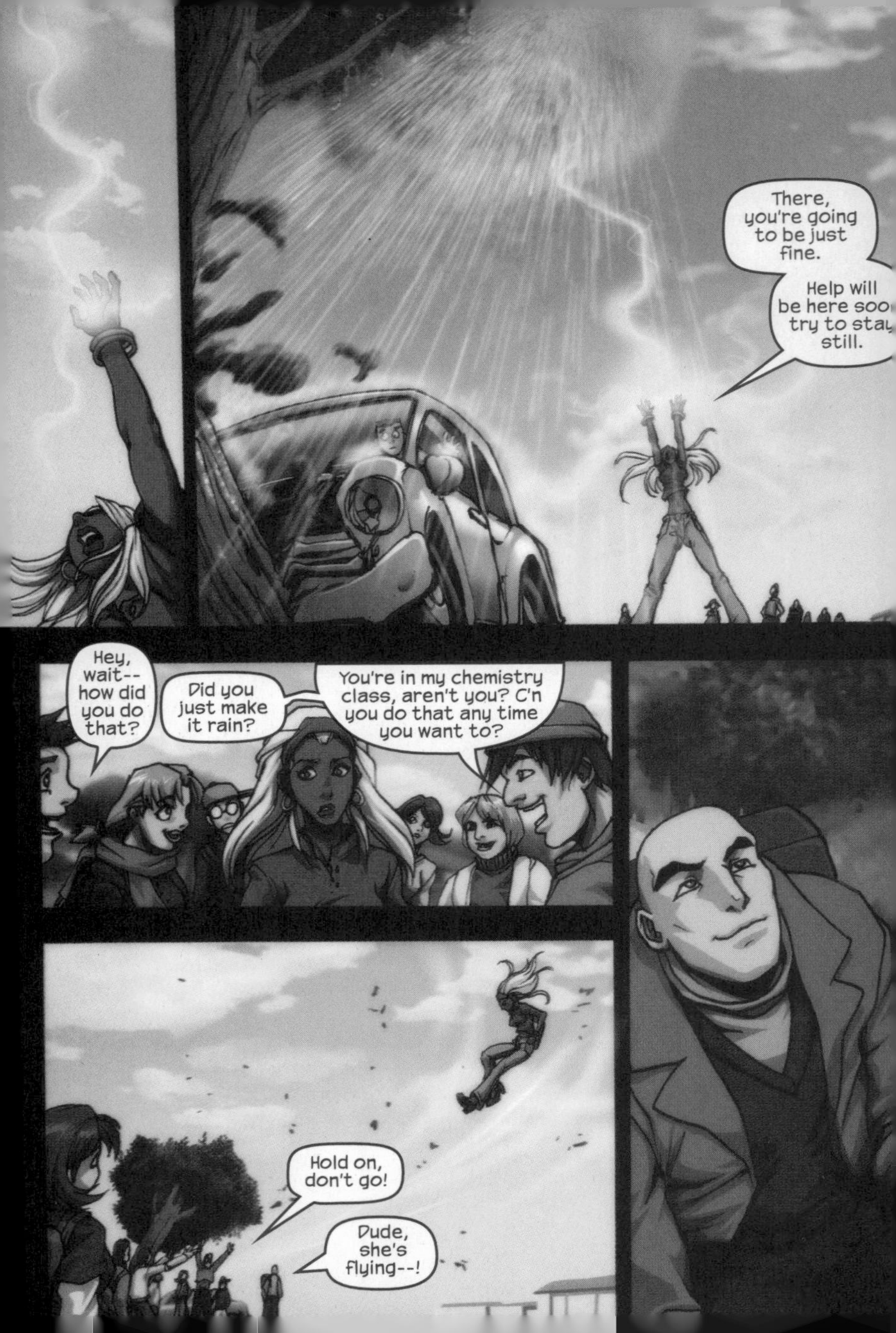
There, you're going to be just fine.
Help will be here soo try to stay still.
Hey, wait-- how did you do that?
Did you just make it rain?
You're in my chemistry class, aren't you? C'n you do that any time you want to?
Hold on, don't go!
Dude, she's flying--!

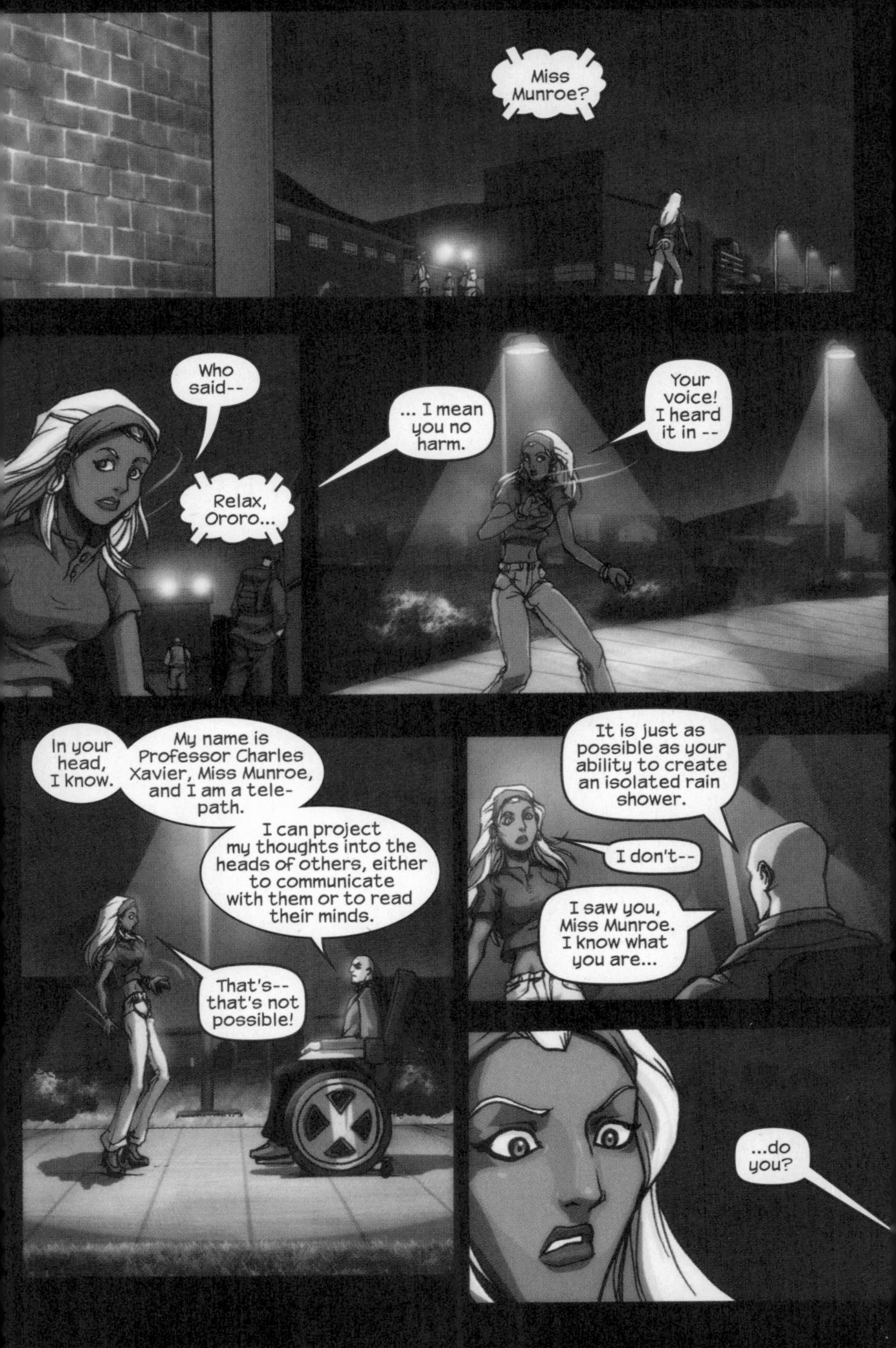
Miss Munroe?
Who said--
Relax, Ororo...
... I mean you no harm.
Your voice! I heard it in --
In your head, I know.
My name is Professor Charles Xavier, Miss Munroe, and I am a tele-path.
I can project my thoughts into the heads of others, either to communicate with them or to read their minds.
That's--that's not possible!
It is just as possible as your ability to create an isolated rain shower.
I don't--
I saw you, Miss Munroe. I know what you are...
...do you?

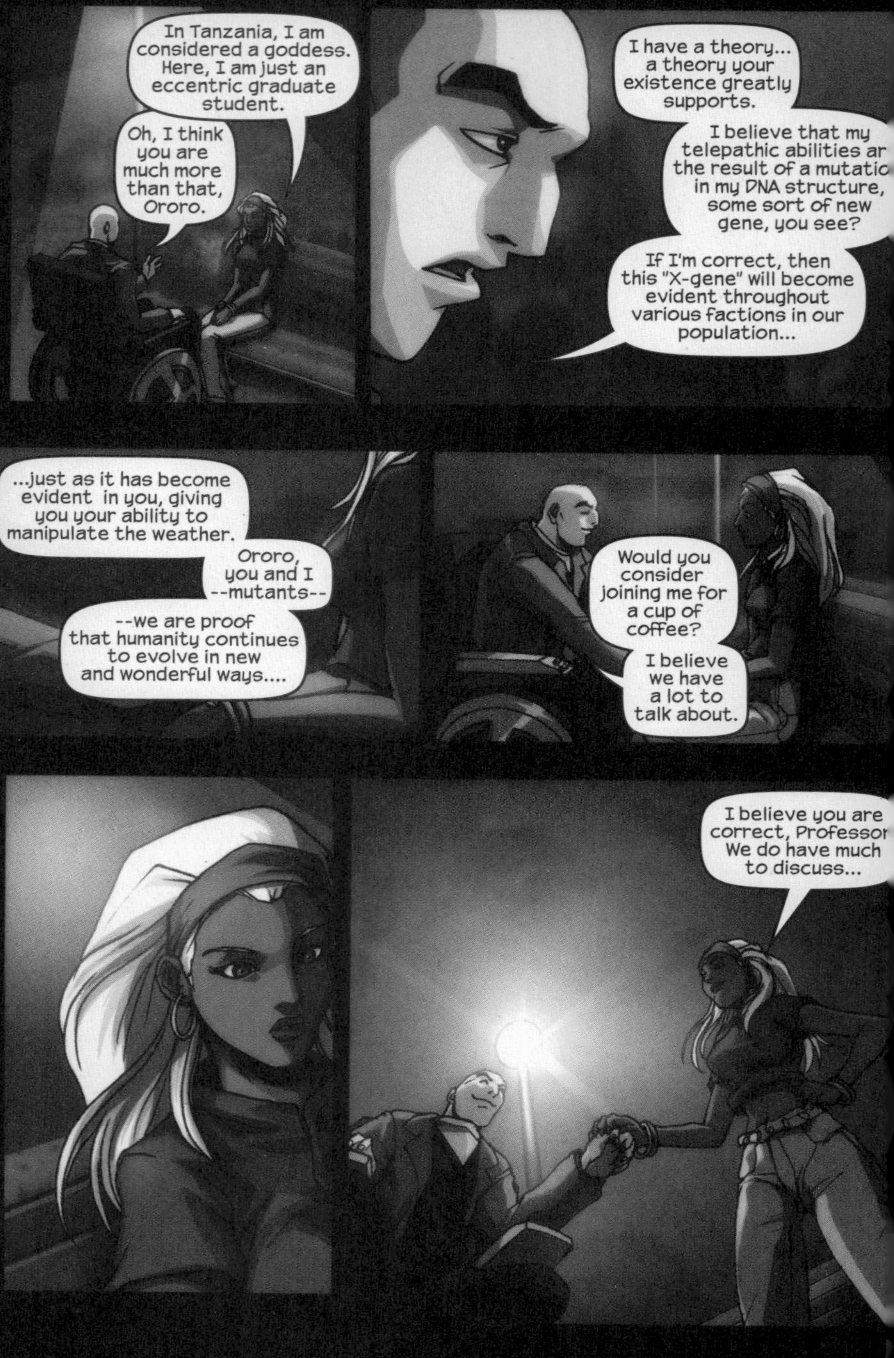
In Tanzania, I am considered a goddess. Here, I am just an eccentric graduate student.
Oh, I think you are much more than that, Ororo.
I have a theory... a theory your existence greatly supports.
I believe that my telepathic abilities ar the result of a mutatio in my DNA structure, some sort of new gene, you see?
If I'm correct, then this "X-gene" will become evident throughout various factions in our population...
...just as it has become evident in you, giving you your ability to manipulate the weather.
Ororo, you and I --mutants--
--we are proof that humanity continues to evolve in new and wonderful ways....
Would you consider joining me for a cup of coffee?
I believe we have a lot to talk about.
I believe you are correct, Professor We do have much to discuss...

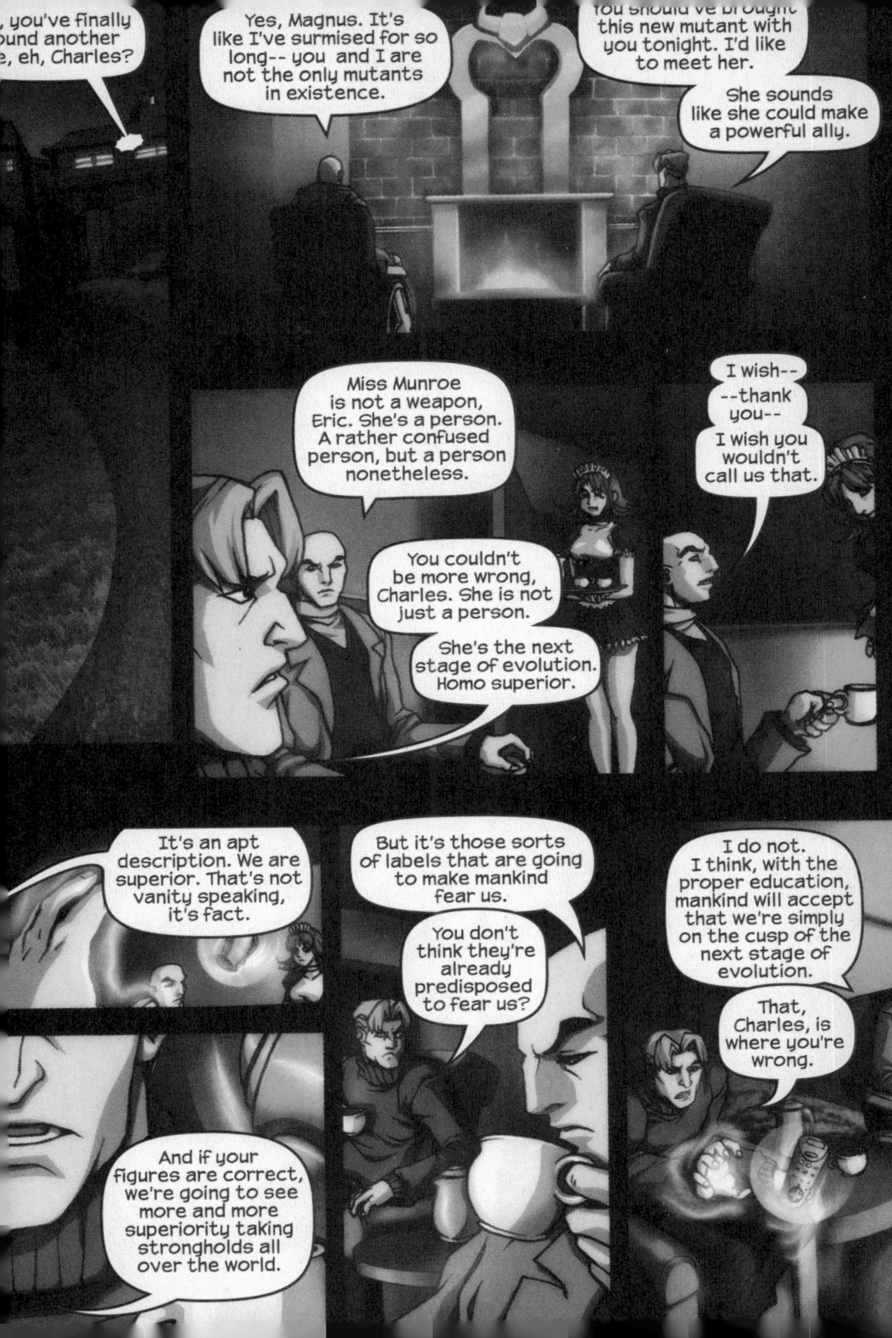

, you've finally
ound another
e, eh, Charles?
Yes, Magnus. It's like I've surmised for so long-- you and I are not the only mutants in existence.
You should've brought this new mutant with you tonight. I'd like to meet her.
She sounds like she could make a powerful ally.
Miss Munroe is not a weapon, Eric. She's a person. A rather confused person, but a person nonetheless.
You couldn't be more wrong, Charles. She is not just a person.
She's the next stage of evolution. Homo superior.
I wish--
--thank you--
I wish you wouldn't call us that.
It's an apt description. We are superior. That's not vanity speaking, it's fact.
And if your figures are correct, we're going to see more and more superiority taking strongholds all over the world.
But it's those sorts of labels that are going to make mankind fear us.
You don't think they're already predisposed to fear us?
I do not. I think, with the proper education, mankind will accept that we're simply on the cusp of the next stage of evolution.
That, Charles, is where you're wrong.

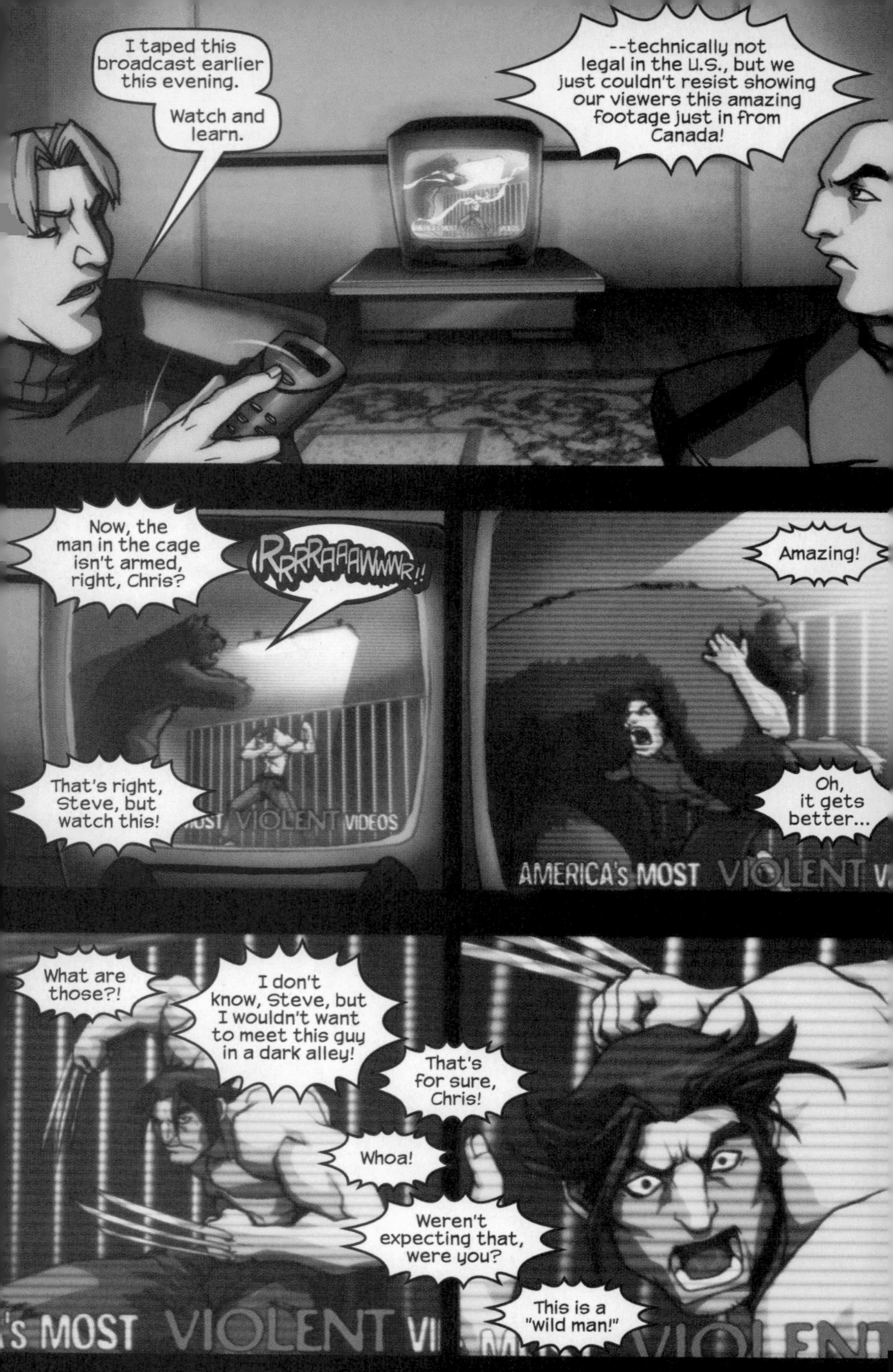
I taped this broadcast earlier this evening.
Watch and learn.
--technically not legal in the U.S., but we just couldn't resist showing our viewers this amazing footage just in from Canada!
Now, the man in the cage isn't armed, right, Chris?
RRRRAAAWWWR!!
That's right, Steve, but watch this!
MOST VIOLENT VIDEOS
Amazing!
Oh, it gets better...
AMERICA's MOST VIOLENT V
What are those?!
I don't know, Steve, but I wouldn't want to meet this guy in a dark alley!
That's for sure, Chris!
Whoa!
Weren't expecting that, were you?
'S MOST VIOLENT VI
This is a "wild man!"
VIOLENT

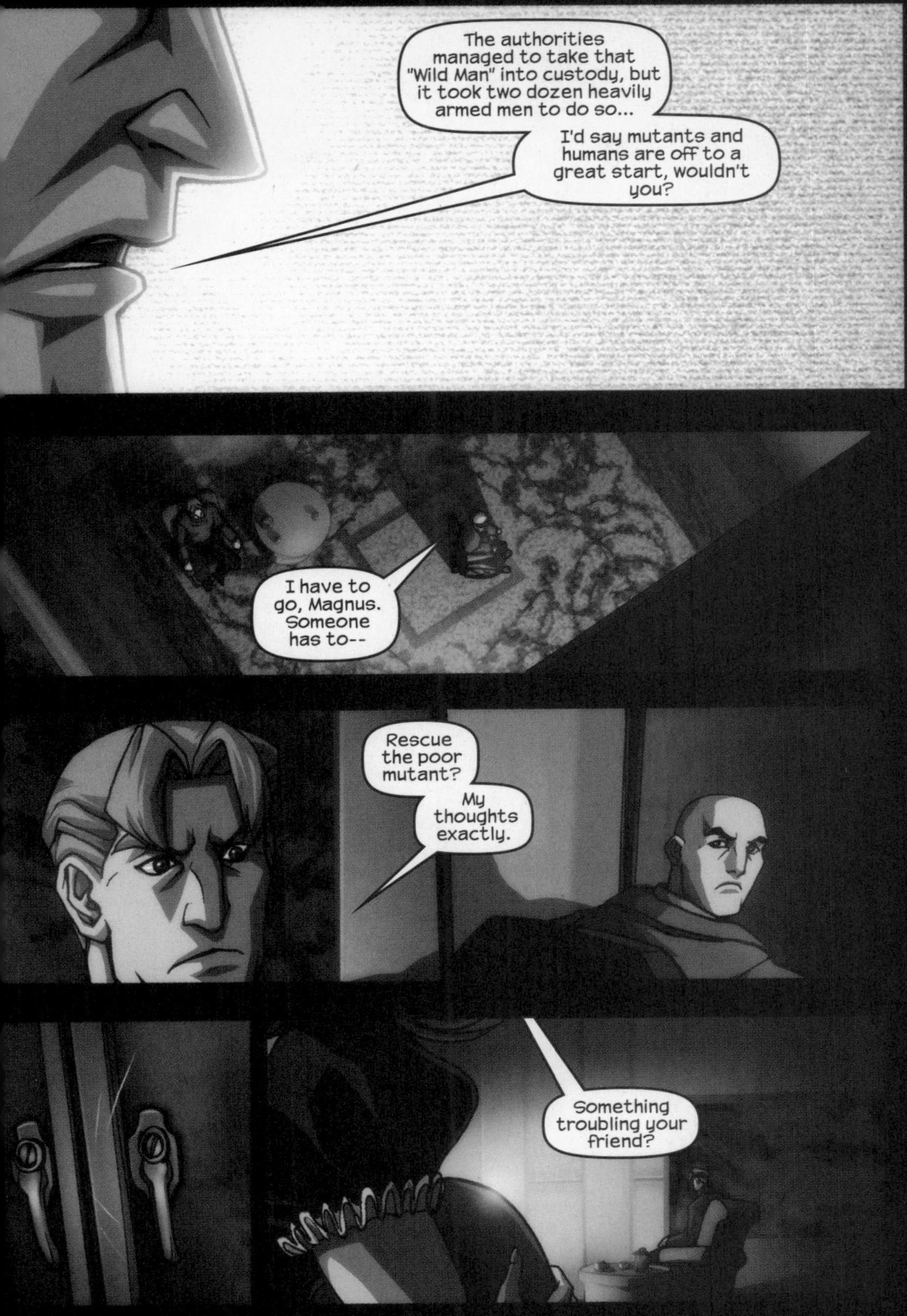
The authorities managed to take that "Wild Man" into custody, but it took two dozen heavily armed men to do so...
I'd say mutants and humans are off to a great start, wouldn't you?
I have to go, Magnus. Someone has to--
Rescue the poor mutant?
My thoughts exactly.
Something troubling your friend?

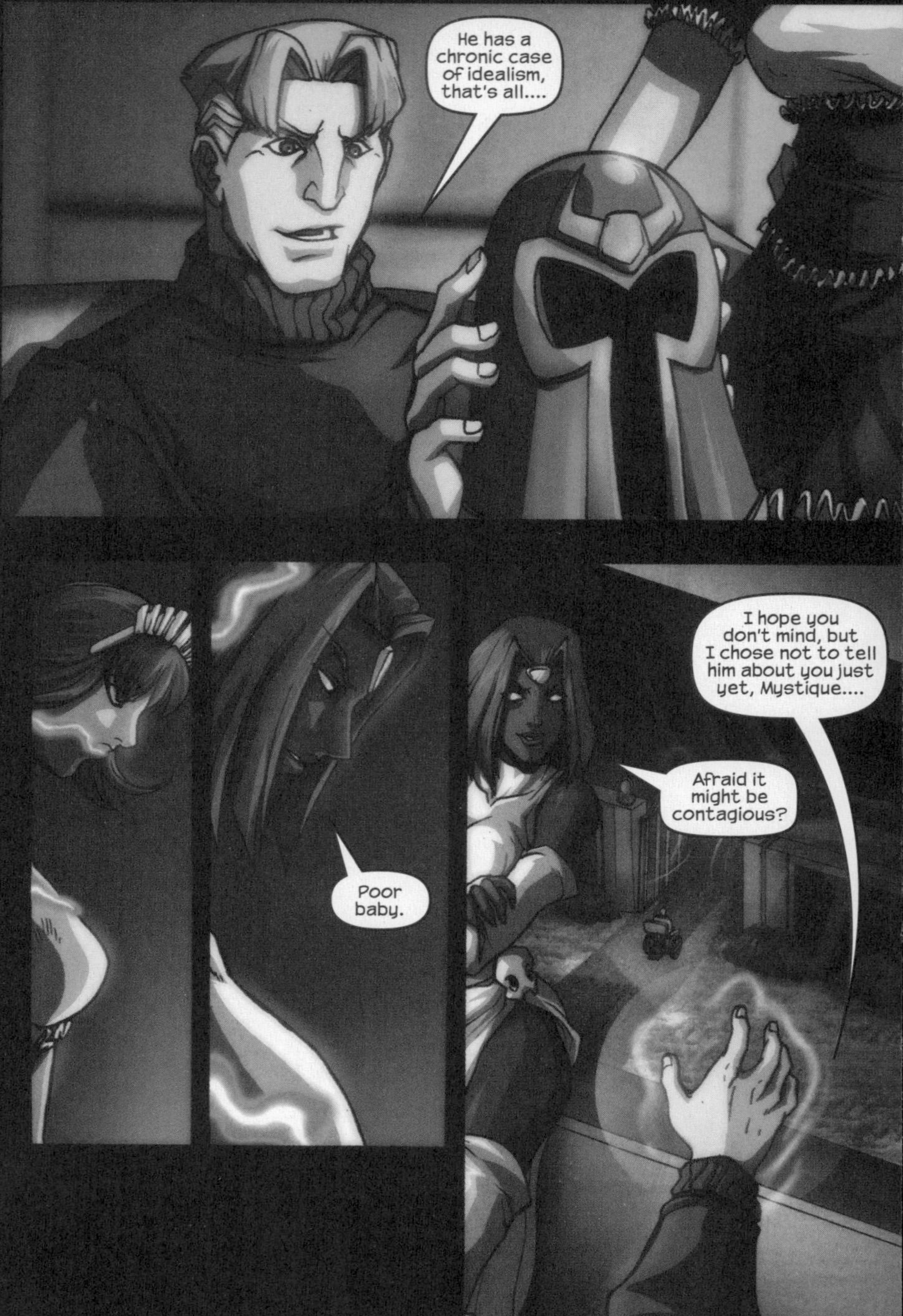
He has a chronic case of idealism, that's all....
Poor baby.
I hope you don't mind, but I chose not to tell him about you just yet, Mystique....
Afraid it might be contagious?

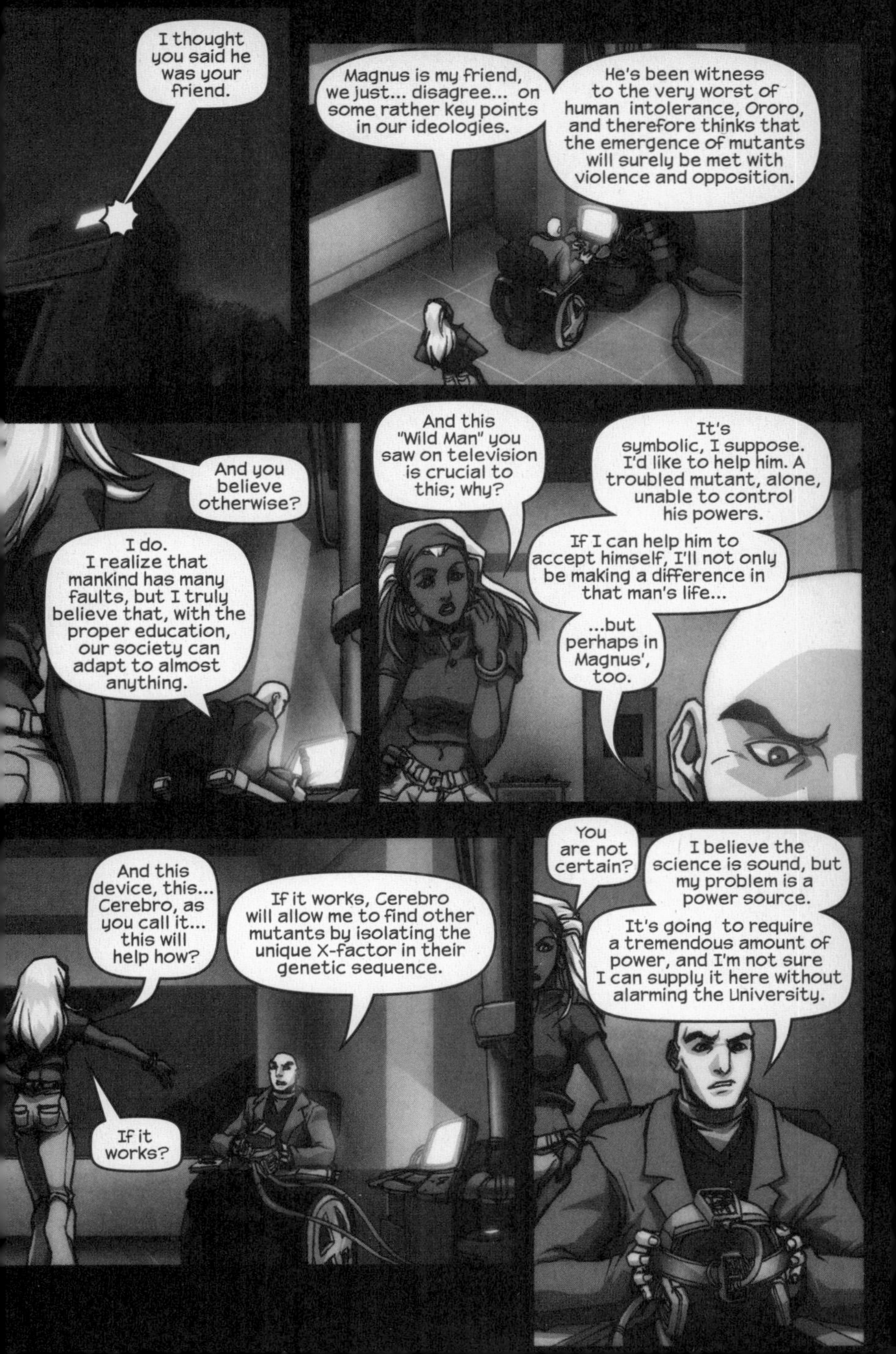

I thought you said he was your friend.
Magnus is my friend, we just... disagree... on some rather key points in our ideologies.
He's been witness to the very worst of human intolerance, Ororo, and therefore thinks that the emergence of mutants will surely be met with violence and opposition.
And you believe otherwise?
I do. I realize that mankind has many faults, but I truly believe that, with the proper education, our society can adapt to almost anything.
And this "Wild Man" you saw on television is crucial to this; why?
It's symbolic, I suppose. I'd like to help him. A troubled mutant, alone, unable to control his powers.
If I can help him to accept himself, I'll not only be making a difference in that man's life...
...but perhaps in Magnus', too.
And this device, this... Cerebro, as you call it... this will help how?
If it works, Cerebro will allow me to find other mutants by isolating the unique X-factor in their genetic sequence.
If it works?
You are not certain?
I believe the science is sound, but my problem is a power source.
It's going to require a tremendous amount of power, and I'm not sure I can supply it here without alarming the University.

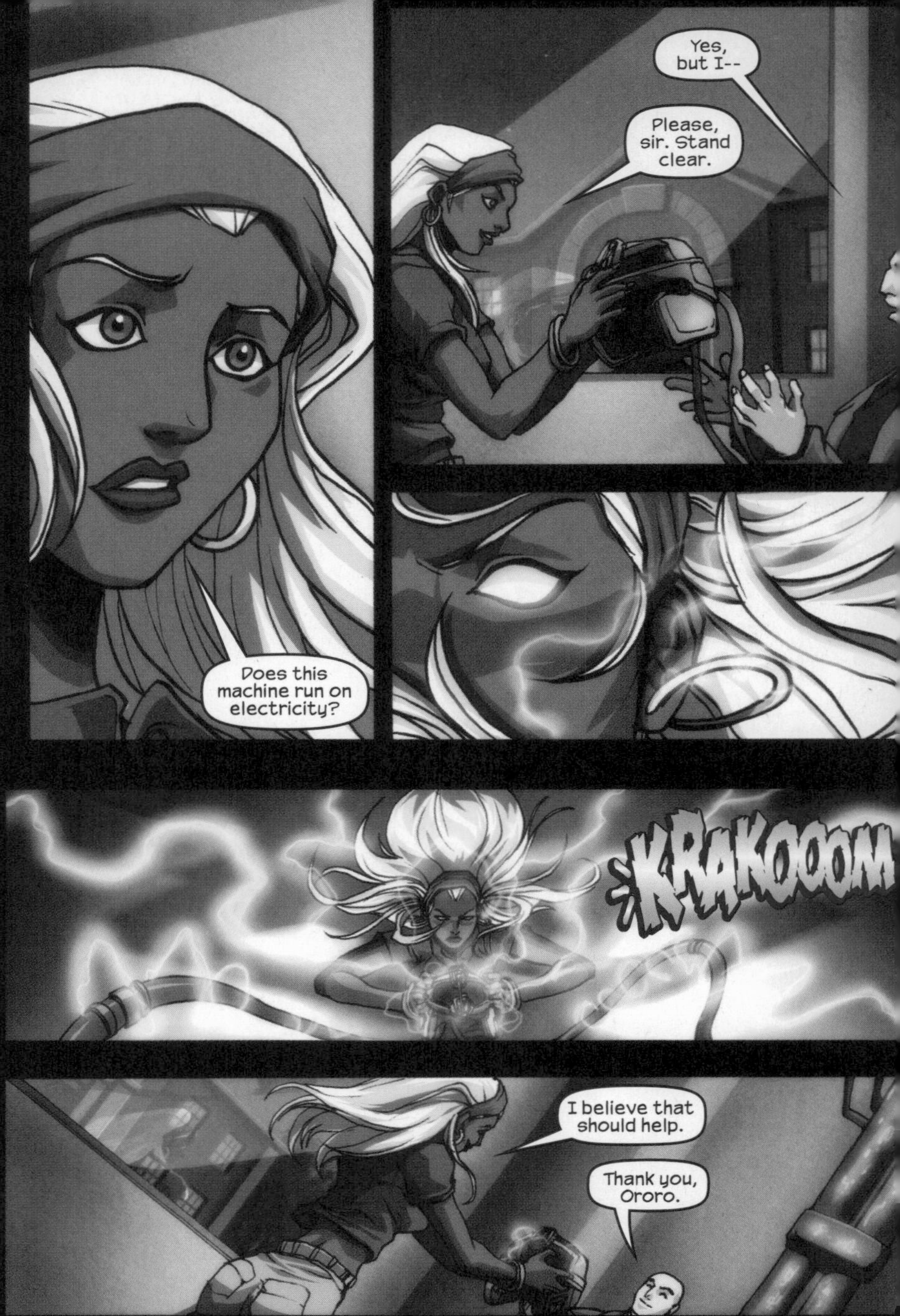
Does this machine run on electricity?
Yes, but I--
Please, sir. Stand clear.
KRAKOOOM
I believe that should help.
Thank you, Ororo.

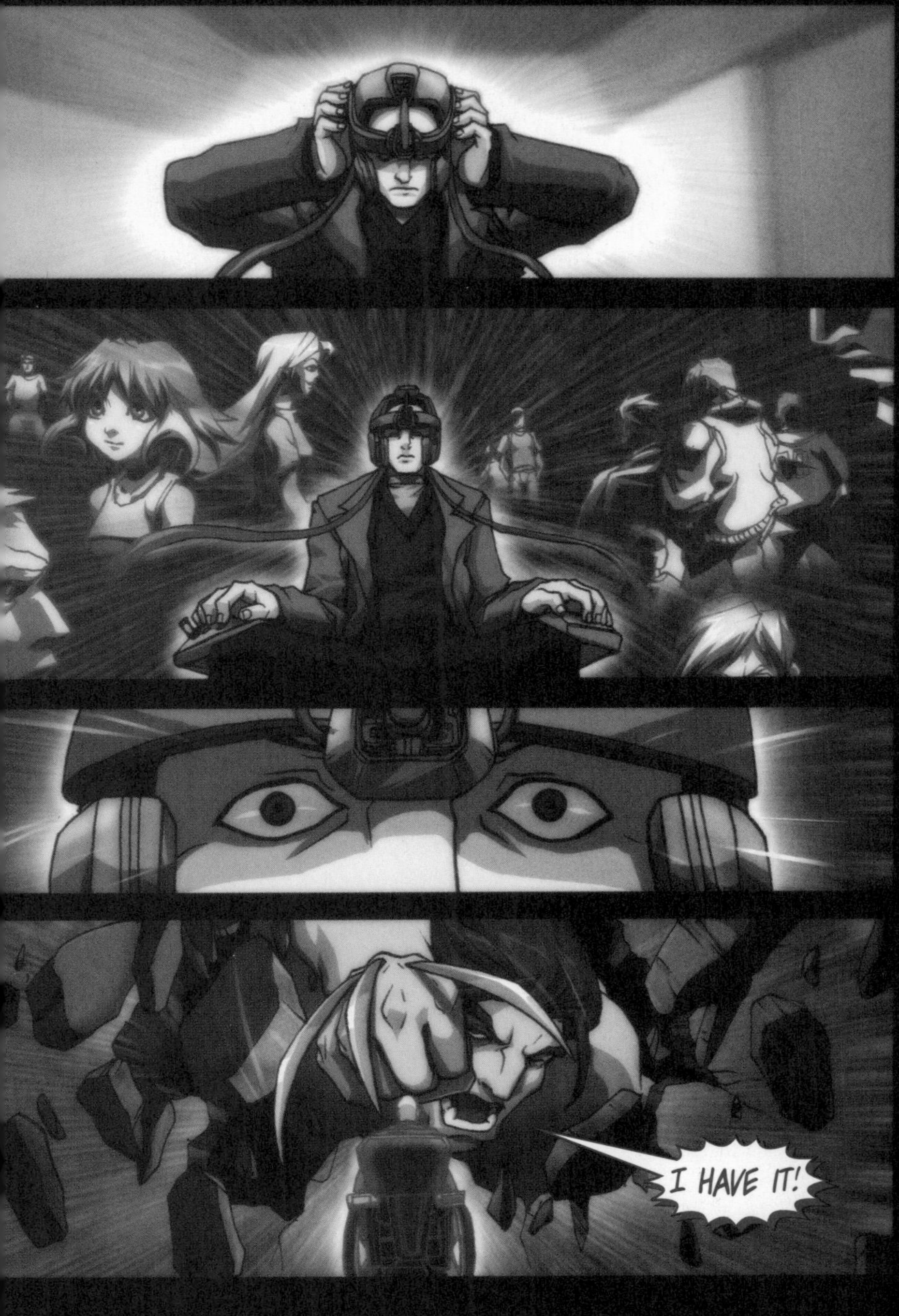
I HAVE IT!

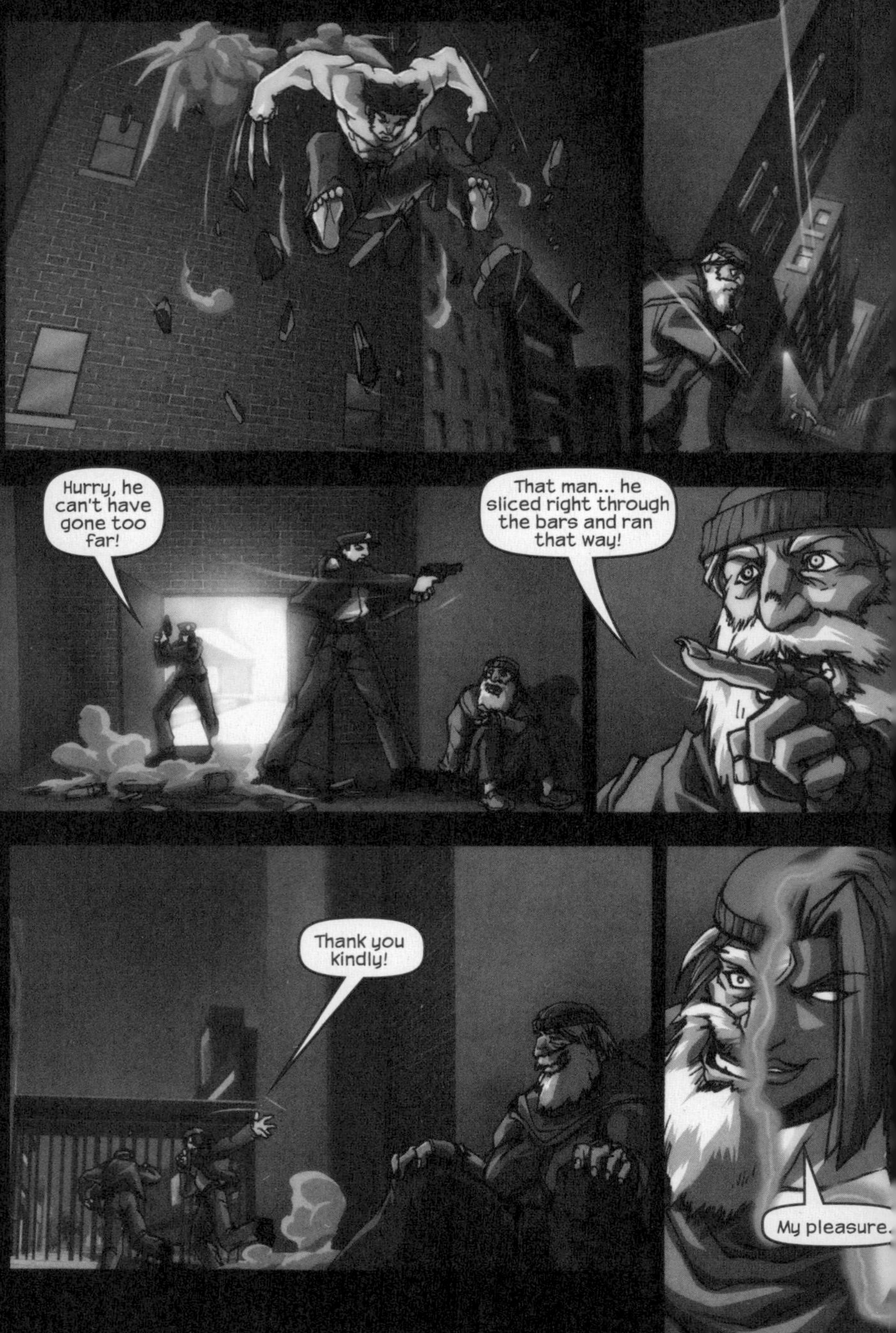

Hurry, he can't have gone too far!
That man... he sliced right through the bars and ran that way!
Thank you kindly!
My pleasure.

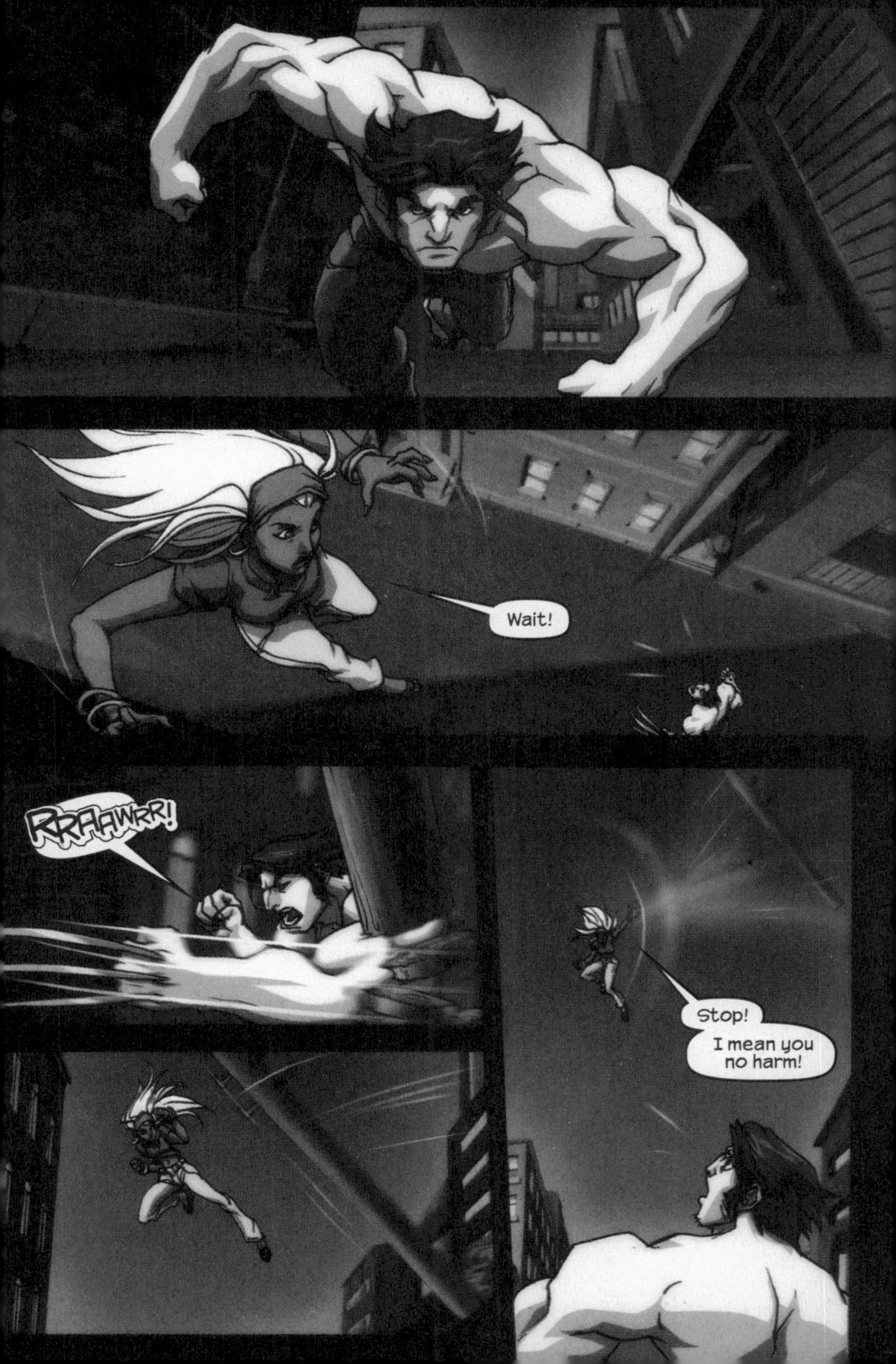
Wait!
RRAAWRR!
Stop!
I mean you no harm!

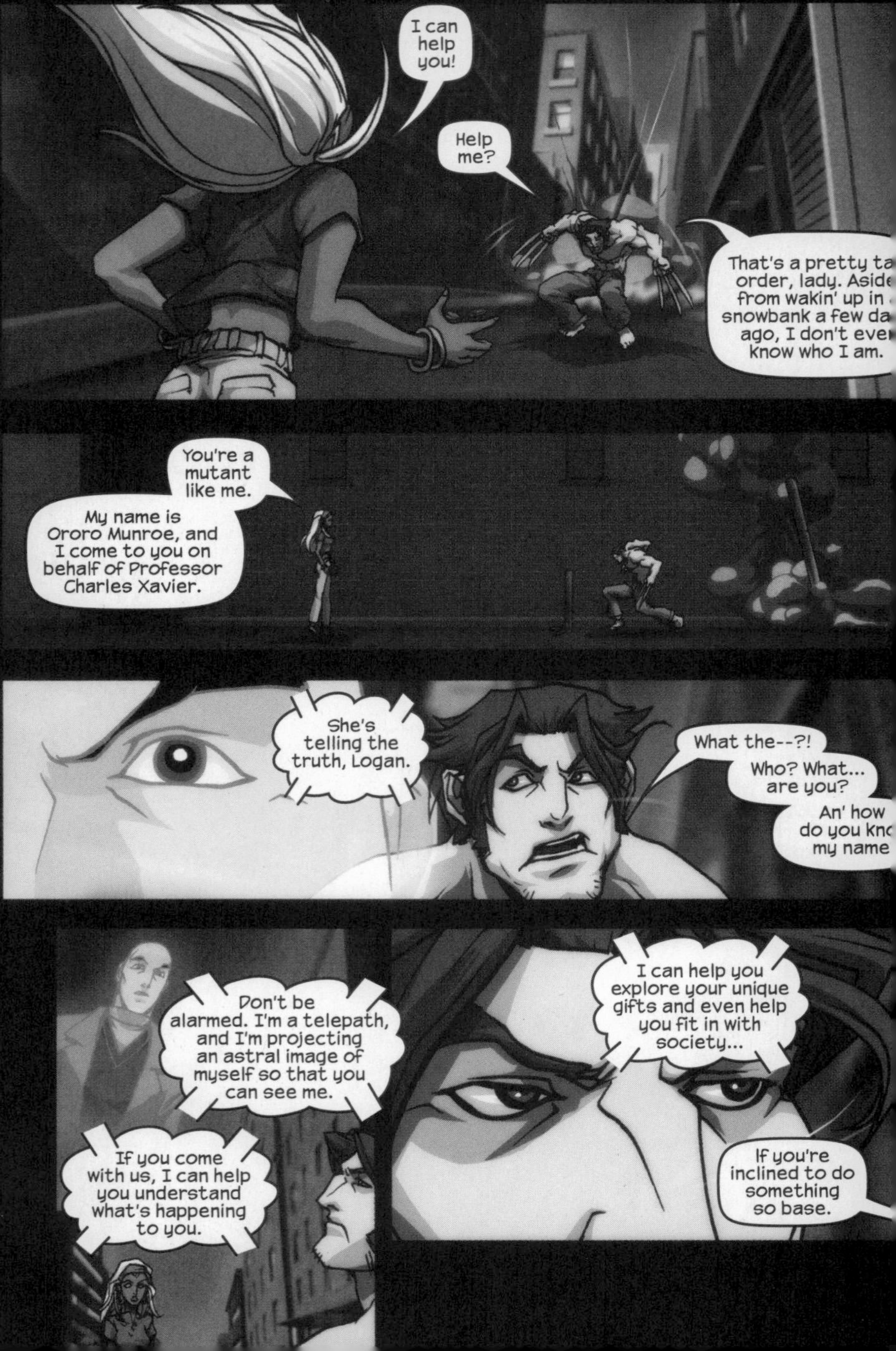
I can help you!
Help me?
That's a pretty ta order, lady. Aside from wakin' up in snowbank a few da ago, I don't eve know who I am.
You're a mutant like me.
My name is Ororo Munroe, and I come to you on behalf of Professor Charles Xavier.
She's telling the truth, Logan.
What the--?!
Who? What... are you?
An' how do you kn my name
Don't be alarmed. I'm a telepath, and I'm projecting an astral image of myself so that you can see me.
I can help you explore your unique gifts and even help you fit in with society...
If you come with us, I can help you understand what's happening to you.
If you're inclined to do something so base.

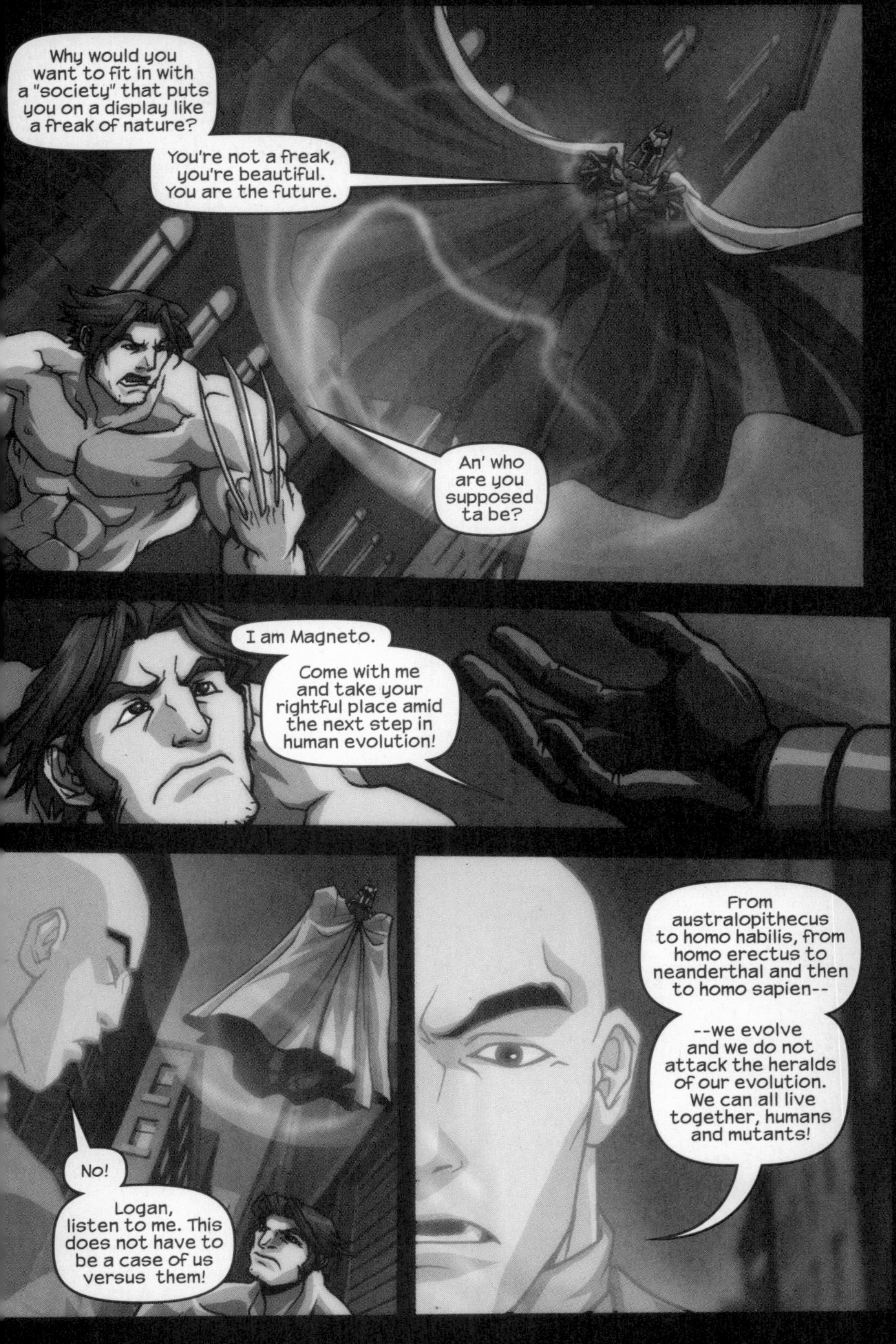
Why would you want to fit in with a "society" that puts you on a display like a freak of nature?
You're not a freak, you're beautiful. You are the future.
An' who are you supposed ta be?
I am Magneto.
Come with me and take your rightful place amid the next step in human evolution!
No!
Logan, listen to me. This does not have to be a case of us versus them!
From australopithecus to homo habilis, from homo erectus to neanderthal and then to homo sapien--
--we evolve and we do not attack the heralds of our evolution. We can all live together, humans and mutants!

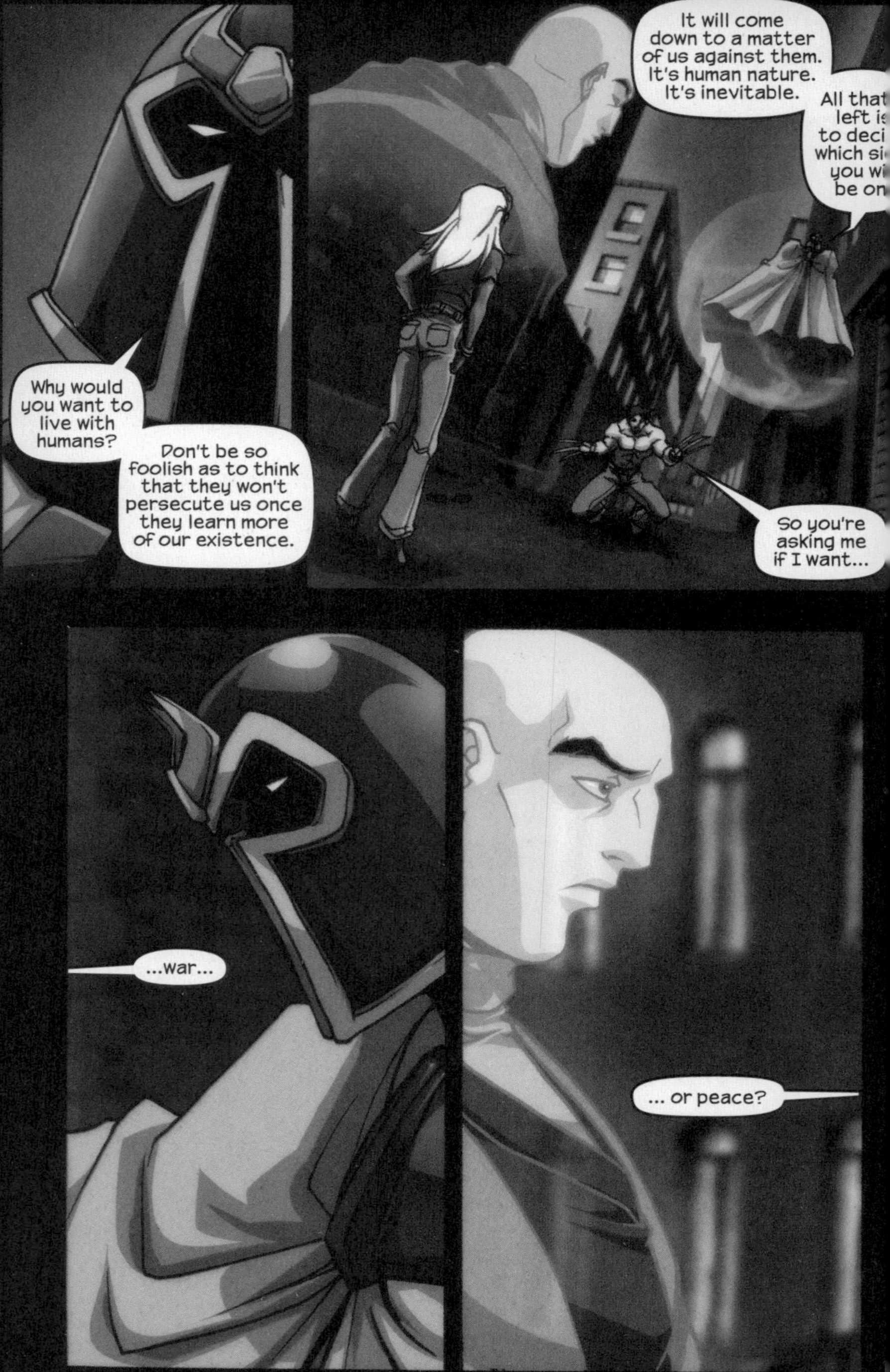
Why would you want to live with humans?
Don't be so foolish as to think that they won't persecute us once they learn more of our existence.
It will come down to a matter of us against them. It's human nature. It's inevitable.
All that left i to deci which si you wi be on
So you're asking me if I want...
...war...
... or peace?

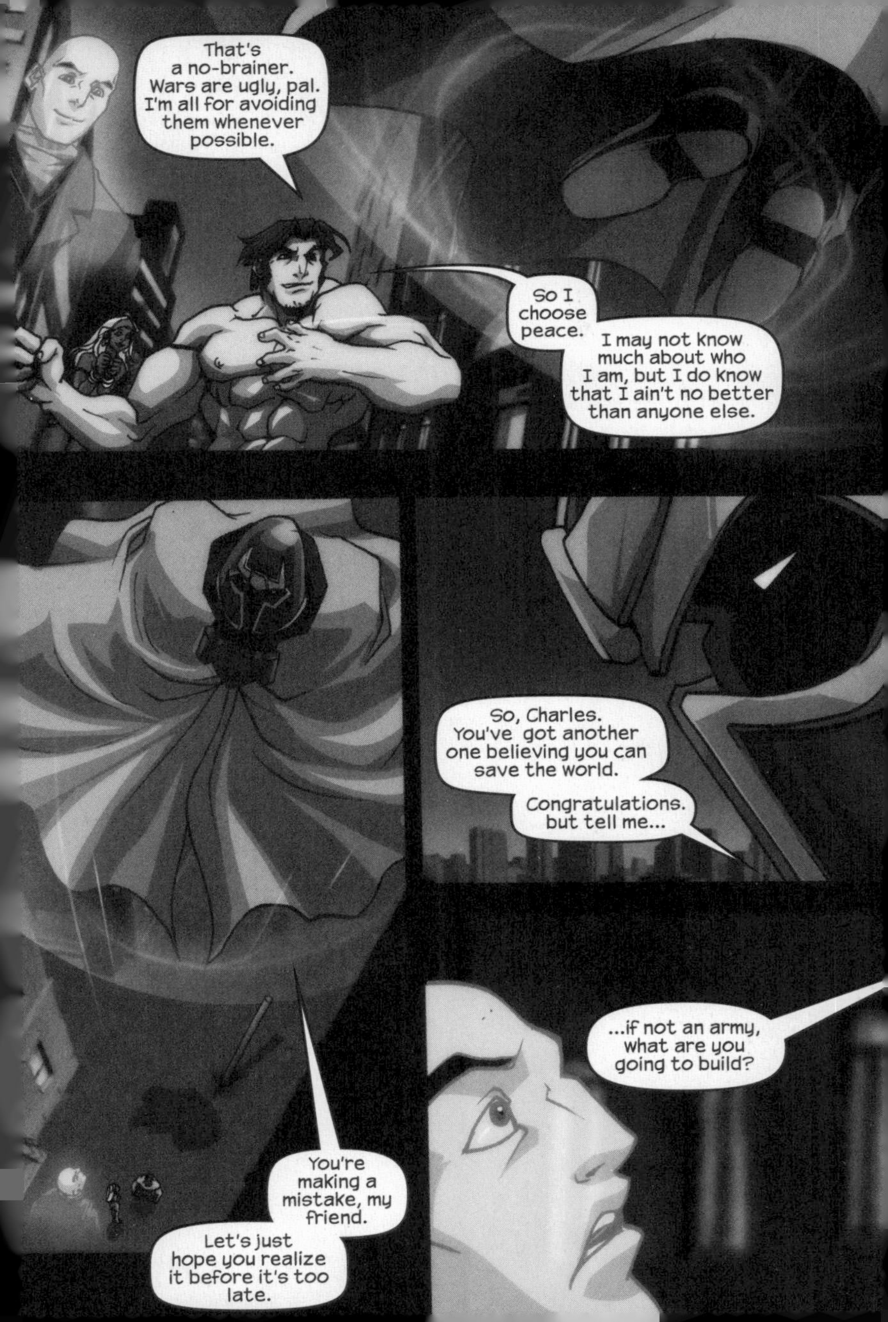
That's a no-brainer. Wars are ugly, pal. I'm all for avoiding them whenever possible.
So I choose peace.
I may not know much about who I am, but I do know that I ain't no better than anyone else.
So, Charles. You've got another one believing you can save the world.
Congratulations. but tell me...
...if not an army, what are you going to build?
You're making a mistake, my friend.
Let's just hope you realize it before it's too late.

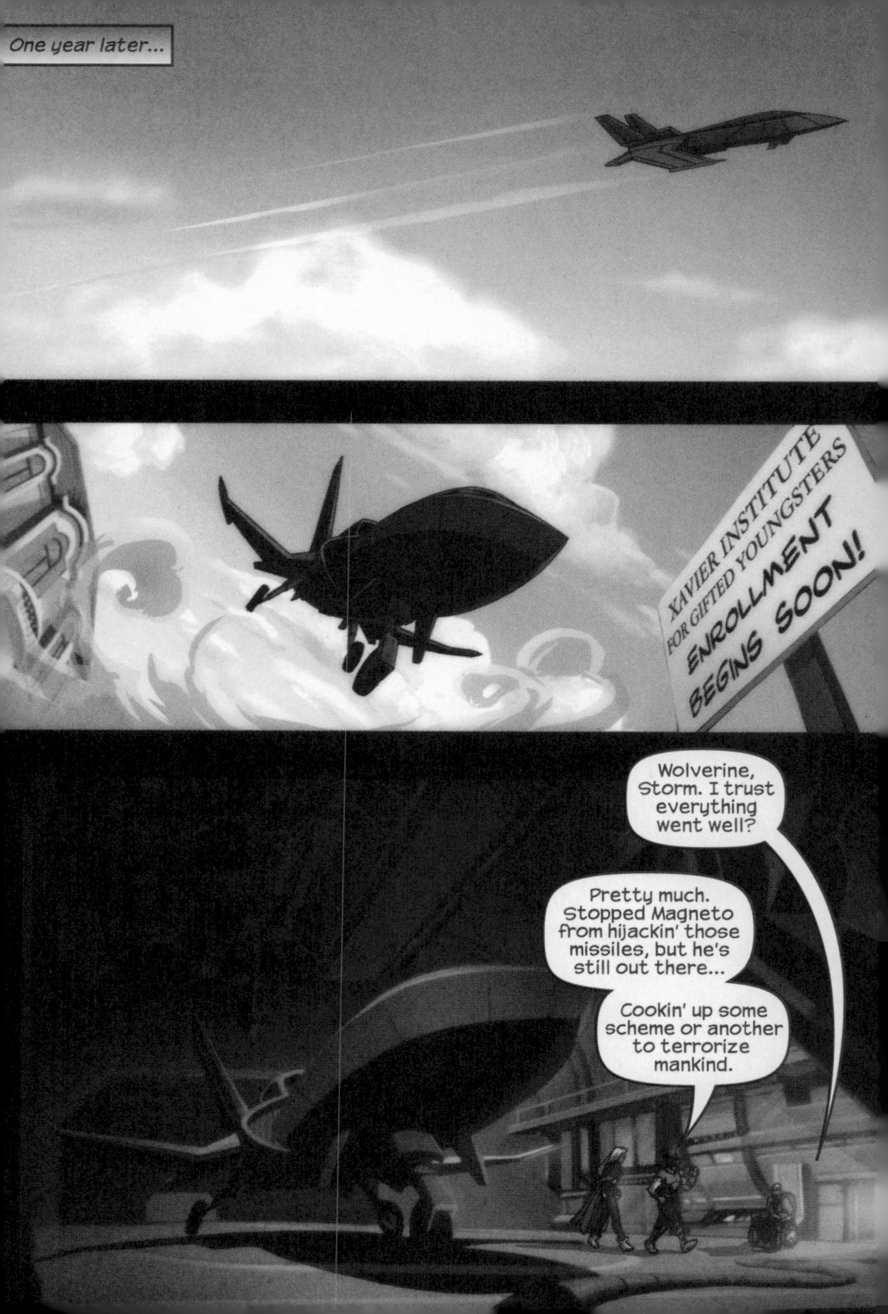

One year later...
XAVIER INSTITUTE FOR GIFTED YOUNGSTERS
ENROLLMENT BEGINS SOON!
Wolverine, Storm. I trust everything went well?
Pretty much. Stopped Magneto from hijackin' those missiles, but he's still out there...
Cookin' up some scheme or another to terrorize mankind.

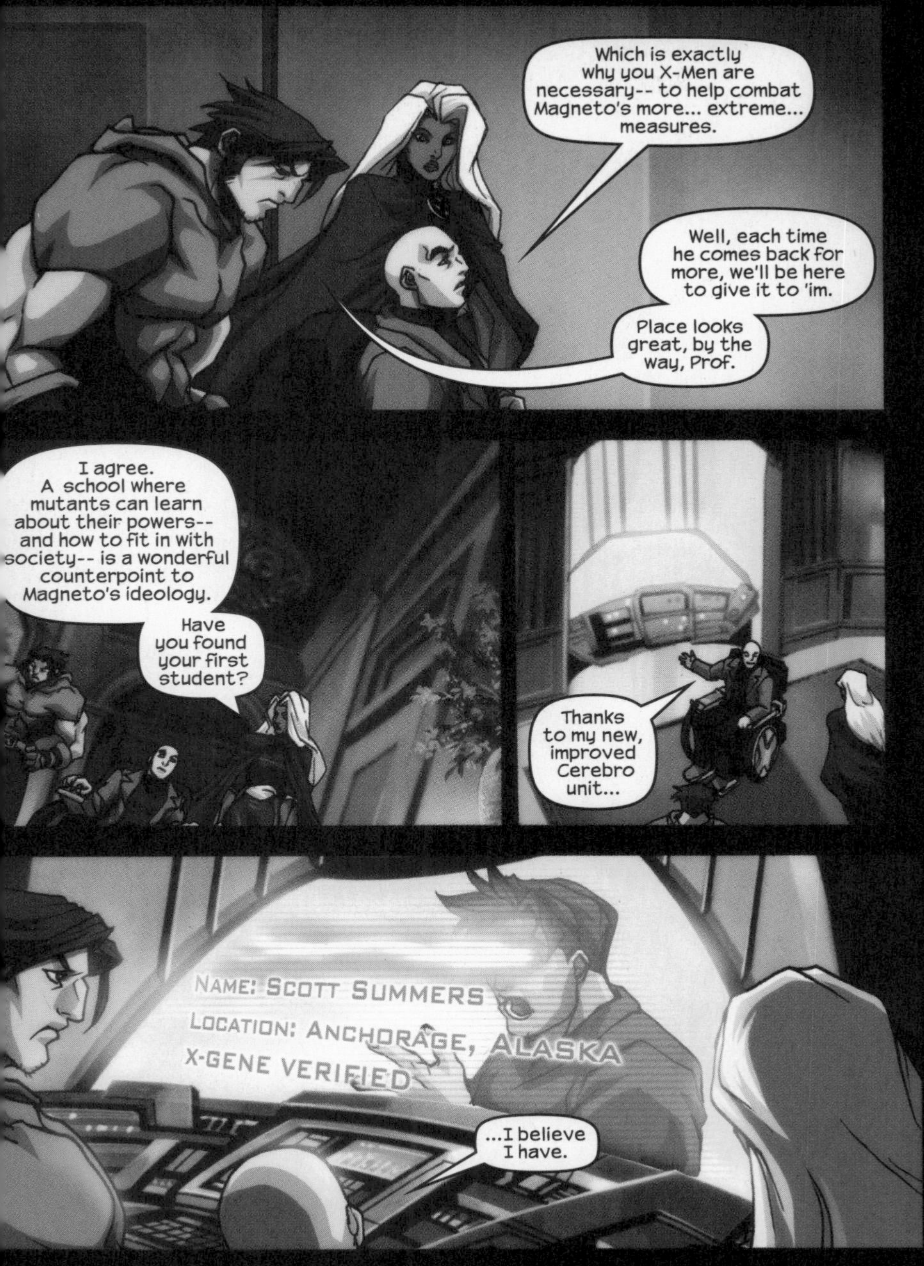
Which is exactly why you X-Men are necessary-- to help combat Magneto's more... extreme... measures.
Well, each time he comes back for more, we'll be here to give it to 'im.
Place looks great, by the way, Prof.
I agree. A school where mutants can learn about their powers-- and how to fit in with society-- is a wonderful counterpoint to Magneto's ideology.
Have you found your first student?
Thanks to my new, improved Cerebro unit...
NAME: SCOTT SUMMERS
LOCATION: ANCHORAGE, ALASKA
X-GENE VERIFIED
...I believe I have.

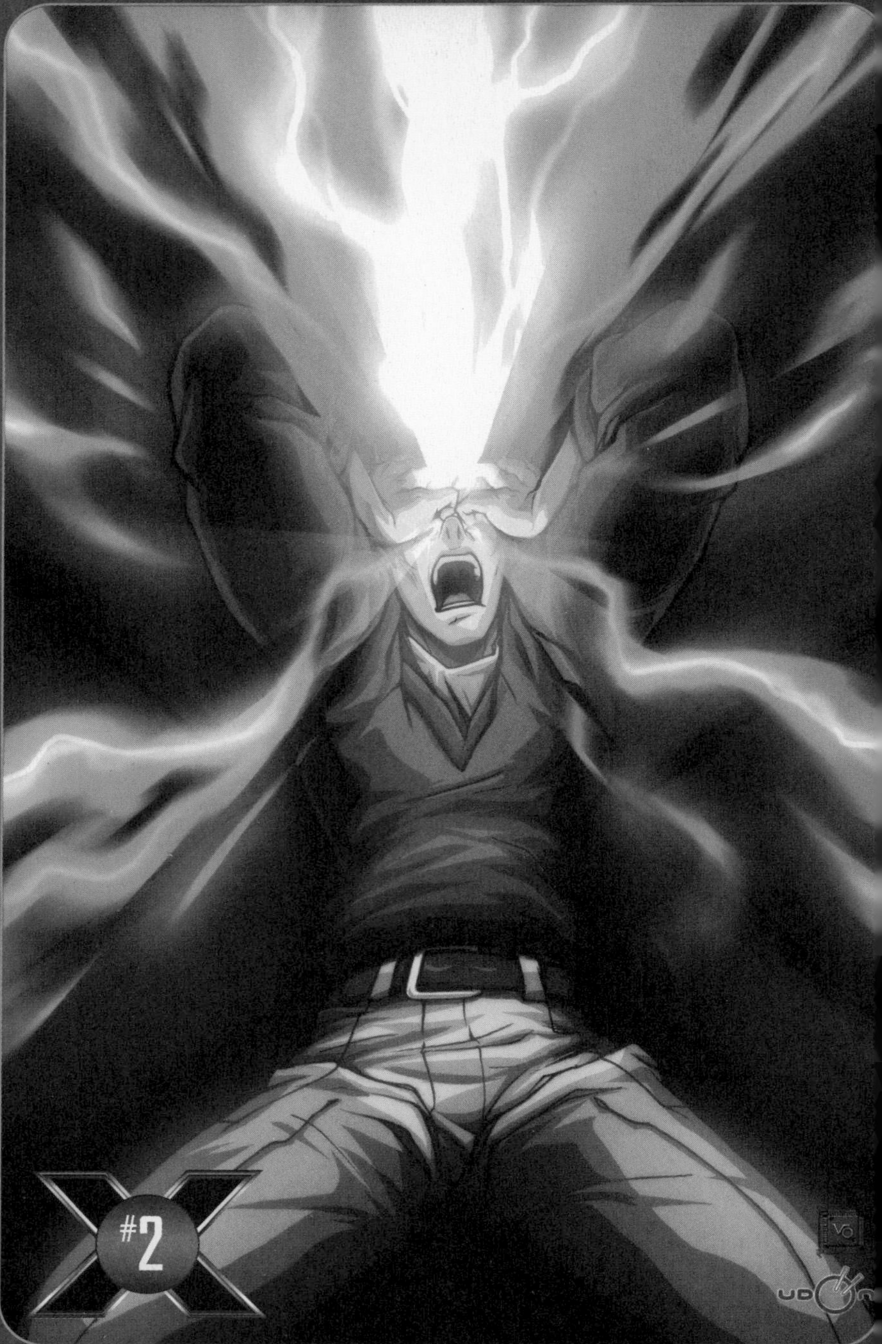
#2

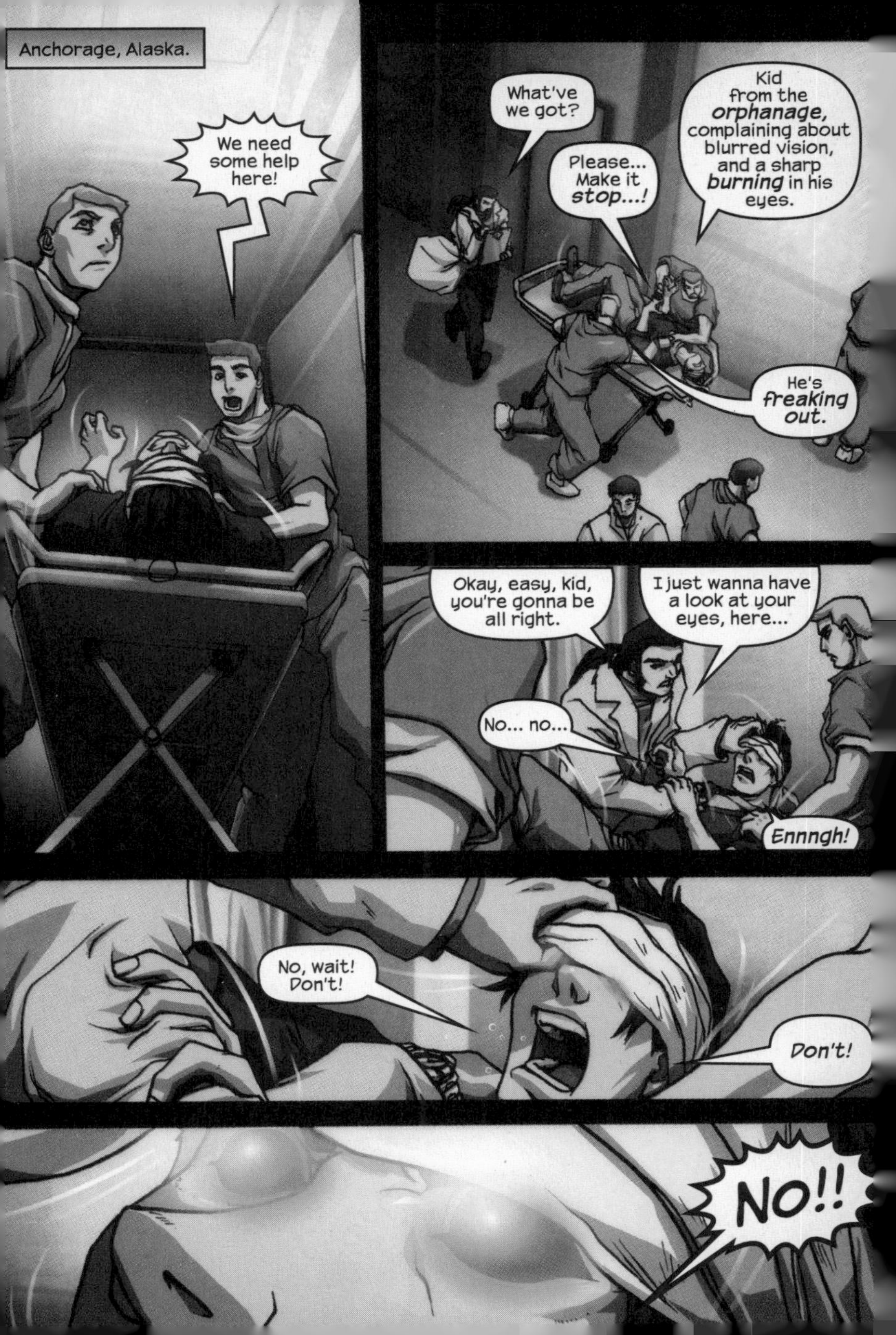
Anchorage, Alaska.
We need some help here!
What've we got?
Please... Make it stop...!
Kid from the orphanage, complaining about blurred vision, and a sharp burning in his eyes.
He's freaking out.
Okay, easy, kid, you're gonna be all right.
I just wanna have a look at your eyes, here...
No... no...
Ennngh!
No, wait! Don't!
Don't!
NO!!

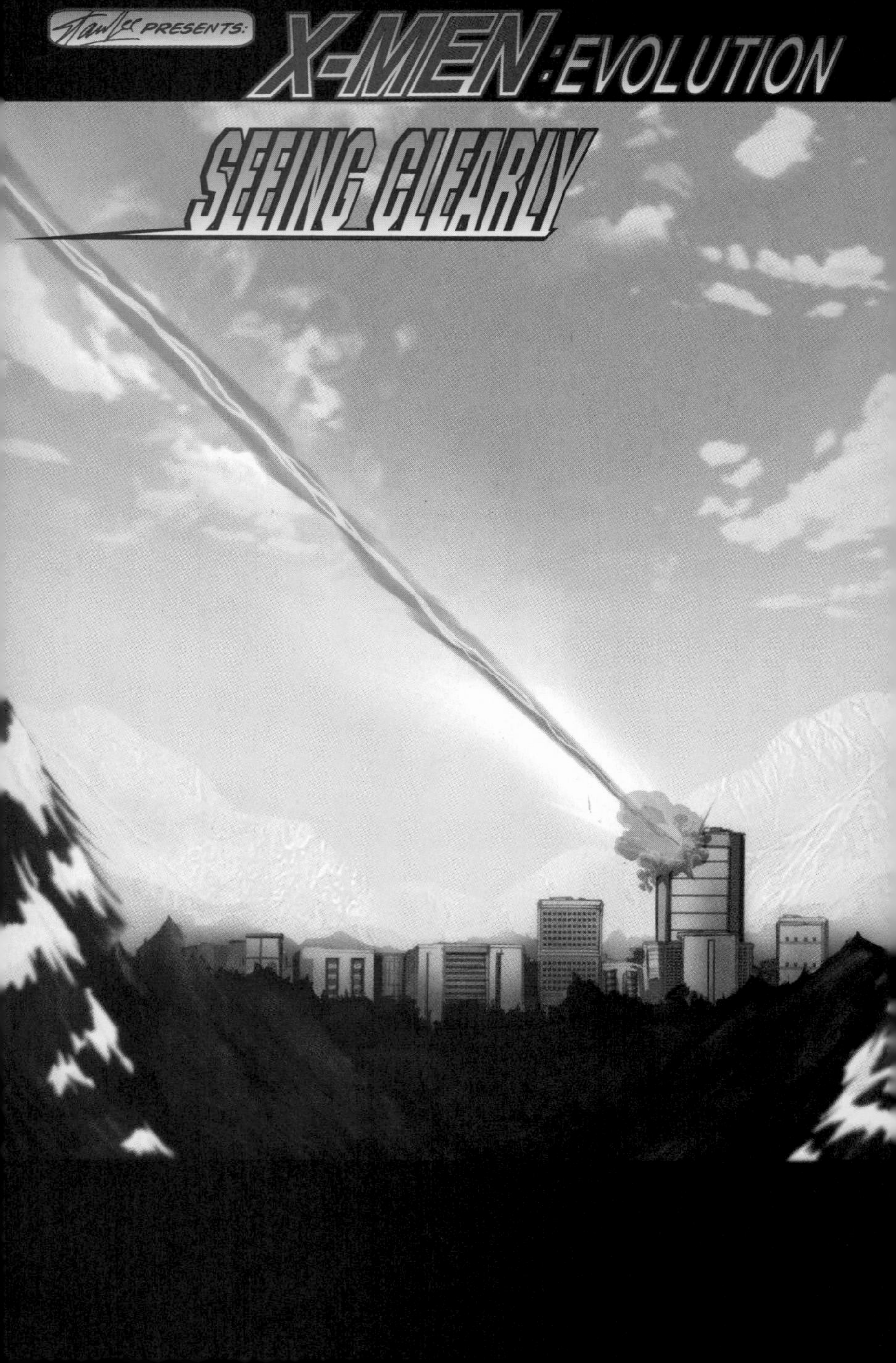
Stan Lee PRESENTS:
X-MEN: EVOLUTION
SEEING CLEARLY

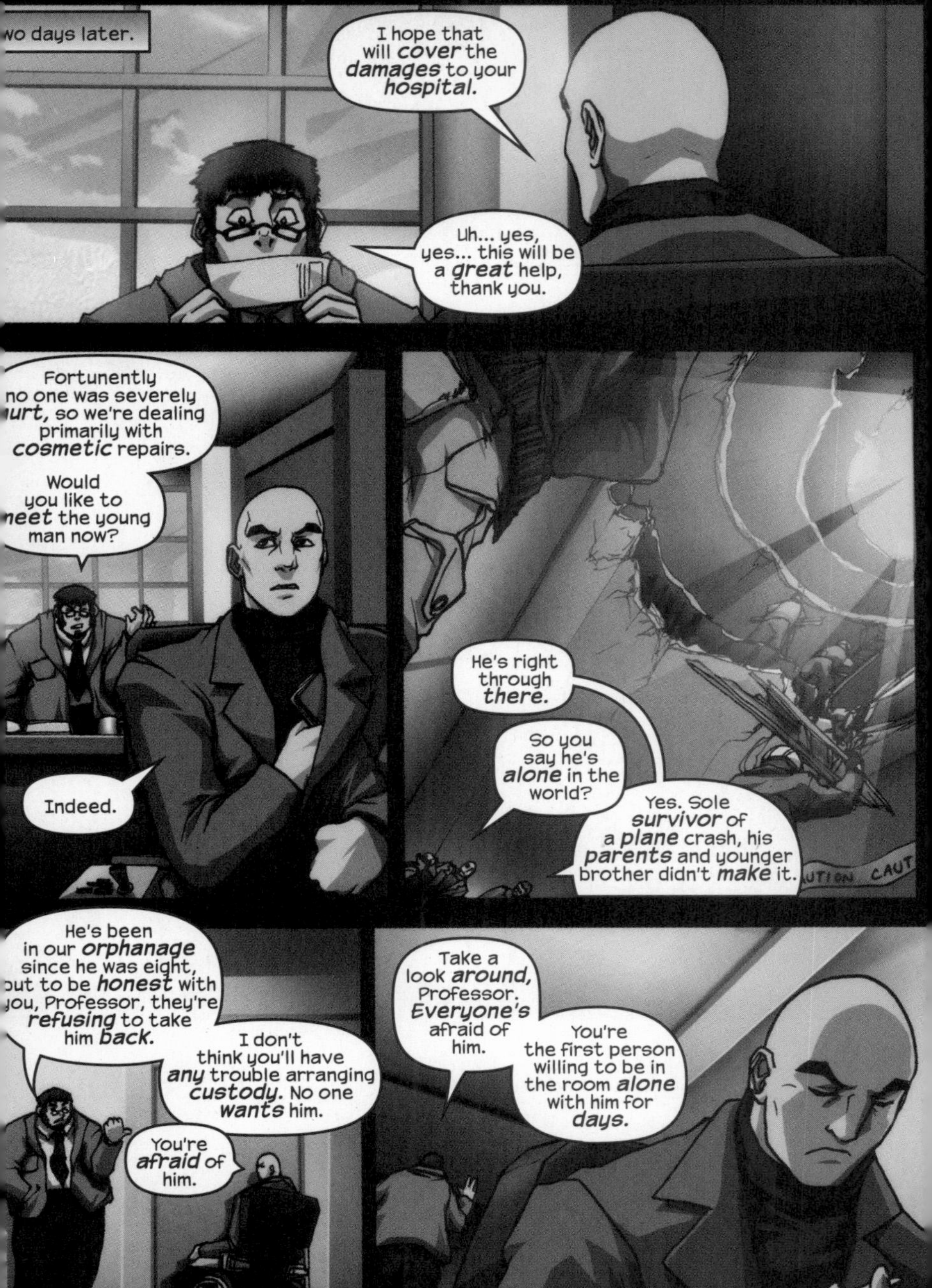
wo days later.
I hope that will cover the damages to your hospital.
Uh... yes, yes... this will be a great help, thank you.
Fortunently no one was severely urt, so we're dealing primarily with cosmetic repairs.
Would you like to neet the young man now?
Indeed.
He's right through there.
So you say he's alone in the world?
Yes. Sole survivor of a plane crash, his parents and younger brother didn't make it.
He's been in our orphanage since he was eight, out to be honest with you, Professor, they're refusing to take him back.
I don't think you'll have any trouble arranging custody. No one wants him.
You're afraid of him.
Take a look around, Professor. Everyone's afraid of him.
You're the first person willing to be in the room alone with him for days.

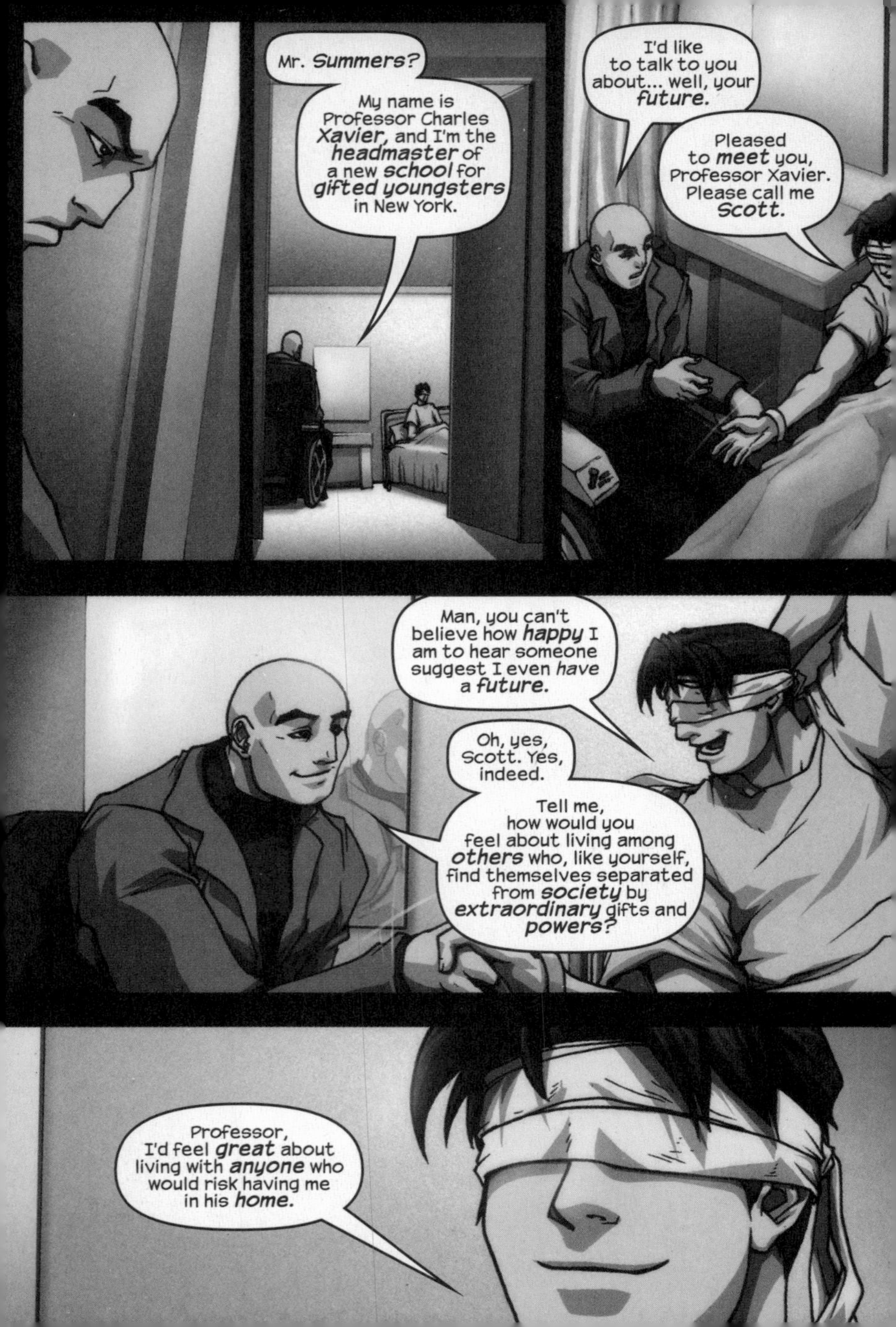
Mr. Summers?
My name is Professor Charles Xavier, and I'm the headmaster of a new school for gifted youngsters in New York.
I'd like to talk to you about... well, your future.
Pleased to meet you, Professor Xavier. Please call me Scott.
Man, you can't believe how happy I am to hear someone suggest I even have a future.
Oh, yes, Scott. Yes, indeed.
Tell me, how would you feel about living among others who, like yourself, find themselves separated from society by extraordinary gifts and powers?
Professor, I'd feel great about living with anyone who would risk having me in his home.

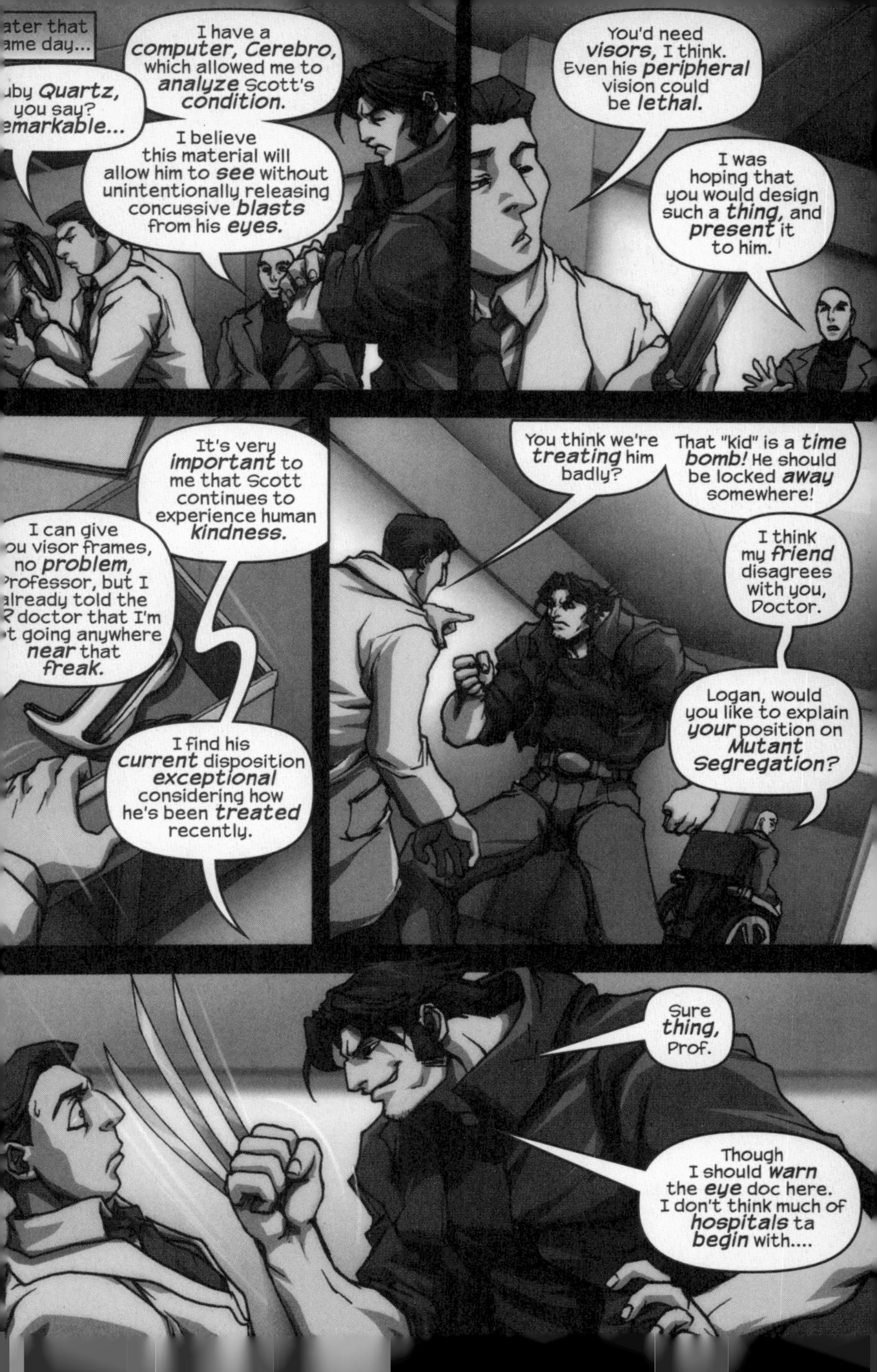

ater that
ame day...
uby Quartz, you say? emarkable...
I have a computer, Cerebro, which allowed me to analyze Scott's condition.
I believe this material will allow him to see without unintentionally releasing concussive blasts from his eyes.
You'd need visors, I think. Even his peripheral vision could be lethal.
I was hoping that you would design such a thing, and present it to him.
I can give ou visor frames, no problem, Professor, but I already told the doctor that I'm t going anywhere near that freak.
It's very important to me that Scott continues to experience human kindness.
I find his current disposition exceptional considering how he's been treated recently.
You think we're treating him badly?
That "kid" is a time bomb! He should be locked away somewhere!
I think my friend disagrees with you, Doctor.
Logan, would you like to explain your position on Mutant Segregation?
Sure thing, Prof.
Though I should warn the eye doc here. I don't think much of hospitals ta begin with....

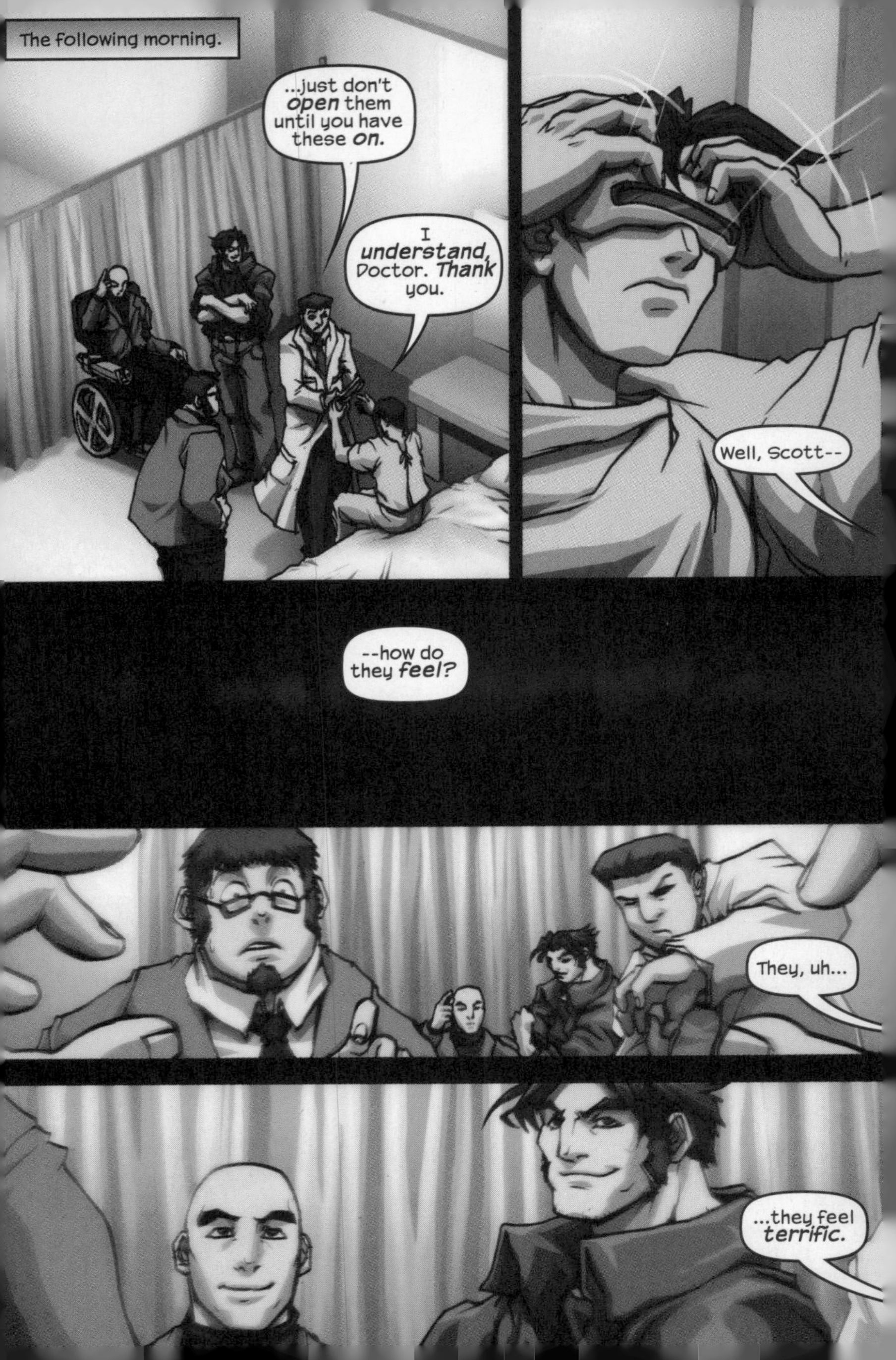
The following morning.
...just don't open them until you have these on.
I understand, Doctor. Thank you.
Well, Scott--
--how do they feel?
They, uh...
...they feel terrific.

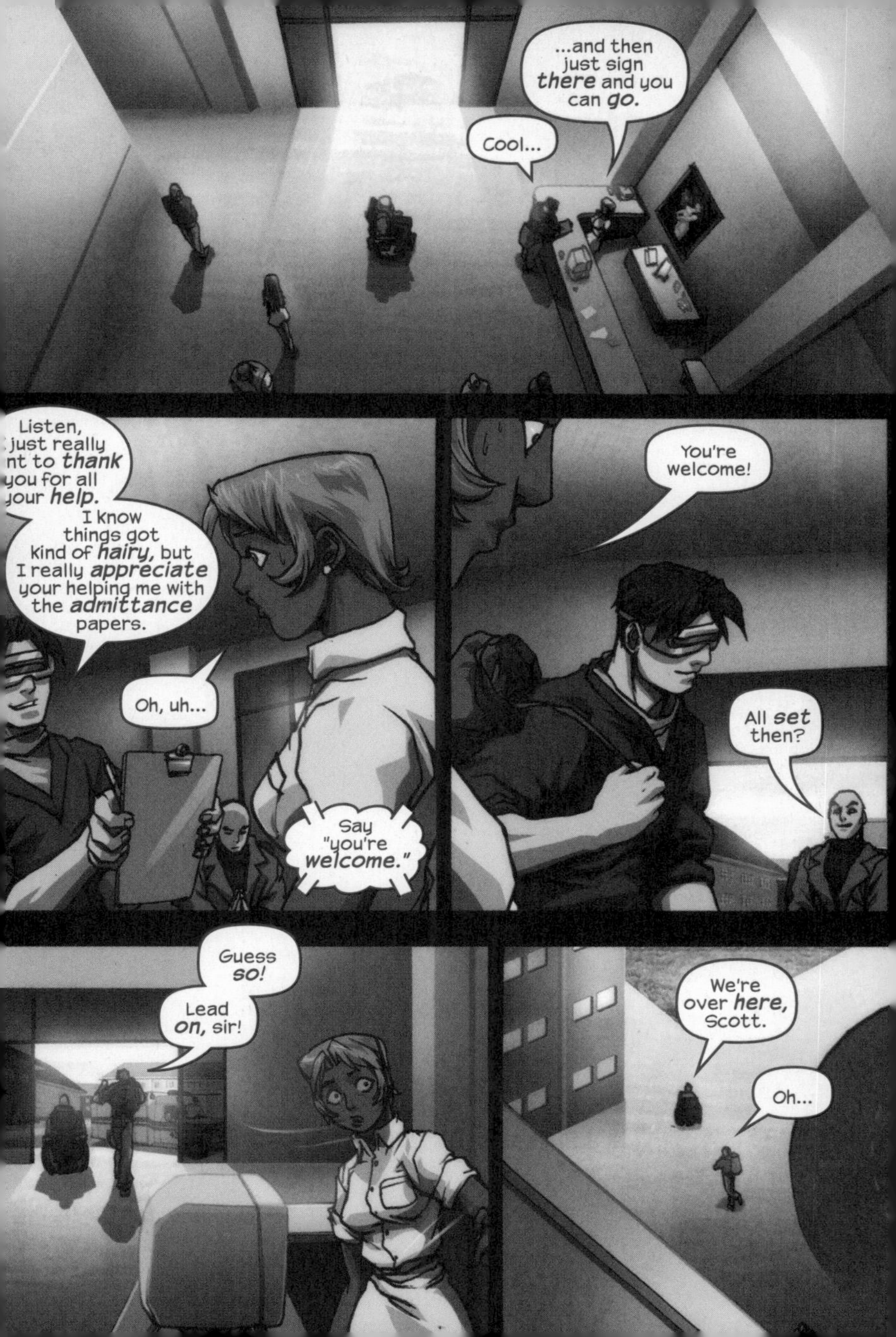
...and then just sign there and you can go.
Cool...
Listen, just really nt to thank you for all your help.
I know things got kind of hairy, but I really appreciate your helping me with the admittance papers.
Oh, uh...
Say "you're welcome."
You're welcome!
All set then?
Guess so!
Lead on, sir!
We're over here, Scott.
Oh...

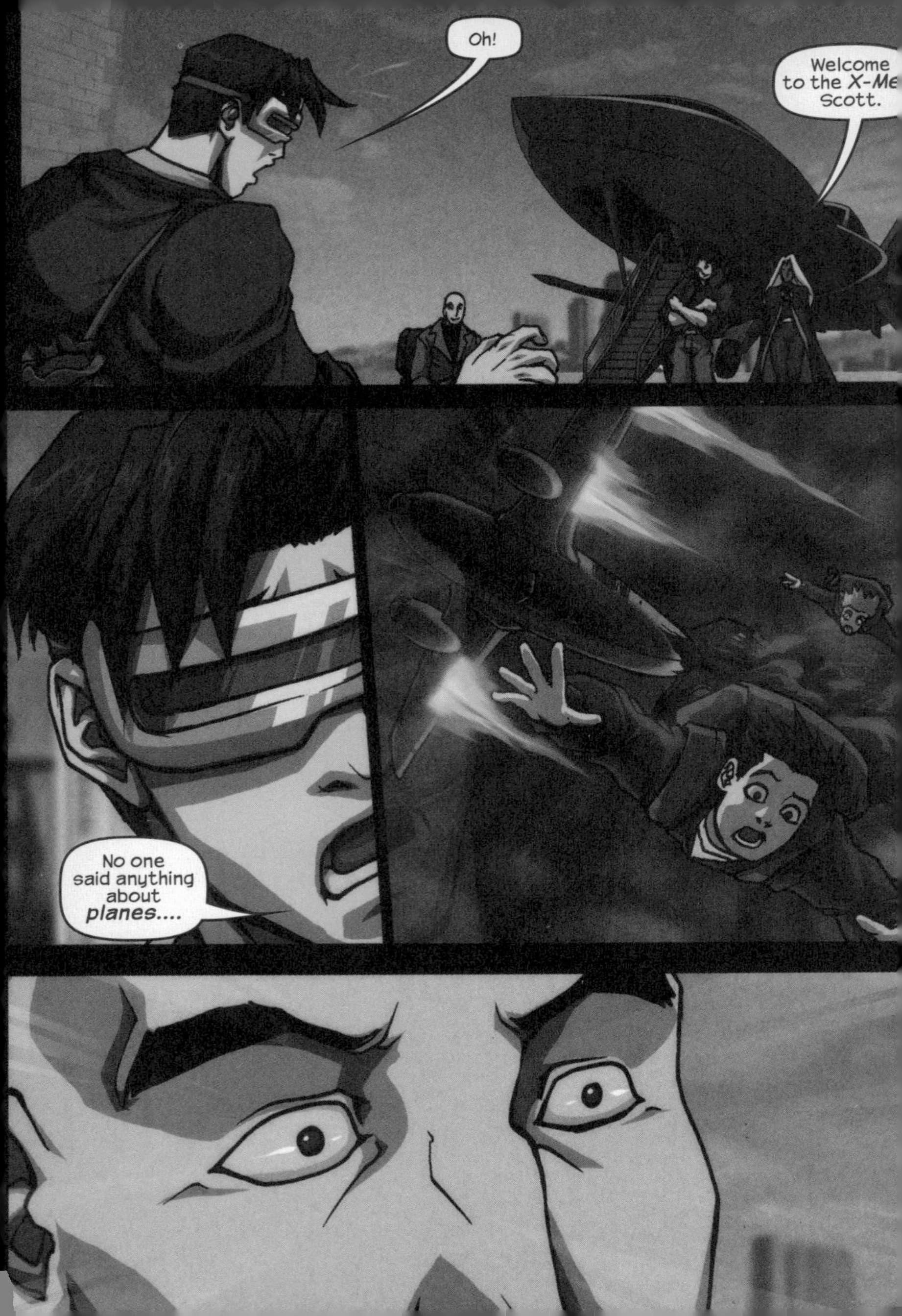
Oh!
Welcome to the X-Me Scott.
No one said anything about planes....

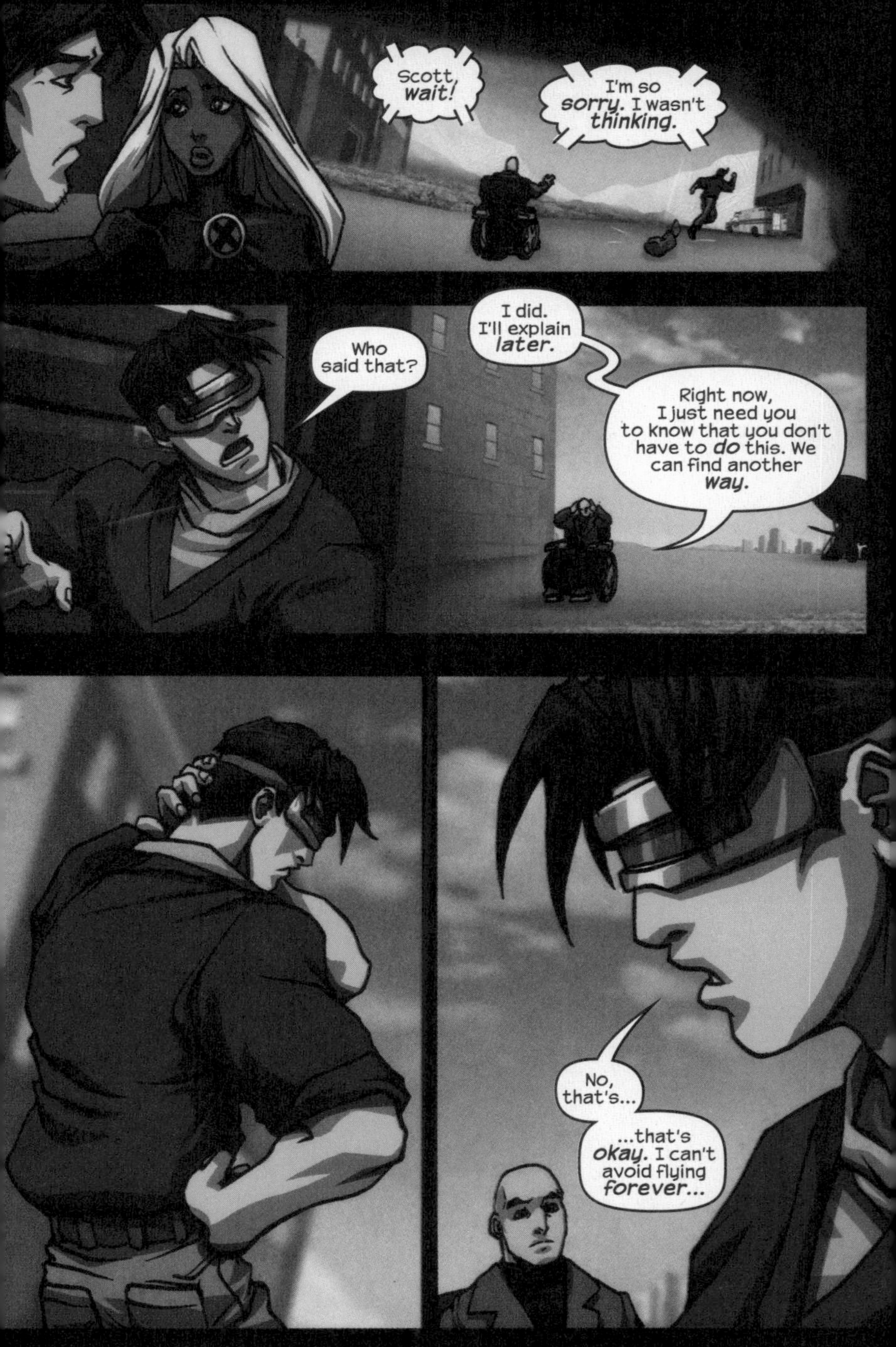
Scott, wait!
I'm so sorry. I wasn't thinking.
Who said that?
I did. I'll explain later.
Right now, I just need you to know that you don't have to do this. We can find another way.
No, that's...
...that's okay. I can't avoid flying forever...

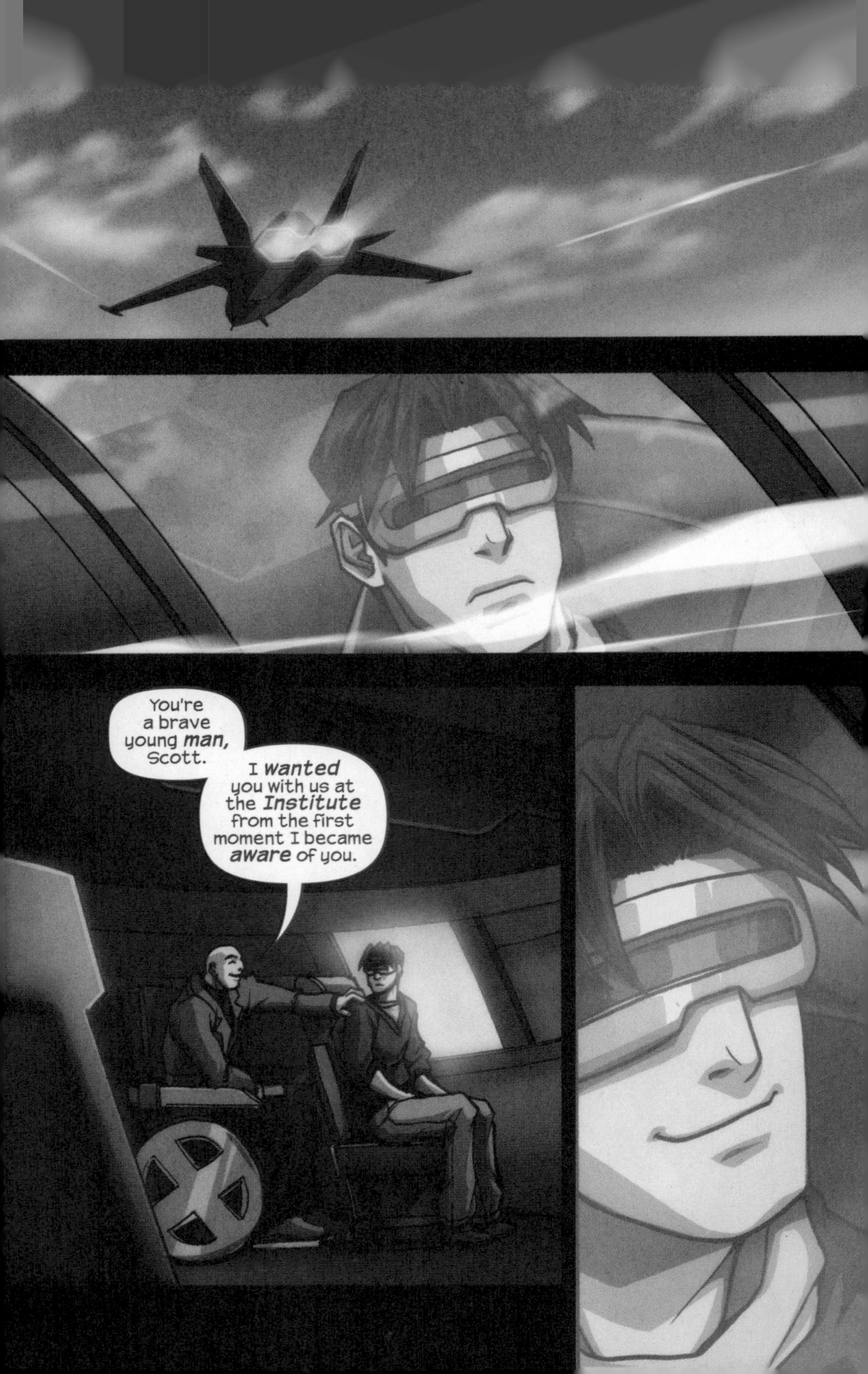
You're a brave young *man,* Scott.
I *wanted* you with us at the *Institute* from the first moment I became *aware* of you.

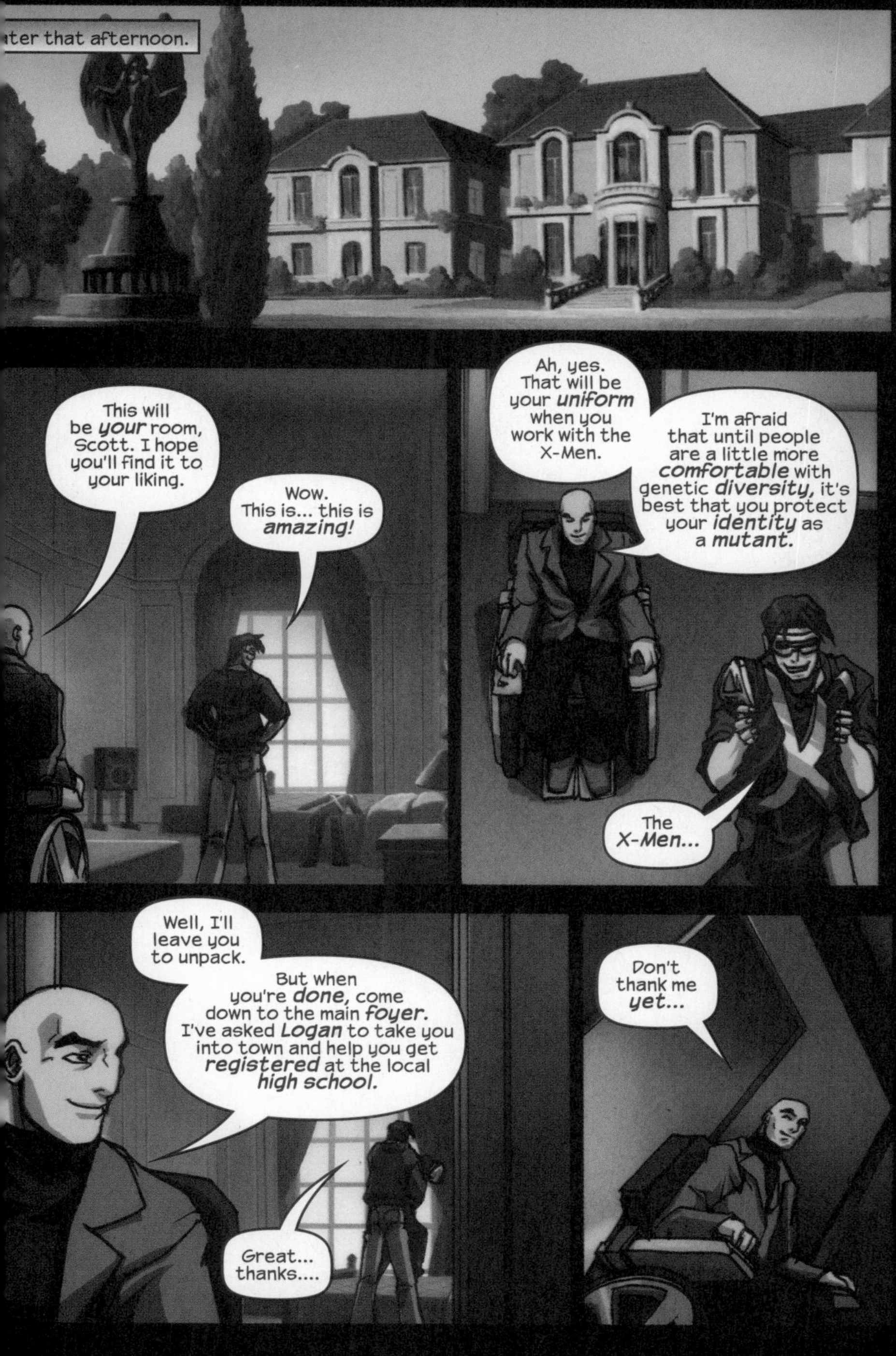

ater that afternoon.
This will be your room, Scott. I hope you'll find it to your liking.
Wow. This is... this is amazing!
Ah, yes. That will be your uniform when you work with the X-Men.
I'm afraid that until people are a little more comfortable with genetic diversity, it's best that you protect your identity as a mutant.
The X-Men...
Well, I'll leave you to unpack.
But when you're done, come down to the main foyer. I've asked Logan to take you into town and help you get registered at the local high school.
Great... thanks....
Don't thank me yet...

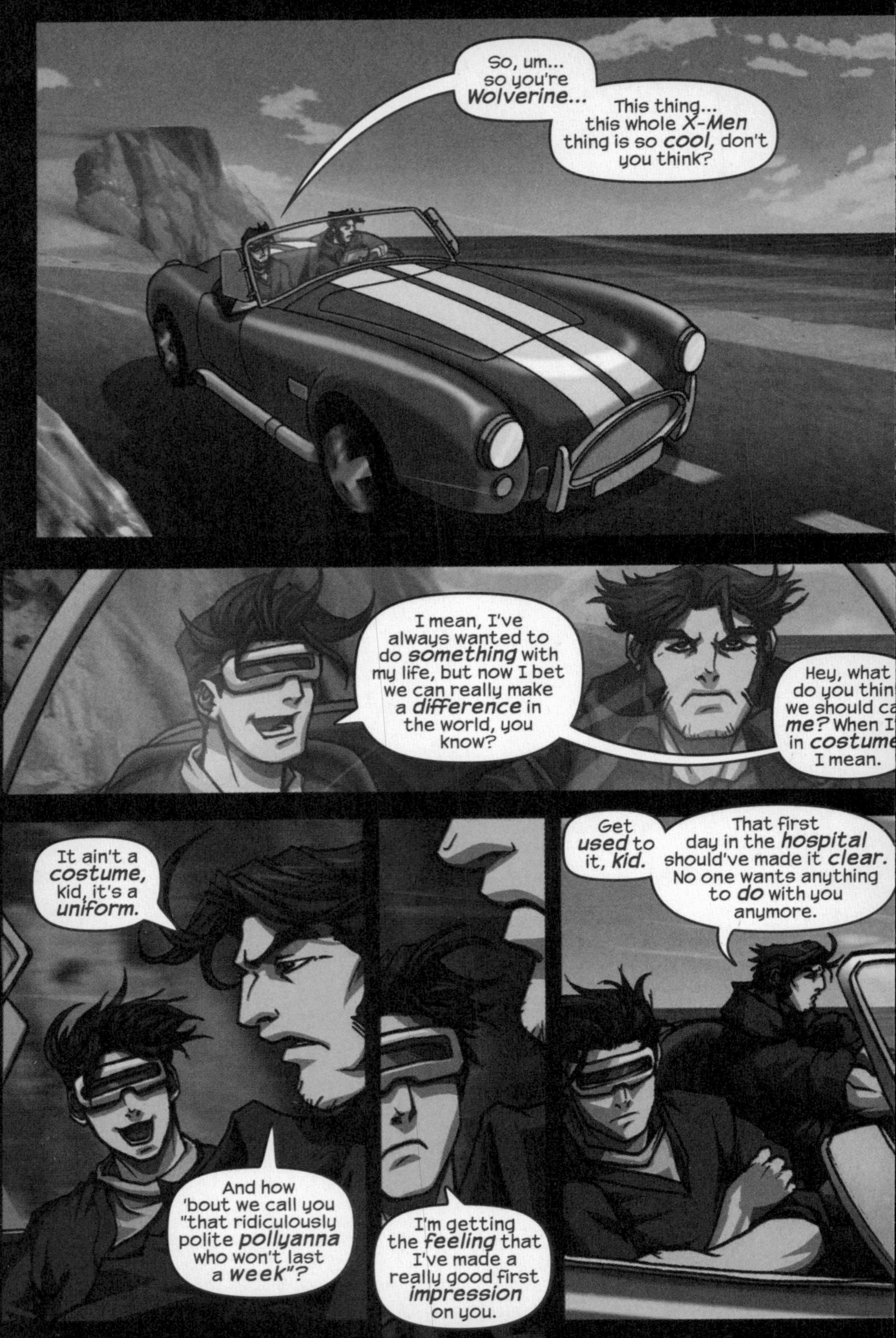
So, um... so you're Wolverine...
This thing... this whole X-Men thing is so cool, don't you think?
I mean, I've always wanted to do something with my life, but now I bet we can really make a difference in the world, you know?
Hey, what do you thin we should ca me? When I in costume I mean.
It ain't a costume, kid, it's a uniform.
And how 'bout we call you "that ridiculously polite pollyanna who won't last a week"?
I'm getting the feeling that I've made a really good first impression on you.
Get used to it, kid.
That first day in the hospital should've made it clear. No one wants anything to do with you anymore.

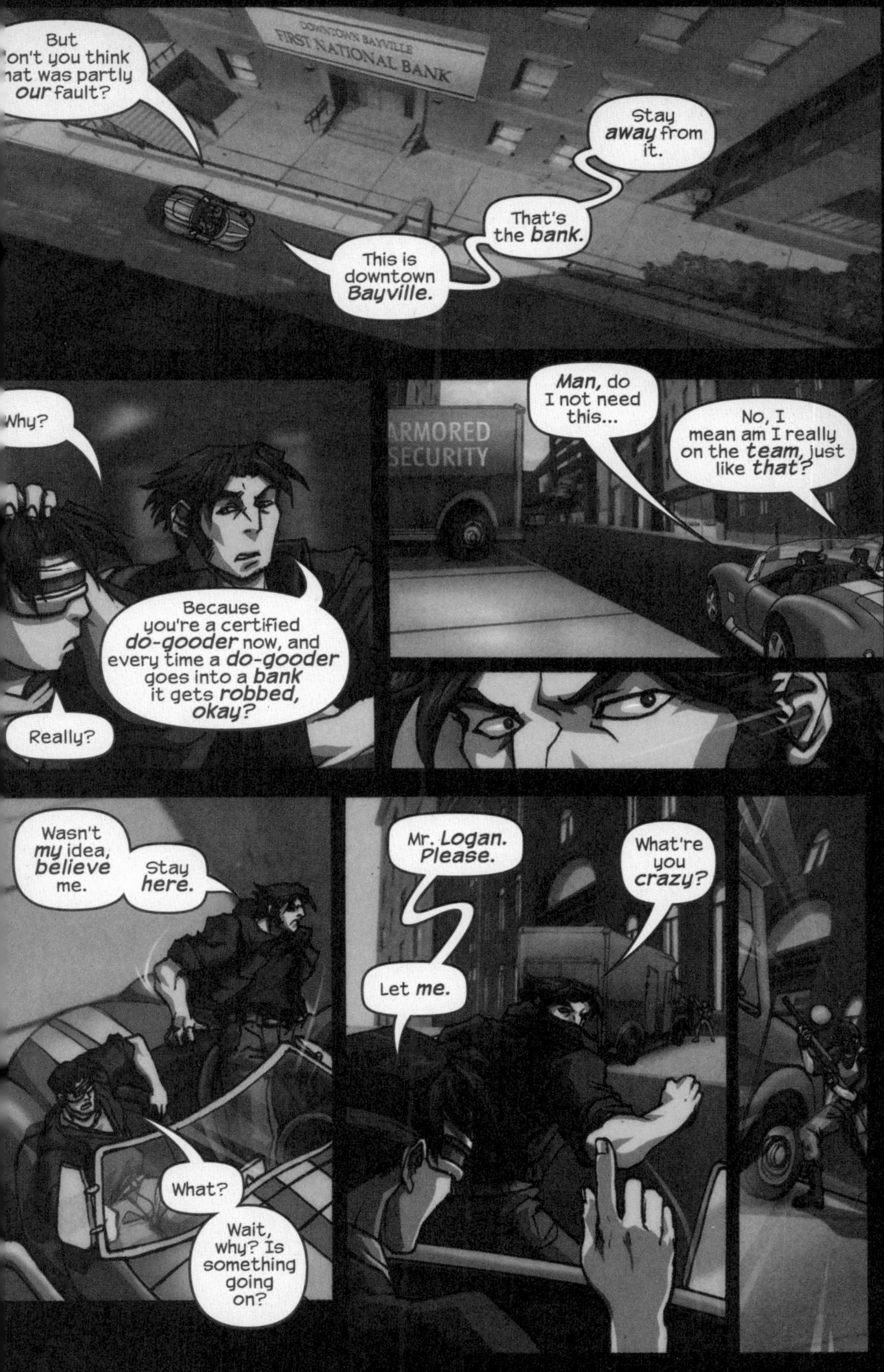

DOWNTOWN BAYVILLE FIRST NATIONAL BANK
But on't you think nat was partly our fault?
This is downtown Bayville.
That's the bank.
Stay away from it.
Why?
Because you're a certified do-gooder now, and every time a do-gooder goes into a bank it gets robbed, okay?
Really?
ARMORED SECURITY
Man, do I not need this...
No, I mean am I really on the team, just like that?
Wasn't my idea, believe me.
Stay here.
What?
Wait, why? Is something going on?
Mr. Logan. Please.
Let me.
What're you crazy?

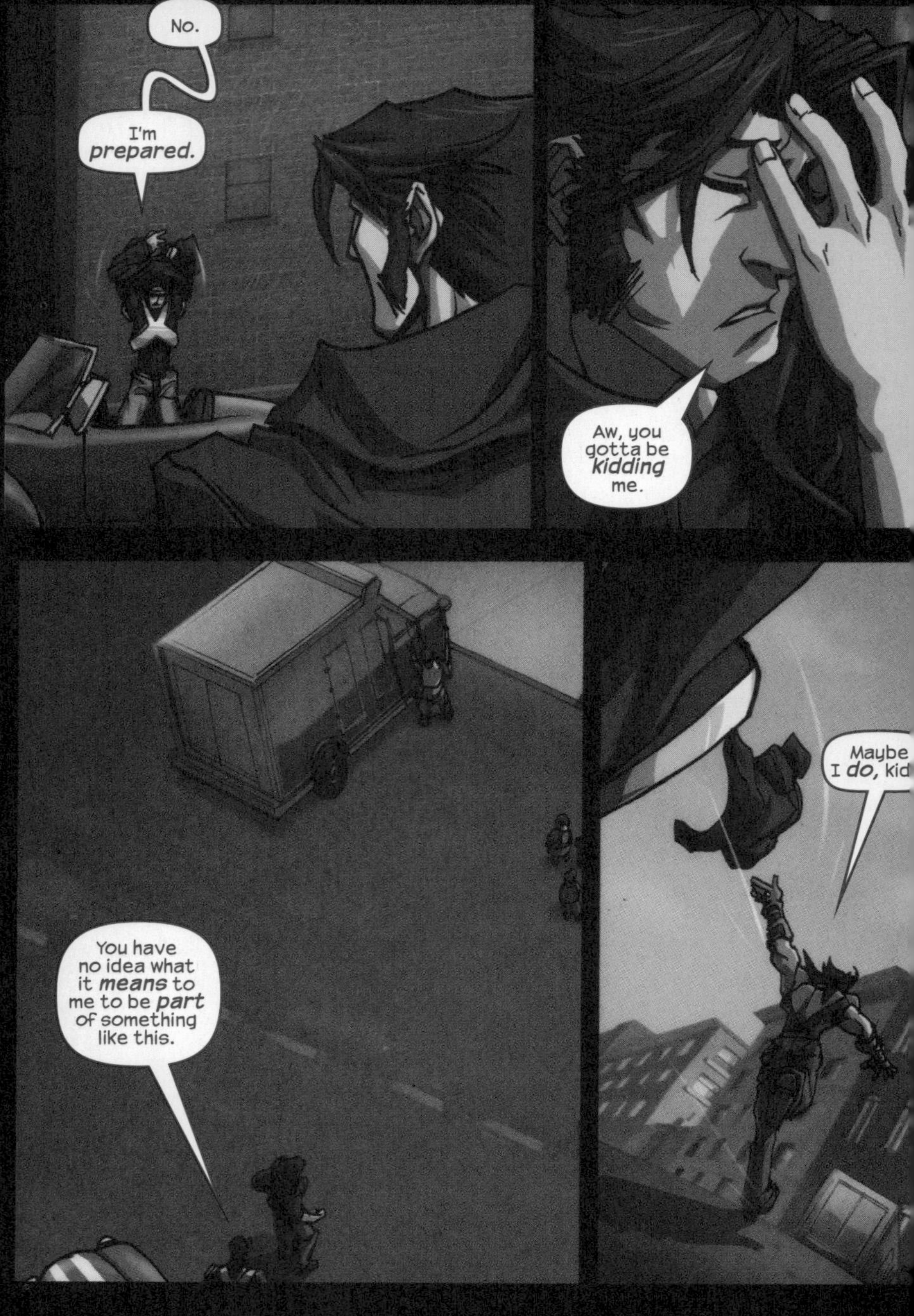
No.
I'm *prepared.*
Aw, you gotta be *kidding* me.
You have no idea what it *means* to me to be *part* of something like this.
Maybe I *do,* kid

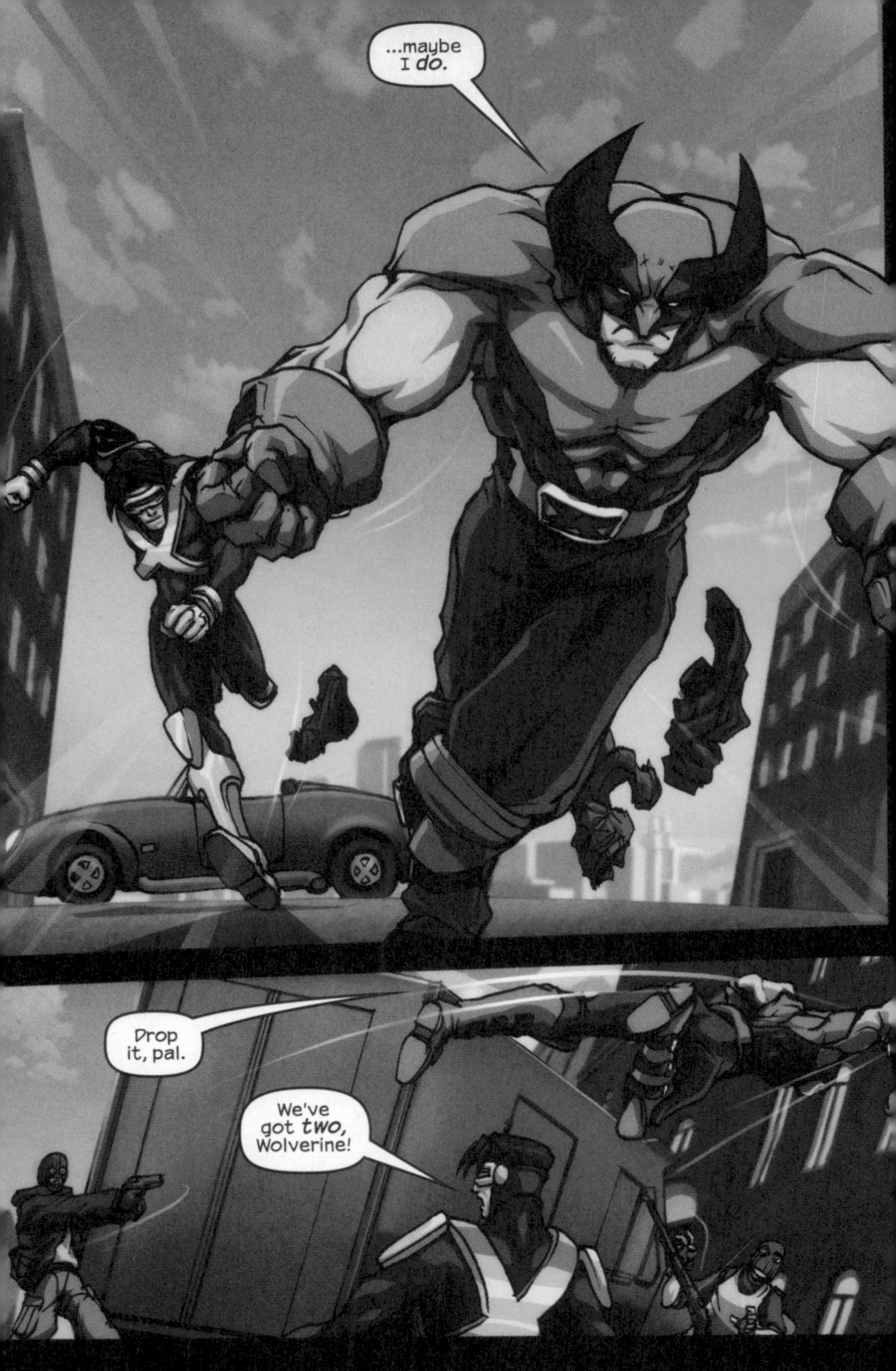
...maybe I *do.*
Drop it, pal.
We've got *two,* Wolverine!

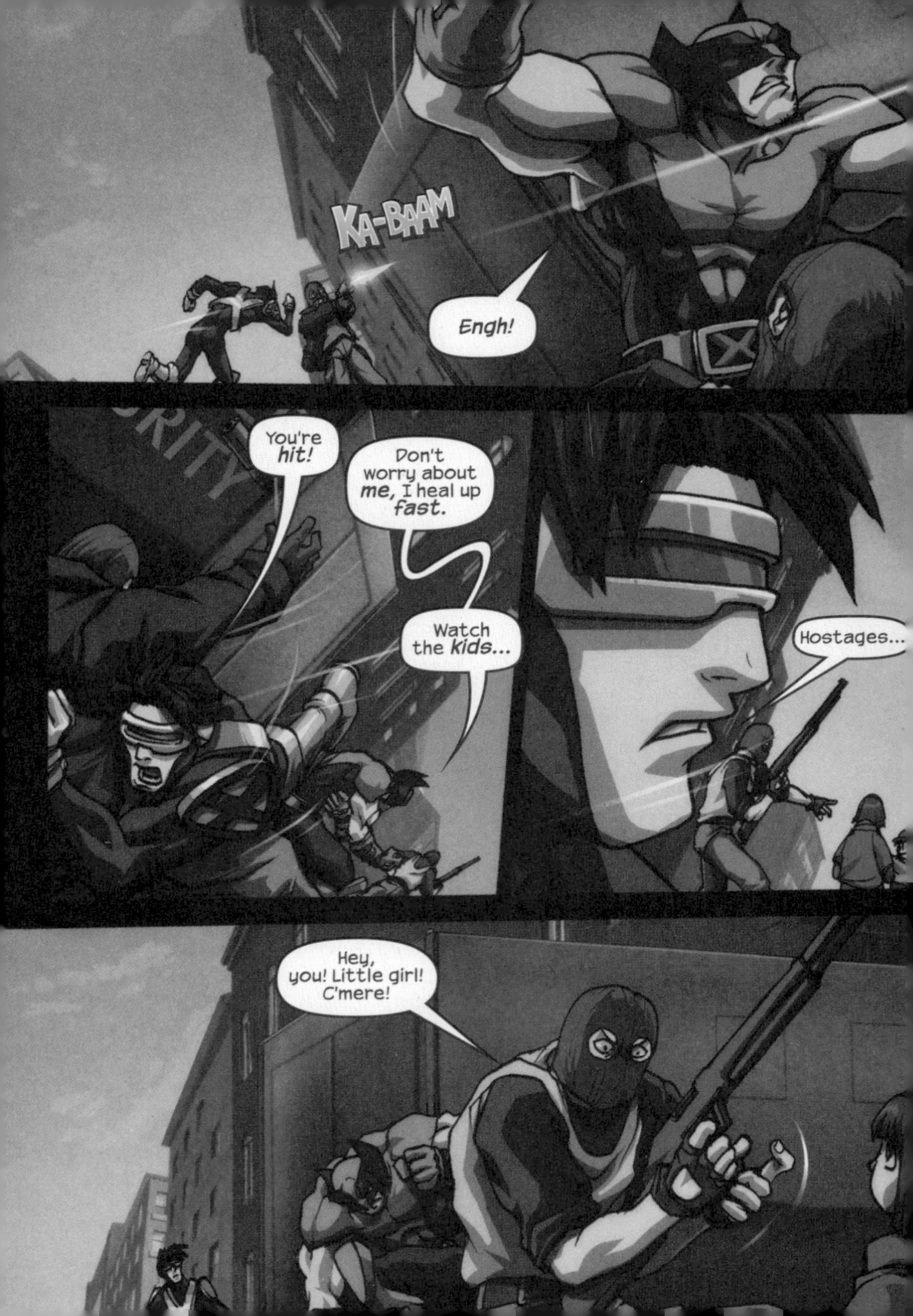
KA-BAAM
Engh!
You're hit!
Don't worry about me, I heal up fast.
Watch the kids...
Hostages...
Hey, you! Little girl! C'mere!

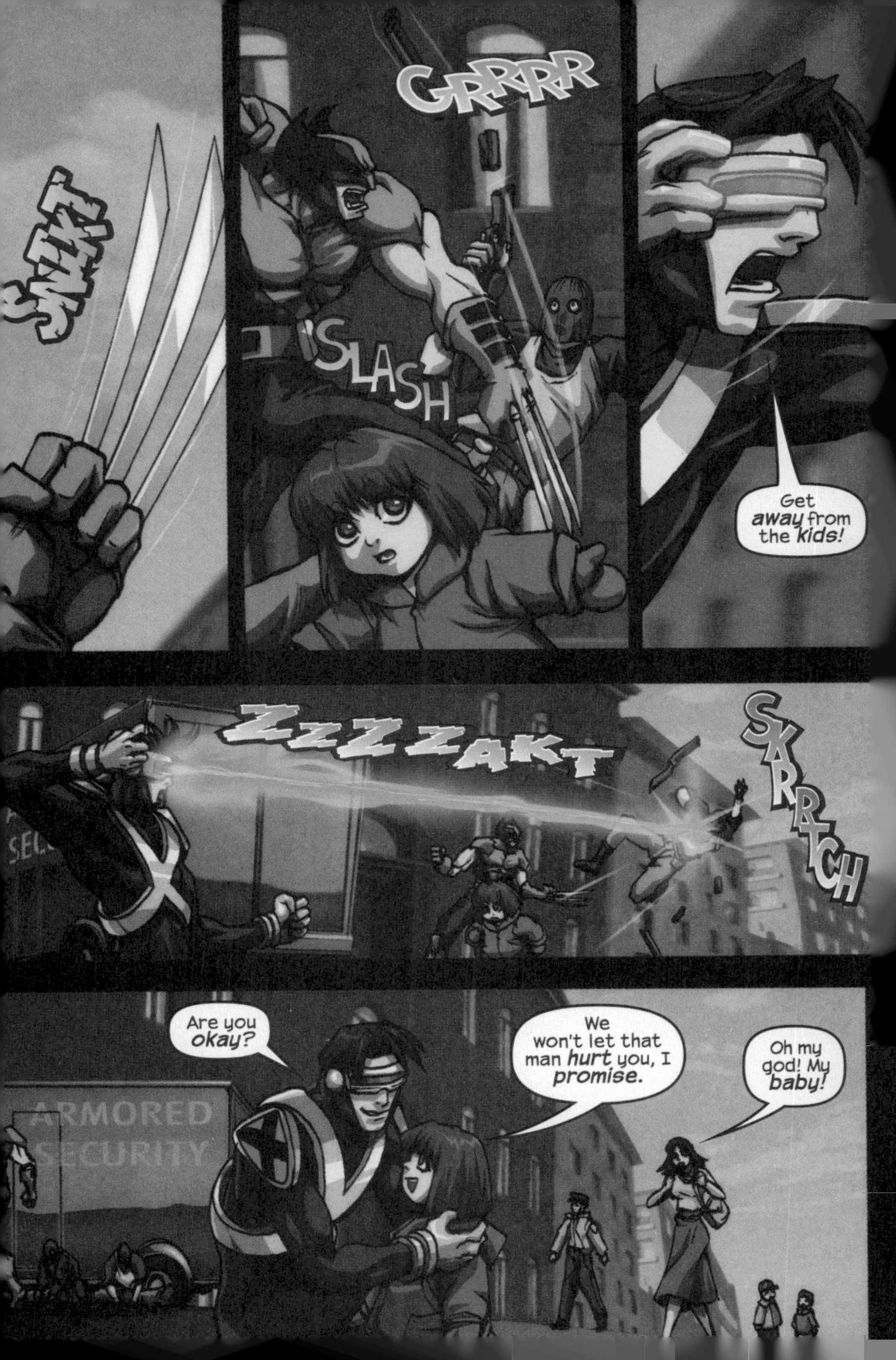
SNIKT
GRRRR
SLASH
Get away from the kids!
ZZZZZAKT
SKRRTCH
Are you okay?
We won't let that man hurt you, I promise.
Oh my god! My baby!
ARMORED SECURITY

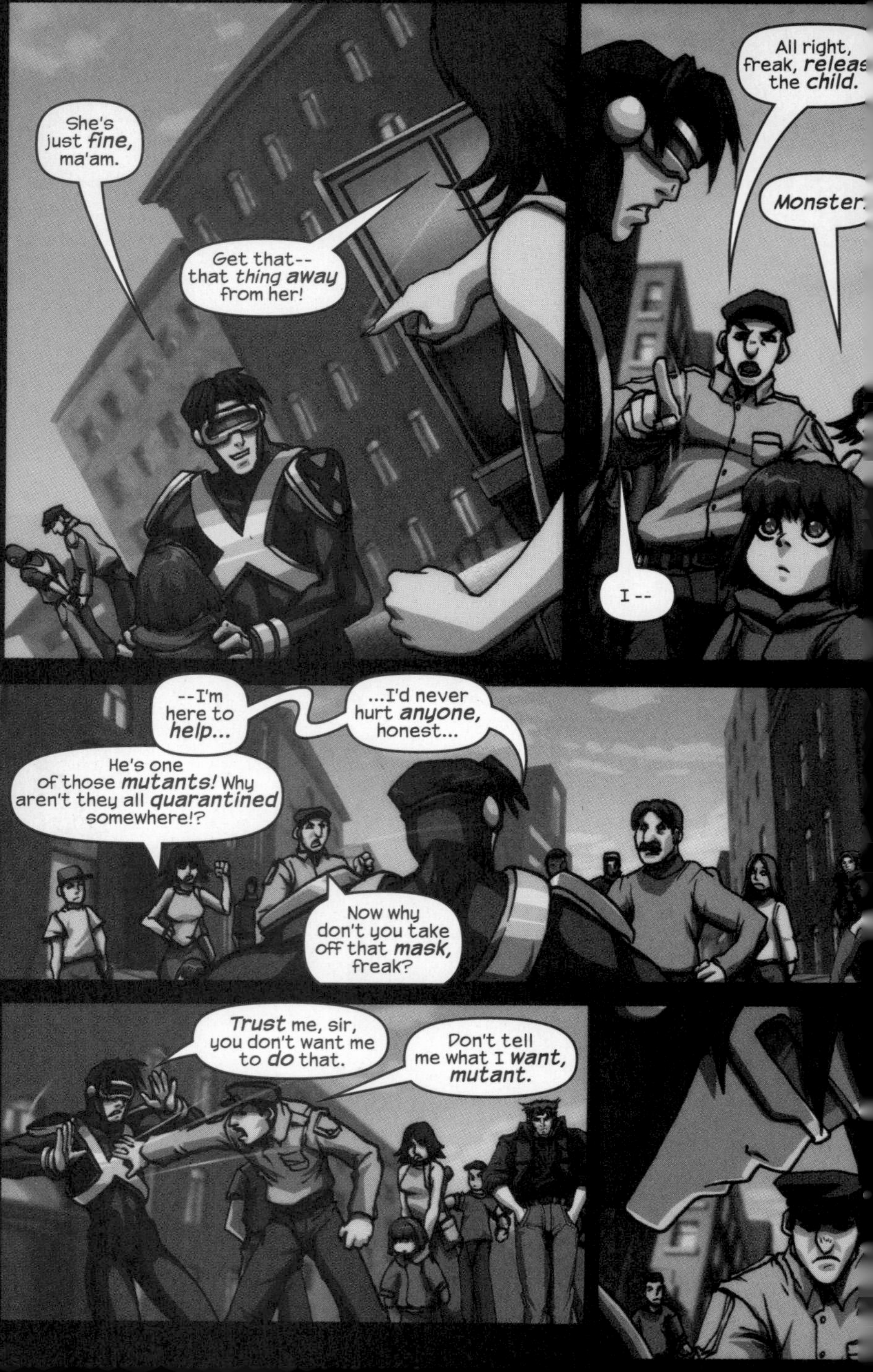
She's just *fine,* ma'am.
Get that-- that *thing away* from her!
All right, freak, *releas* the *child.*
Monster
I --
--I'm here to *help...*
...I'd never hurt *anyone,* honest...
He's one of those *mutants!* Why aren't they all *quarantined* somewhere!?
Now why don't you take off that *mask,* freak?
Trust me, sir, you don't want me to *do* that.
Don't tell me what I *want,* ***mutant.***

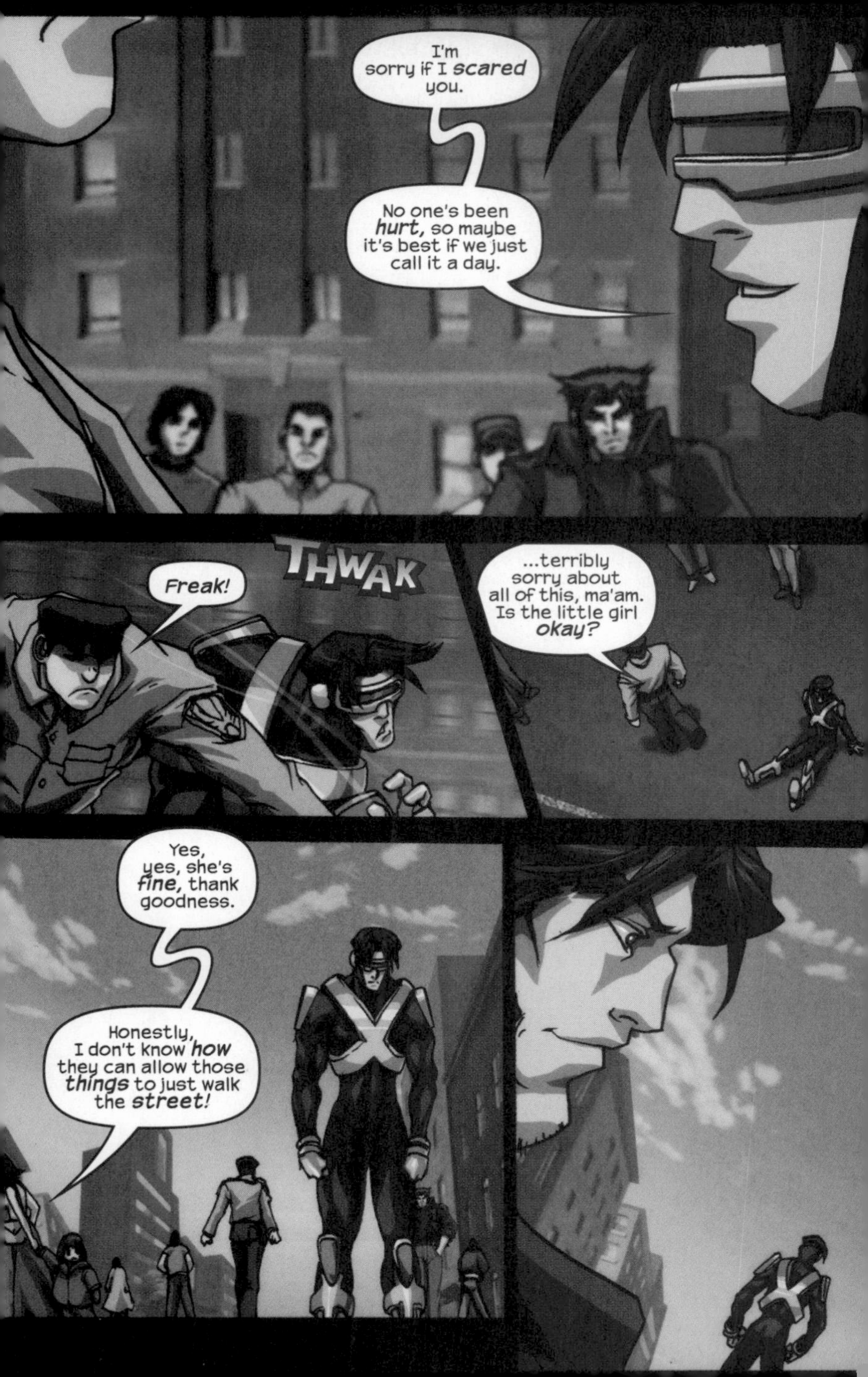
I'm sorry if I scared you.
No one's been hurt, so maybe it's best if we just call it a day.
THWAK
Freak!
...terribly sorry about all of this, ma'am. Is the little girl okay?
Yes, yes, she's fine, thank goodness.
Honestly, I don't know how they can allow those things to just walk the street!

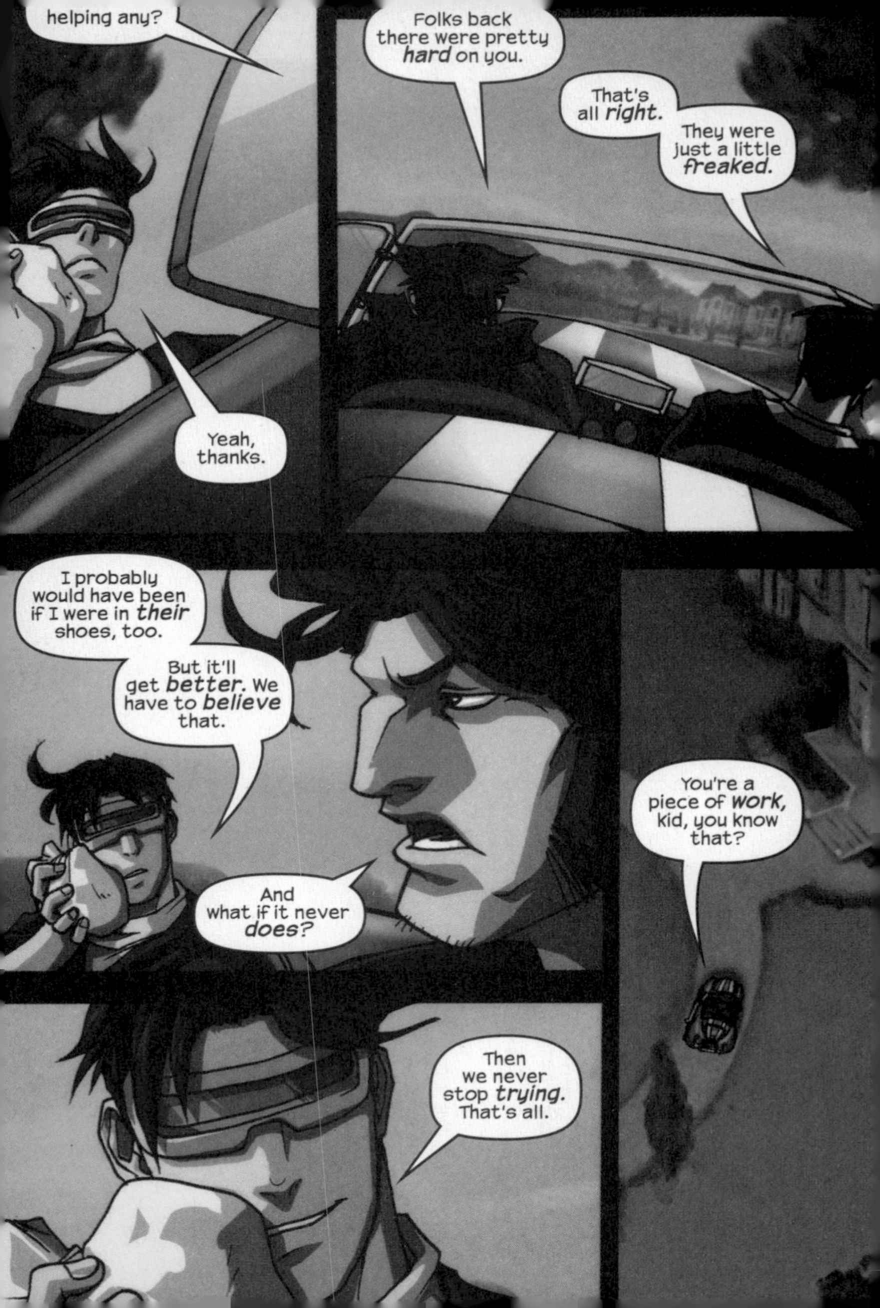
helping any?
Yeah, thanks.
Folks back there were pretty *hard* on you.
That's all *right*.
They were just a little *freaked*.
I probably would have been if I were in *their* shoes, too.
But it'll get *better*. We have to *believe* that.
And what if it never *does*?
Then we never stop *trying*. That's all.
You're a piece of *work*, kid, you know that?

Doesn't happen often, but I can admit when I'm wrong.
The kid's *good,* Charles.
You shoulda seen him today. He's the *real thing.*
I think you're telling this to the wrong person, my friend.
It's okay. I heard it all.
Let it go to your *head* and I'll have to knock it back *out.*
Fair *enough.*

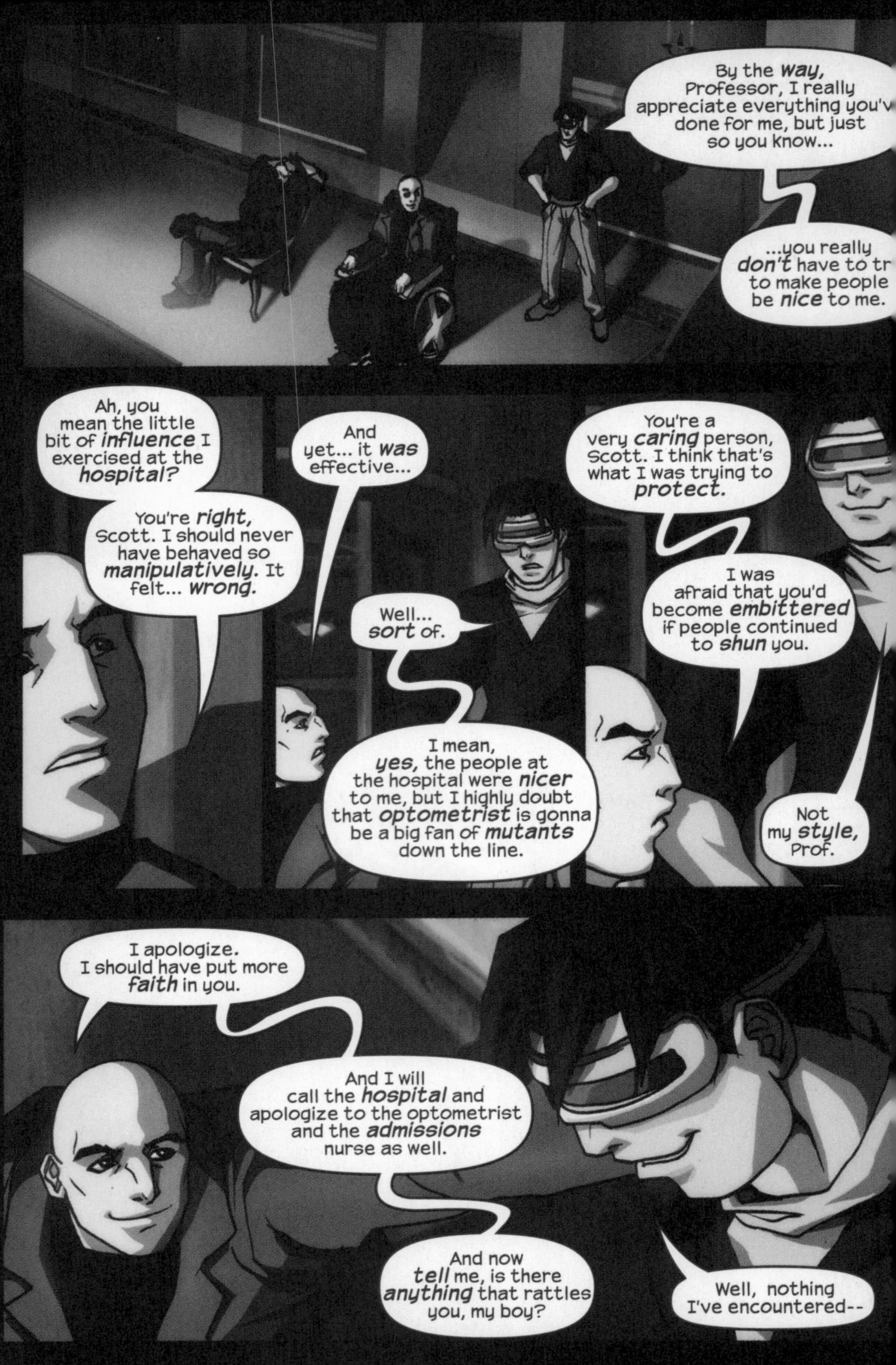
By the way, Professor, I really appreciate everything you'v done for me, but just so you know...
...you really don't have to tr to make people be nice to me.
Ah, you mean the little bit of influence I exercised at the hospital?
You're right, Scott. I should never have behaved so manipulatively. It felt... wrong.
And yet... it was effective...
Well... sort of.
I mean, yes, the people at the hospital were nicer to me, but I highly doubt that optometrist is gonna be a big fan of mutants down the line.
You're a very caring person, Scott. I think that's what I was trying to protect.
I was afraid that you'd become embittered if people continued to shun you.
Not my style, Prof.
I apologize. I should have put more faith in you.
And I will call the hospital and apologize to the optometrist and the admissions nurse as well.
And now tell me, is there anything that rattles you, my boy?
Well, nothing I've encountered--

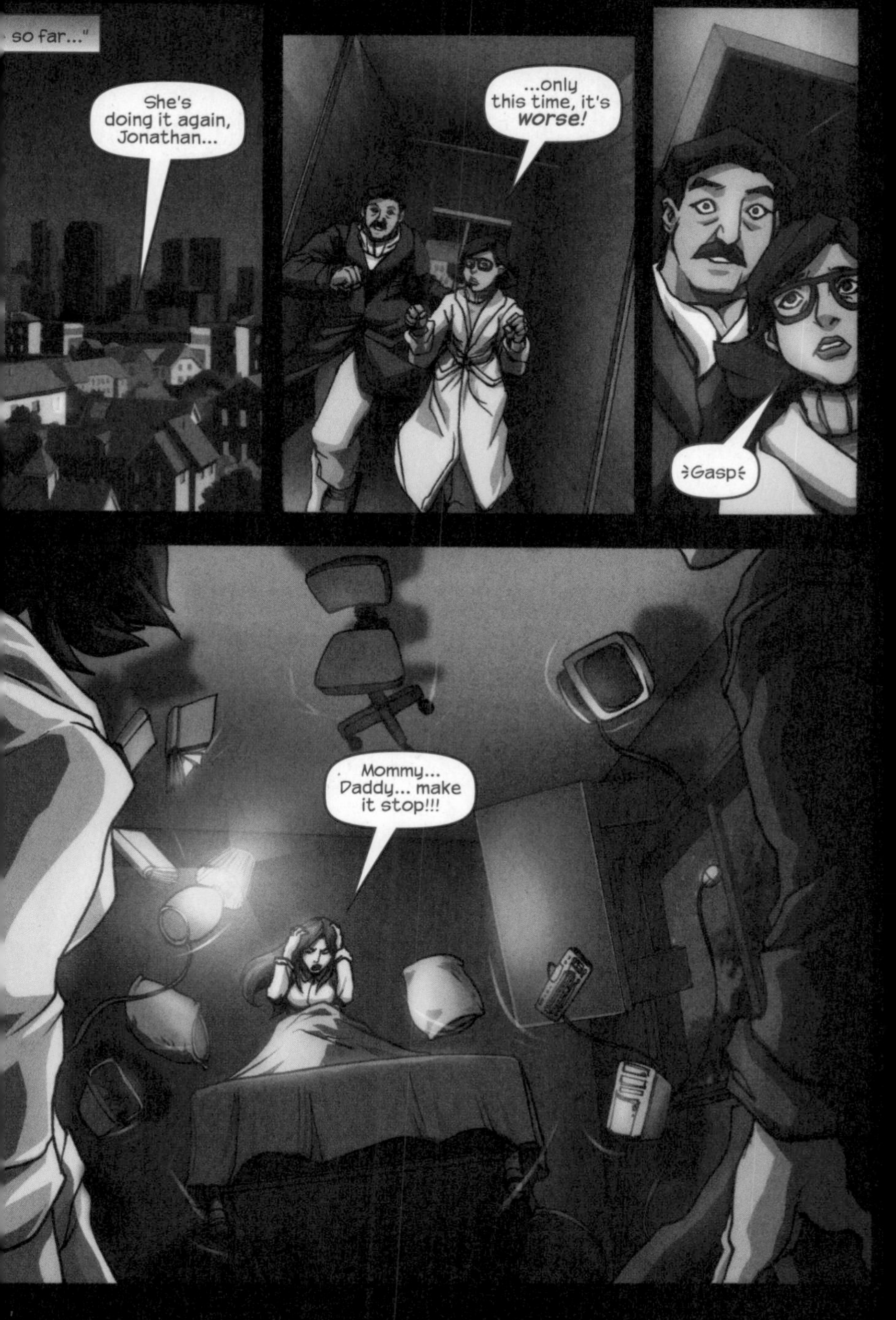
so far..."
She's doing it again, Jonathan...
...only this time, it's *worse!*
Gasp
Mommy... Daddy... make it stop!!!

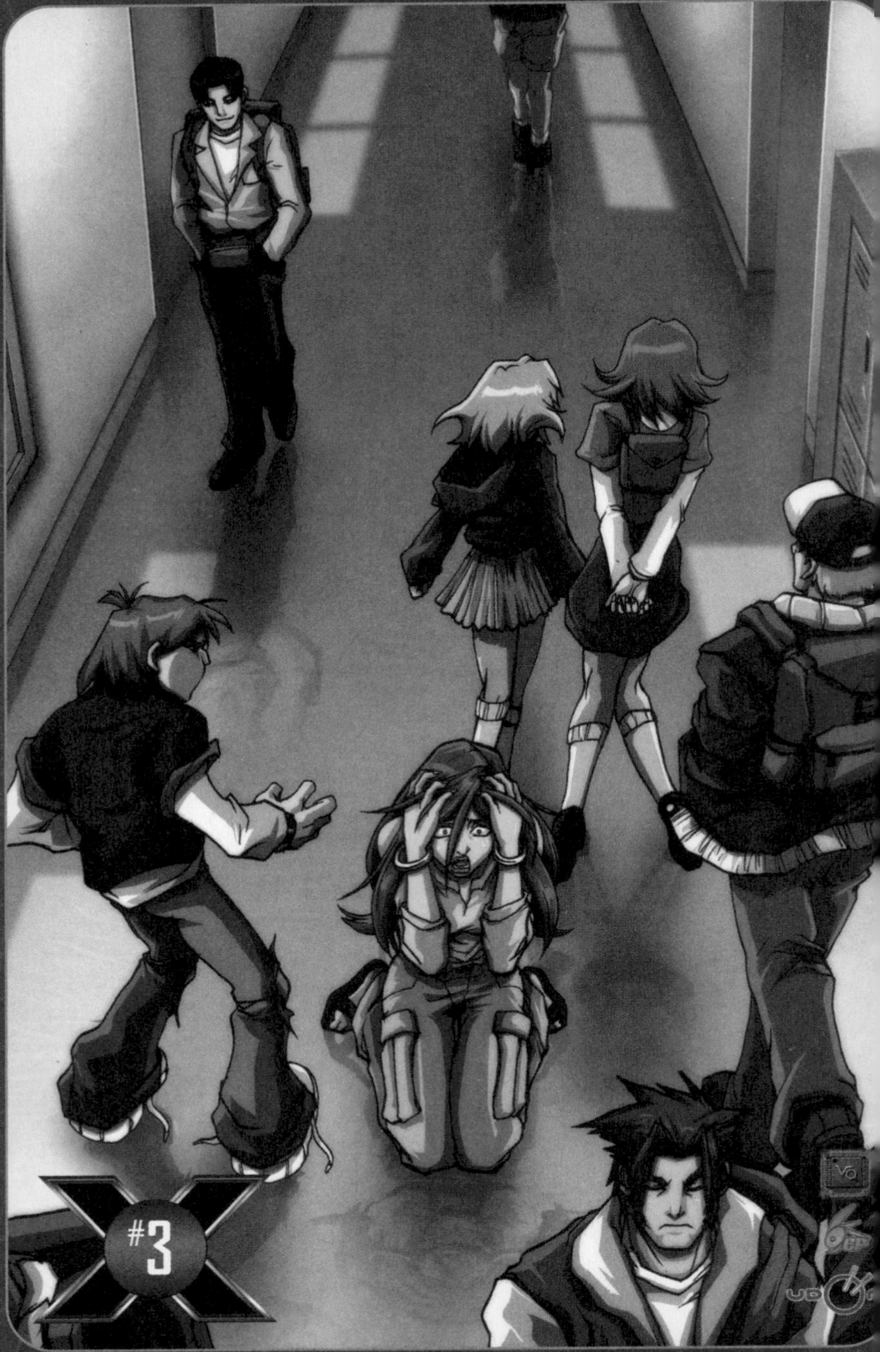
#3

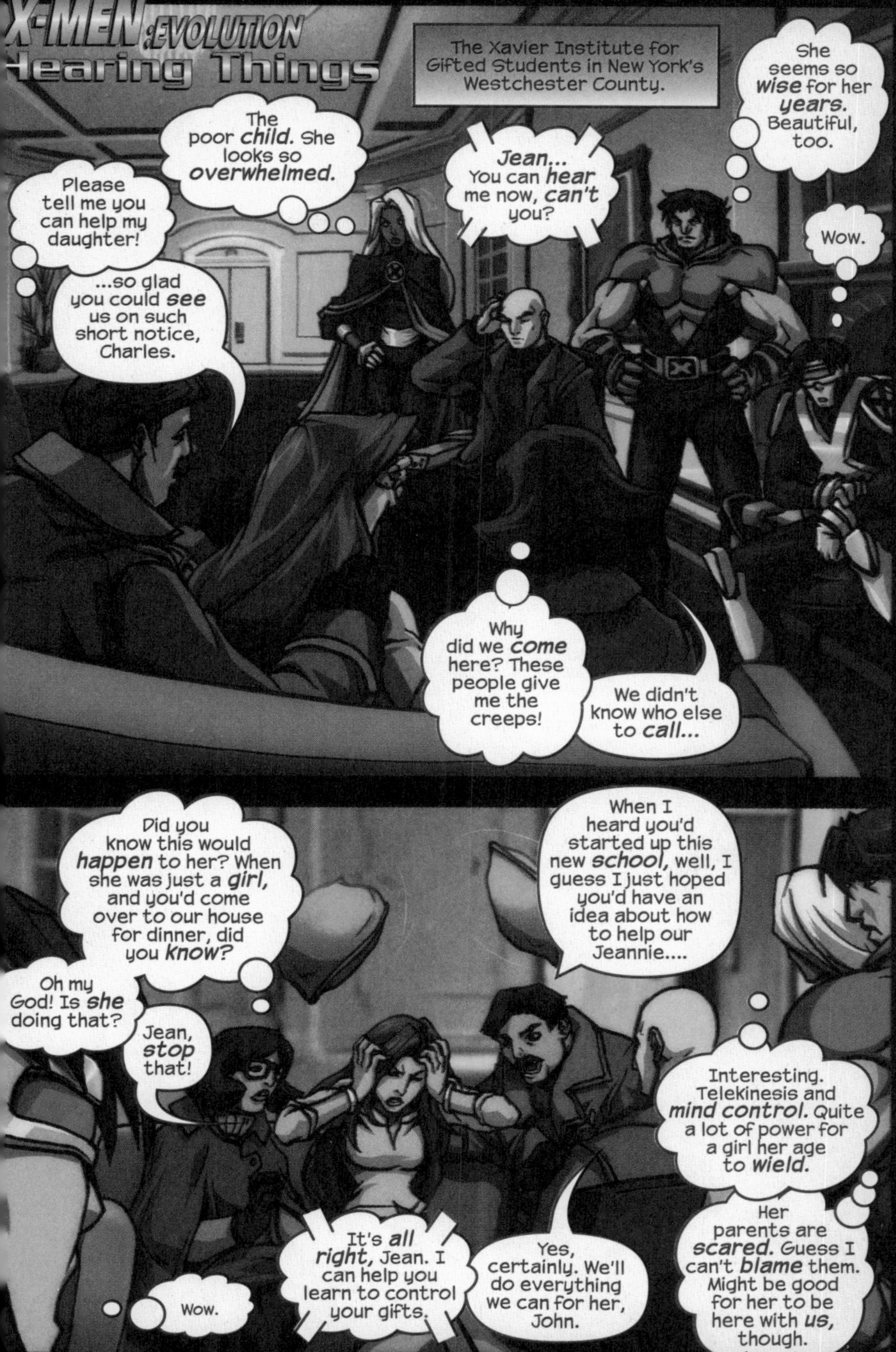
X-MEN: EVOLUTION
Hearing Things
The Xavier Institute for Gifted Students in New York's Westchester County.
Please tell me you can help my daughter!
The poor child. She looks so overwhelmed.
Jean... You can hear me now, can't you?
She seems so wise for her years. Beautiful, too.
Wow.
...so glad you could see us on such short notice, Charles.
Why did we come here? These people give me the creeps!
We didn't know who else to call...
Did you know this would happen to her? When she was just a girl, and you'd come over to our house for dinner, did you know?
When I heard you'd started up this new school, well, I guess I just hoped you'd have an idea about how to help our Jeannie....
Oh my God! Is she doing that?
Jean, stop that!
Interesting. Telekinesis and mind control. Quite a lot of power for a girl her age to wield.
Wow.
It's all right, Jean. I can help you learn to control your gifts.
Yes, certainly. We'll do everything we can for her, John.
Her parents are scared. Guess I can't blame them. Might be good for her to be here with us, though.

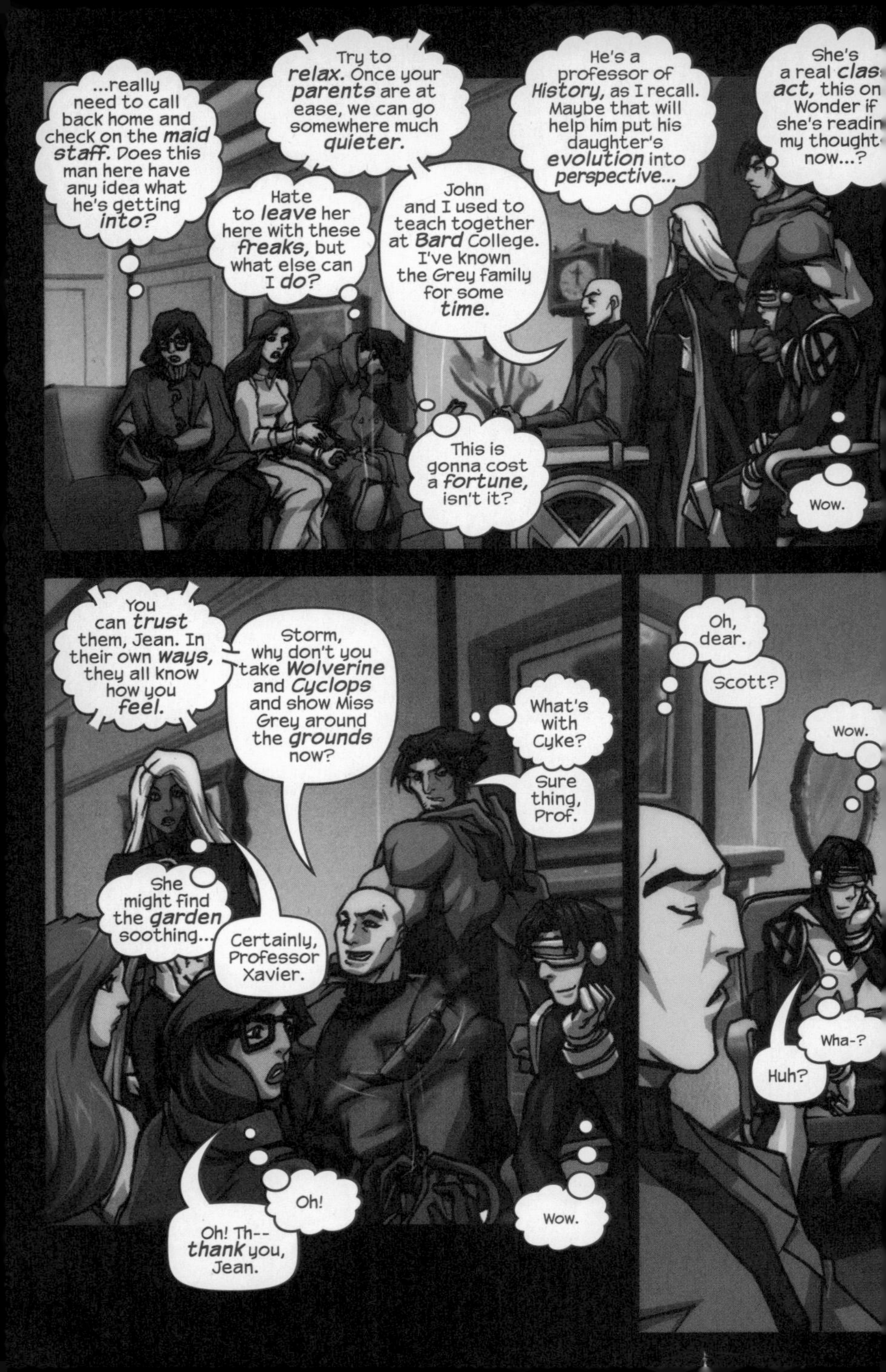

...really need to call back home and check on the maid staff. Does this man here have any idea what he's getting into?
Try to relax. Once your parents are at ease, we can go somewhere much quieter.
Hate to leave her here with these freaks, but what else can I do?
John and I used to teach together at Bard College. I've known the Grey family for some time.
He's a professor of History, as I recall. Maybe that will help him put his daughter's evolution into perspective...
She's a real clas act, this on Wonder if she's readin my thought now...?
This is gonna cost a fortune, isn't it?
Wow.
You can trust them, Jean. In their own ways, they all know how you feel.
Storm, why don't you take Wolverine and Cyclops and show Miss Grey around the grounds now?
What's with Cyke?
Sure thing, Prof.
She might find the garden soothing...
Certainly, Professor Xavier.
Oh!
Oh! Th--thank you, Jean.
Wow.
Oh, dear.
Scott?
Wow.
Wha-?
Huh?

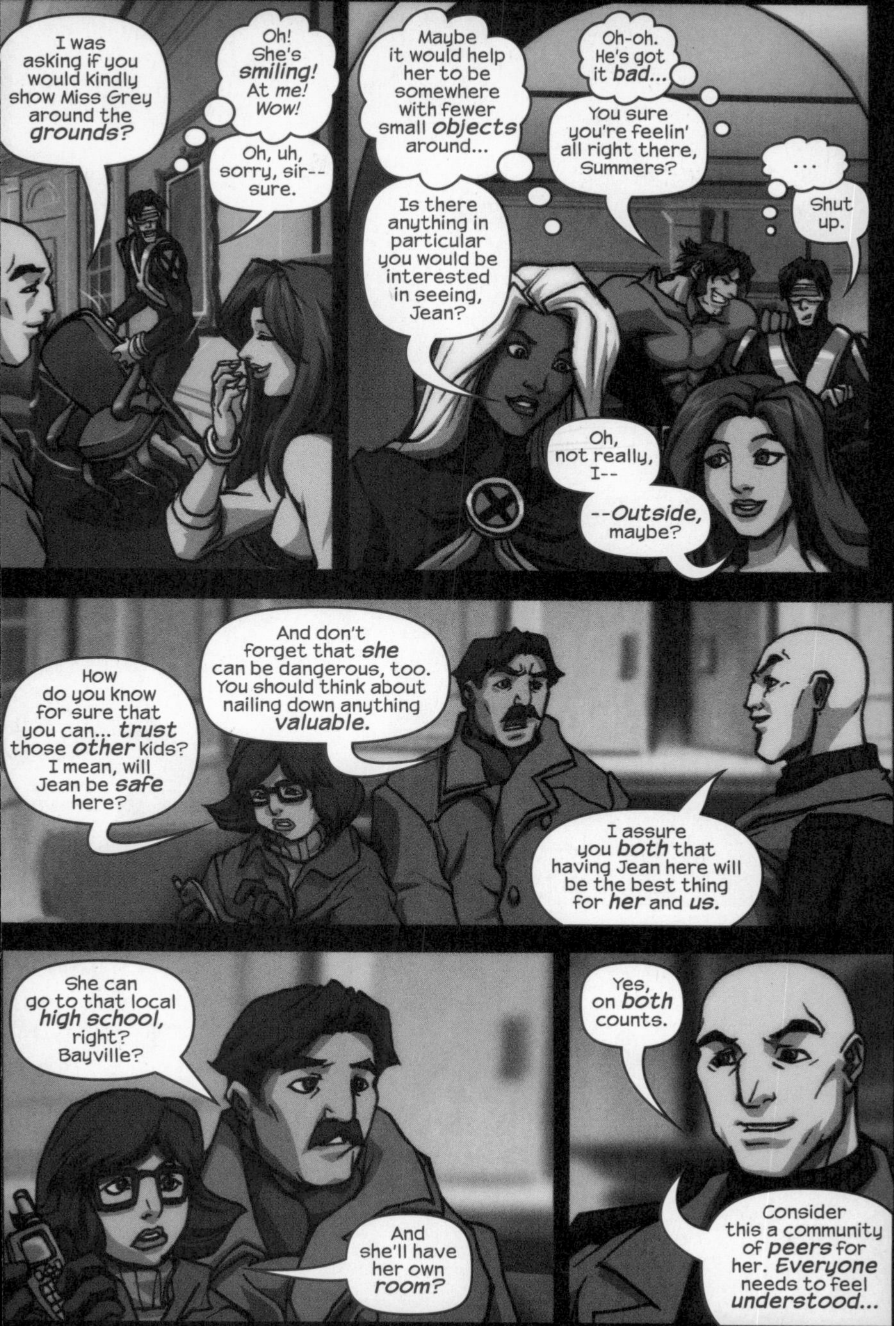
I was asking if you would kindly show Miss Grey around the grounds?
Oh! She's smiling! At me! Wow!
Oh, uh, sorry, sir-- sure.
Maybe it would help her to be somewhere with fewer small objects around...
Is there anything in particular you would be interested in seeing, Jean?
Oh-oh. He's got it bad...
You sure you're feelin' all right there, Summers?
...
Shut up.
Oh, not really, I--
--Outside, maybe?
How do you know for sure that you can... trust those other kids? I mean, will Jean be safe here?
And don't forget that she can be dangerous, too. You should think about nailing down anything valuable.
I assure you both that having Jean here will be the best thing for her and us.
She can go to that local high school, right? Bayville?
And she'll have her own room?
Yes, on both counts.
Consider this a community of peers for her. Everyone needs to feel understood...

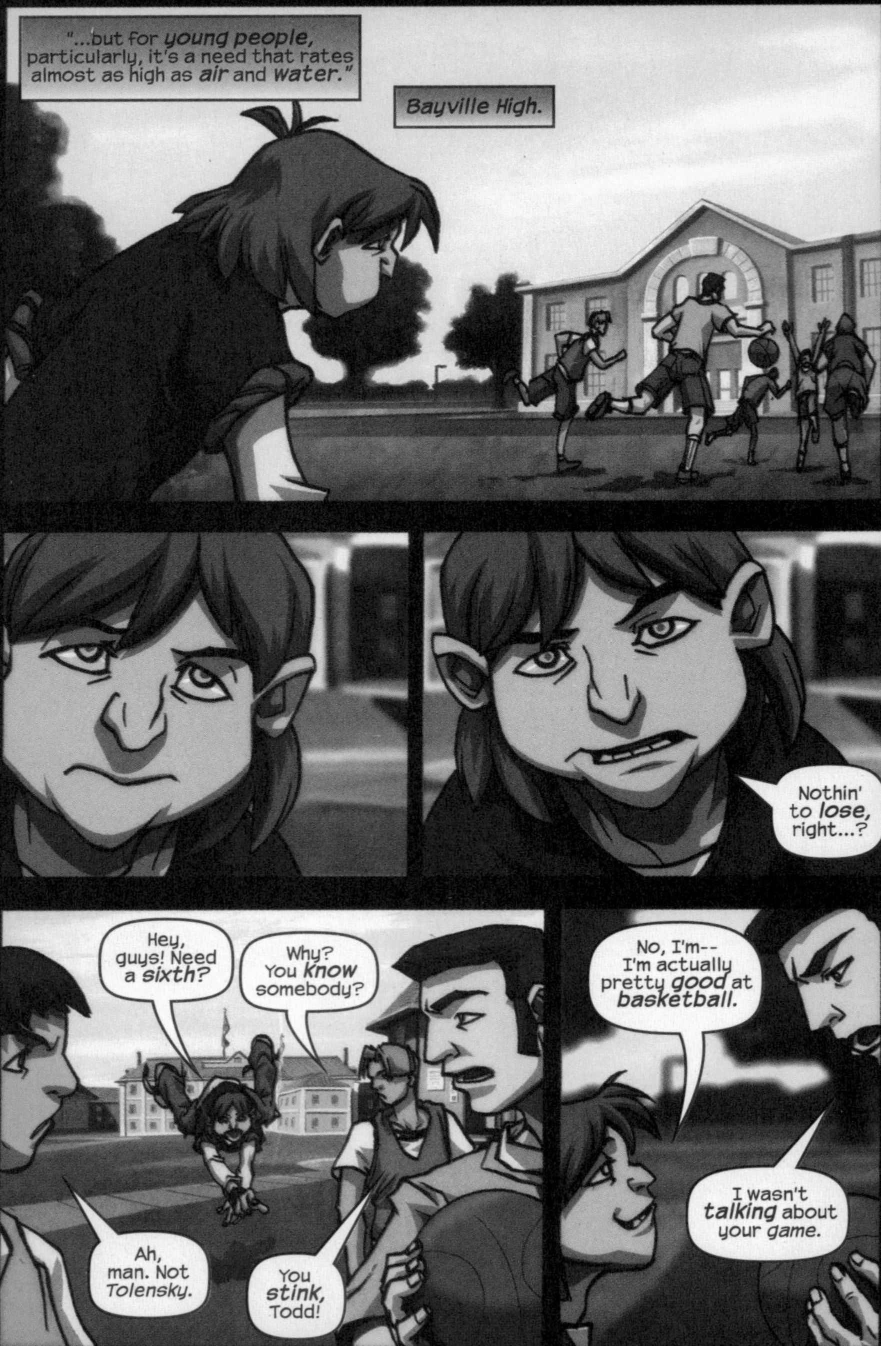
"...but for young people, particularly, it's a need that rates almost as high as air and water."
Bayville High.
Nothin' to lose, right...?
Hey, guys! Need a sixth?
Why? You know somebody?
Ah, man. Not Tolensky.
You stink, Todd!
No, I'm-- I'm actually pretty good at basketball.
I wasn't talking about your game.

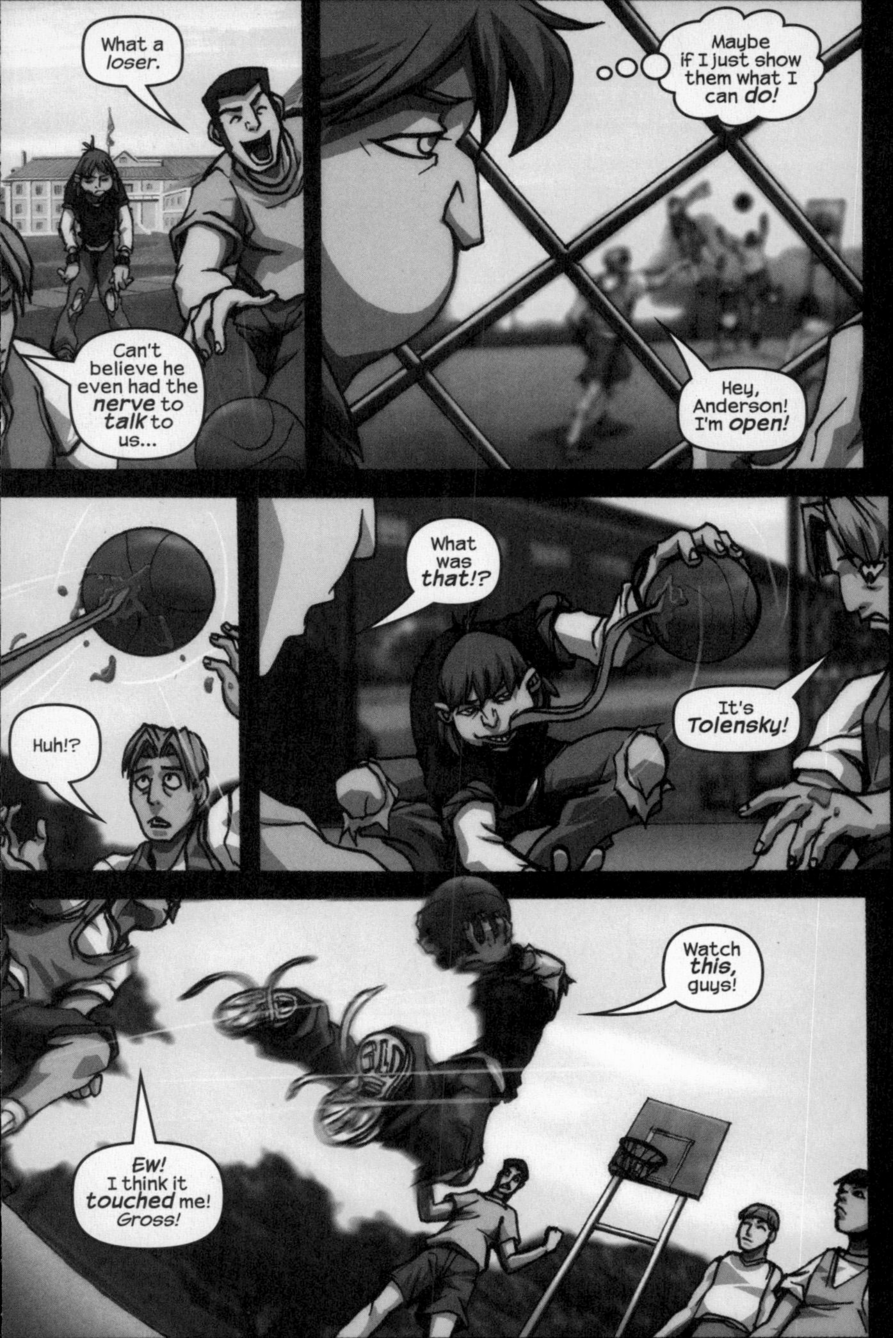
What a *loser.*
Can't believe he even had the ***nerve*** to ***talk*** to us...
Maybe if I just show them what I can ***do!***
Hey, Anderson! I'm ***open!***
Huh!?
What was ***that!?***
It's ***Tolensky!***
Watch ***this,*** guys!
Ew! I think it ***touched*** me! *Gross!*

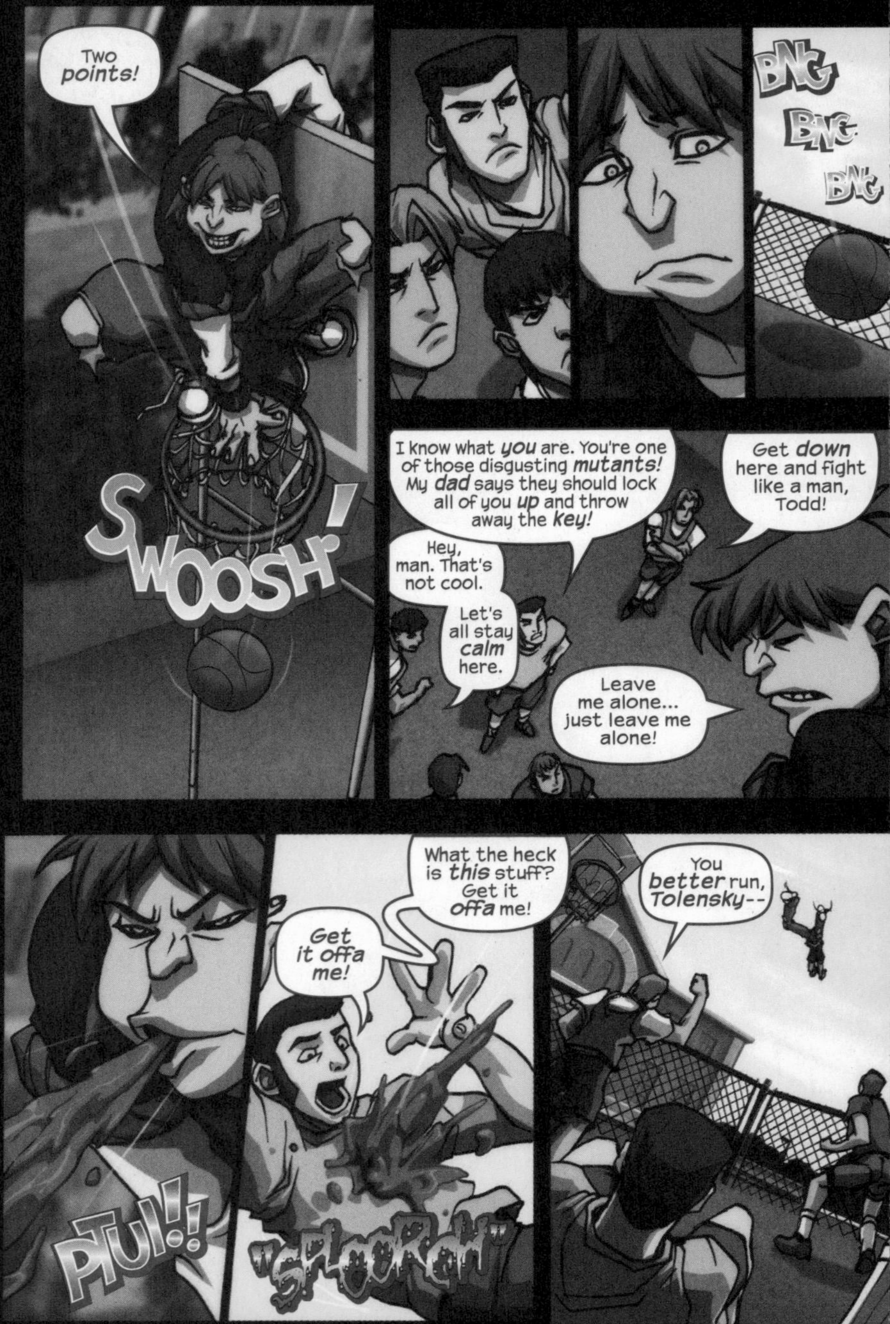
Two points!
SWOOSH!
BANG
BANG
BANG
I know what you are. You're one of those disgusting mutants! My dad says they should lock all of you up and throw away the key!
Get down here and fight like a man, Todd!
Hey, man. That's not cool.
Let's all stay calm here.
Leave me alone... just leave me alone!
PTUI!!
What the heck is this stuff? Get it offa me!
Get it offa me!
SPLOORCH
You better run, Tolensky--

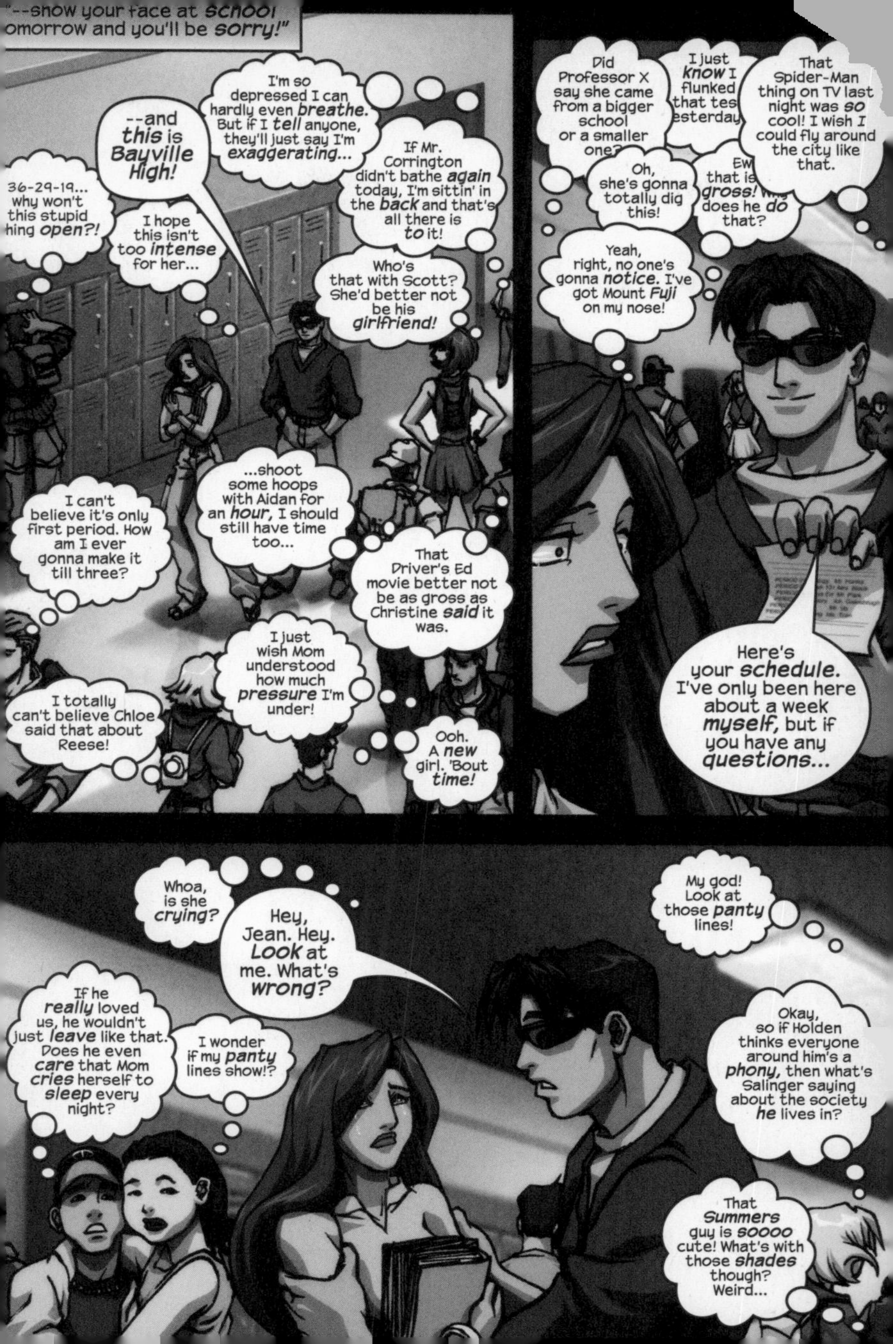
"--show your face at school
omorrow and you'll be sorry!"
--and this is Bayville High!
I'm so depressed I can hardly even breathe. But if I tell anyone, they'll just say I'm exaggerating...
36-29-19... why won't this stupid hing open?!
I hope this isn't too intense for her...
If Mr. Corrington didn't bathe again today, I'm sittin' in the back and that's all there is to it!
Who's that with Scott? She'd better not be his girlfriend!
I can't believe it's only first period. How am I ever gonna make it till three?
...shoot some hoops with Aidan for an hour, I should still have time too...
That Driver's Ed movie better not be as gross as Christine said it was.
I just wish Mom understood how much pressure I'm under!
I totally can't believe Chloe said that about Reese!
Ooh. A new girl. 'Bout time!
Did Professor X say she came from a bigger school or a smaller one?
I just know I flunked that tes esterday
That Spider-Man thing on TV last night was so cool! I wish I could fly around the city like that.
Oh, she's gonna totally dig this!
Ew that is gross! does he do that?
Yeah, right, no one's gonna notice. I've got Mount Fuji on my nose!
Here's your schedule. I've only been here about a week myself, but if you have any questions...
Whoa, is she crying?
Hey, Jean. Hey. Look at me. What's wrong?
My god! Look at those panty lines!
If he really loved us, he wouldn't just leave like that. Does he even care that Mom cries herself to sleep every night?
I wonder if my panty lines show!?
Okay, so if Holden thinks everyone around him's a phony, then what's Salinger saying about the society he lives in?
That Summers guy is soooo cute! What's with those shades though? Weird...

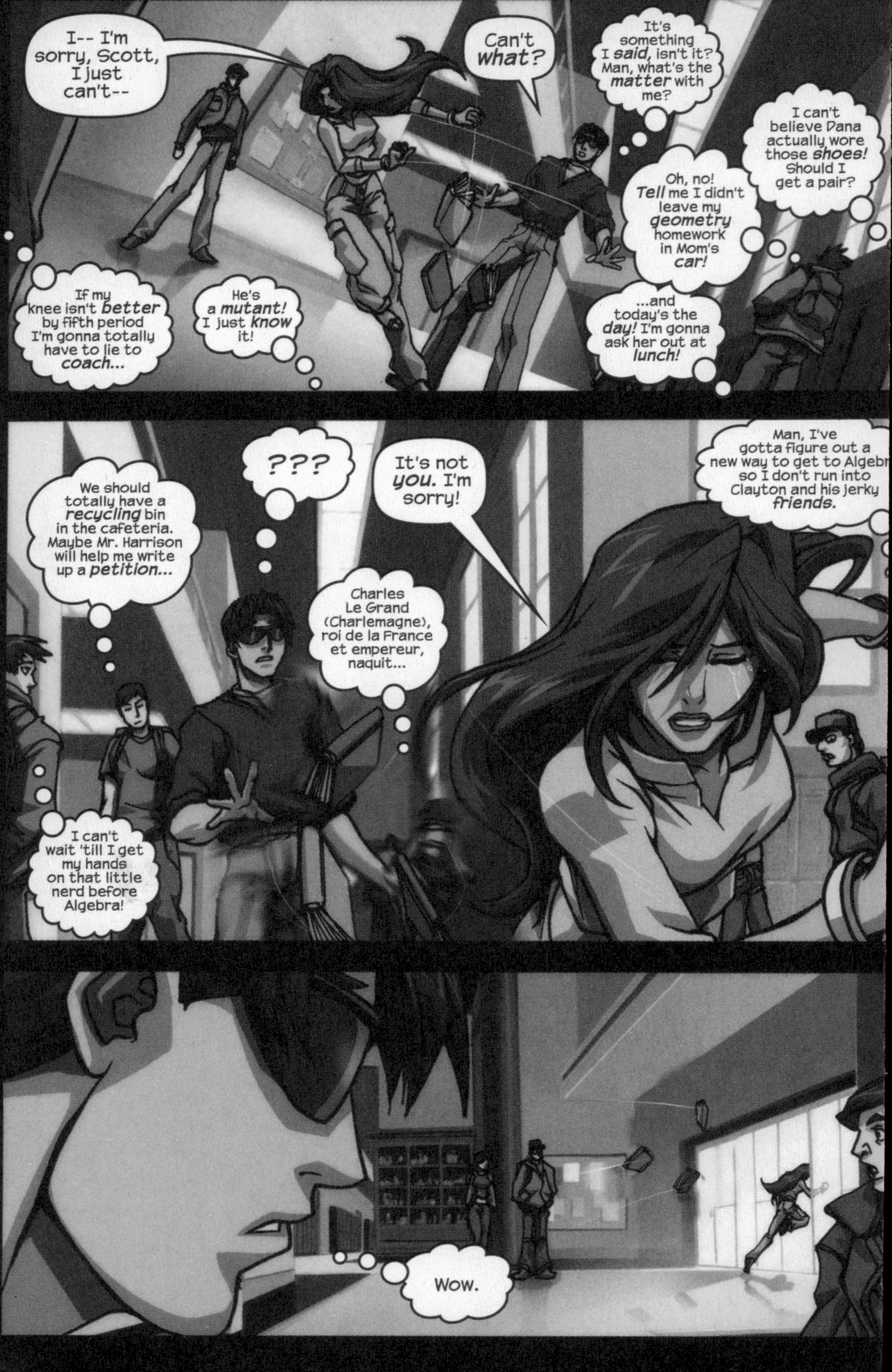
I-- I'm sorry, Scott, I just can't--
Can't what?
It's something I said, isn't it? Man, what's the matter with me?
I can't believe Dana actually wore those shoes! Should I get a pair?
Oh, no! Tell me I didn't leave my geometry homework in Mom's car!
If my knee isn't better by fifth period I'm gonna totally have to lie to coach...
He's a mutant! I just know it!
...and today's the day! I'm gonna ask her out at lunch!
We should totally have a recycling bin in the cafeteria. Maybe Mr. Harrison will help me write up a petition...
???
It's not you. I'm sorry!
Man, I've gotta figure out a new way to get to Algebr so I don't run into Clayton and his jerky friends.
Charles Le Grand (Charlemagne), roi de la France et empereur, naquit...
I can't wait 'till I get my hands on that little nerd before Algebra!
Wow.

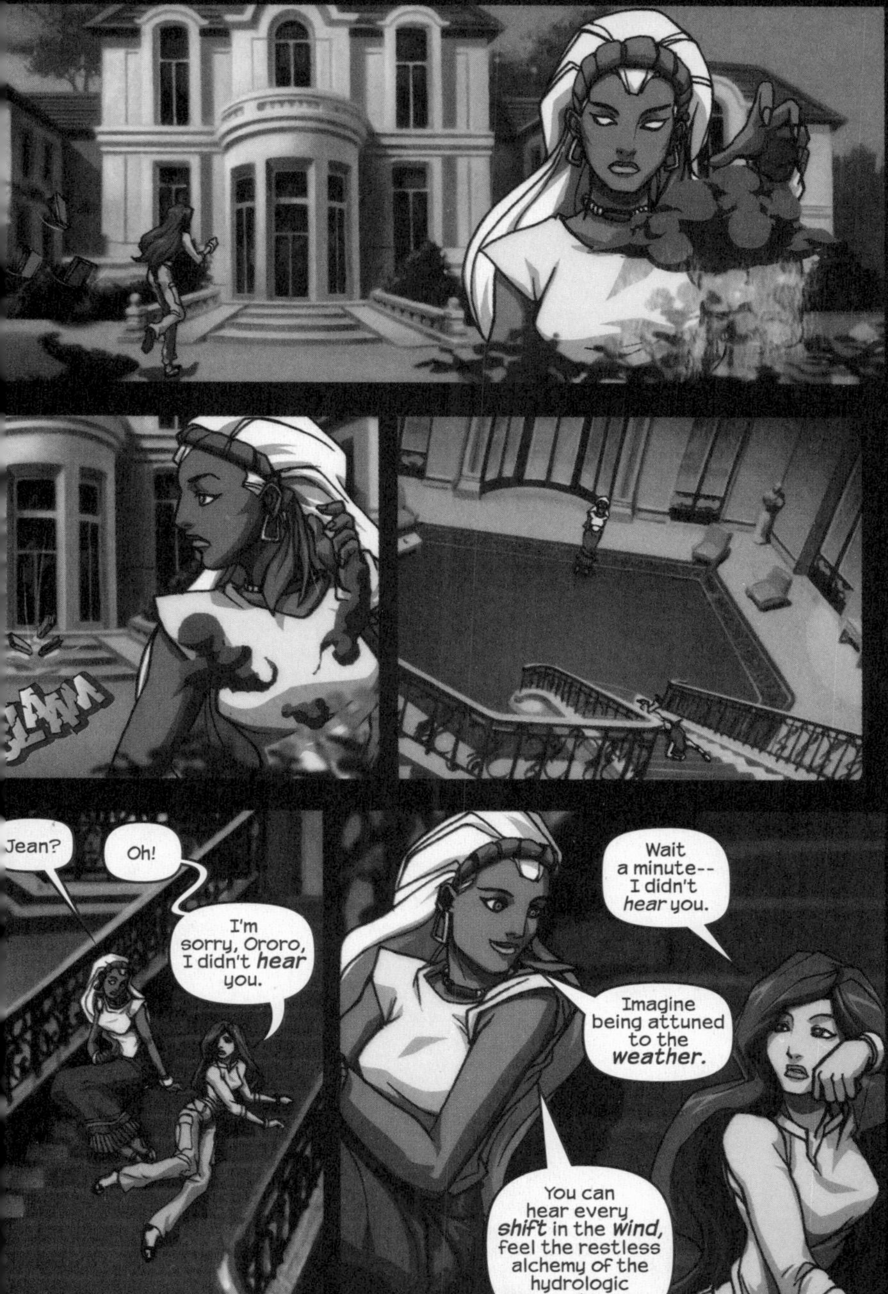
SLAMM
Jean?
Oh!
I'm sorry, Ororo, I didn't *hear* you.
Wait a minute-- I didn't *hear* you.
Imagine being attuned to the *weather.*
You can hear every *shift* in the *wind,* feel the restless alchemy of the hydrologic cycle...

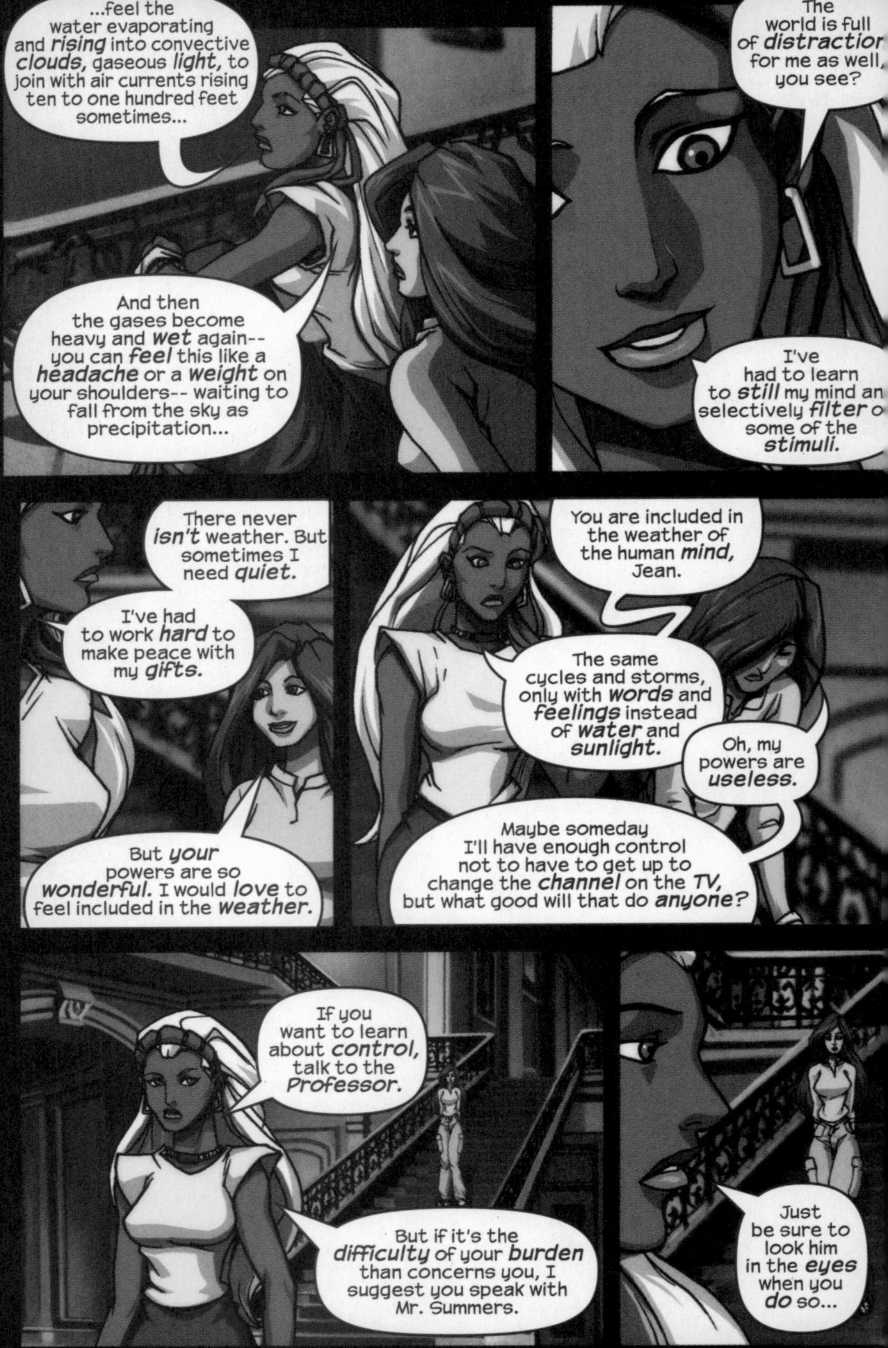
...feel the water evaporating and rising into convective clouds, gaseous light, to join with air currents rising ten to one hundred feet sometimes...
And then the gases become heavy and wet again-- you can feel this like a headache or a weight on your shoulders-- waiting to fall from the sky as precipitation...
The world is full of distractior for me as well, you see?
I've had to learn to still my mind an selectively filter o some of the stimuli.
There never isn't weather. But sometimes I need quiet.
I've had to work hard to make peace with my gifts.
But your powers are so wonderful. I would love to feel included in the weather.
You are included in the weather of the human mind, Jean.
The same cycles and storms, only with words and feelings instead of water and sunlight.
Oh, my powers are useless.
Maybe someday I'll have enough control not to have to get up to change the channel on the TV, but what good will that do anyone?
If you want to learn about control, talk to the Professor.
But if it's the difficulty of your burden than concerns you, I suggest you speak with Mr. Summers.
Just be sure to look him in the eyes when you do so...

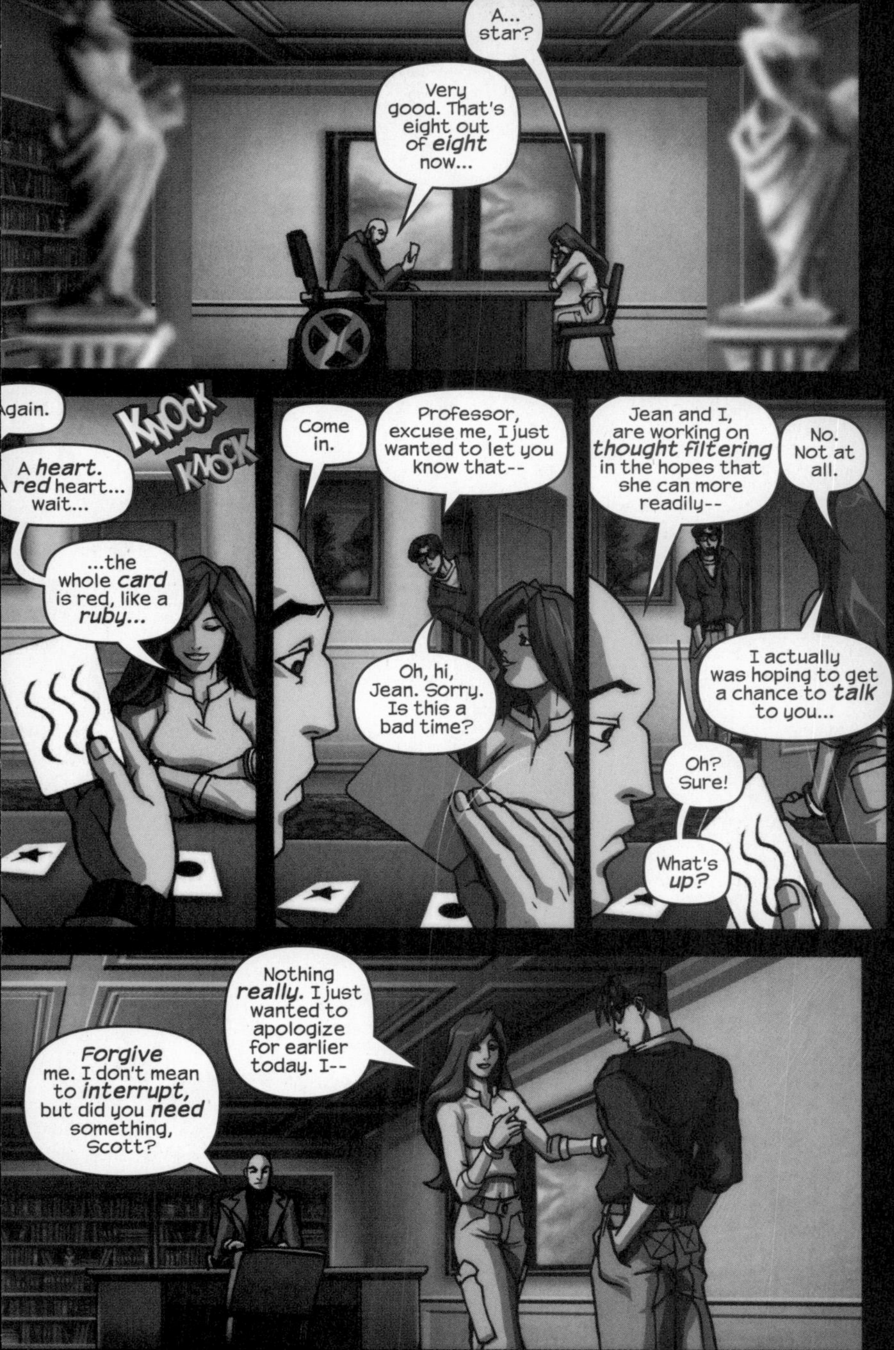
A... star?
Very good. That's eight out of *eight* now...
Again.
KNOCK KNOCK
A *heart.* A *red* heart... wait...
...the whole *card* is red, like a *ruby...*
Come in.
Professor, excuse me, I just wanted to let you know that--
Oh, hi, Jean. Sorry. Is this a bad time?
Jean and I, are working on *thought filtering* in the hopes that she can more readily--
No. Not at all.
I actually was hoping to get a chance to *talk* to you...
Oh? Sure!
What's *up?*
Nothing *really.* I just wanted to apologize for earlier today. I--
Forgive me. I don't mean to *interrupt,* but did you *need* something, Scott?

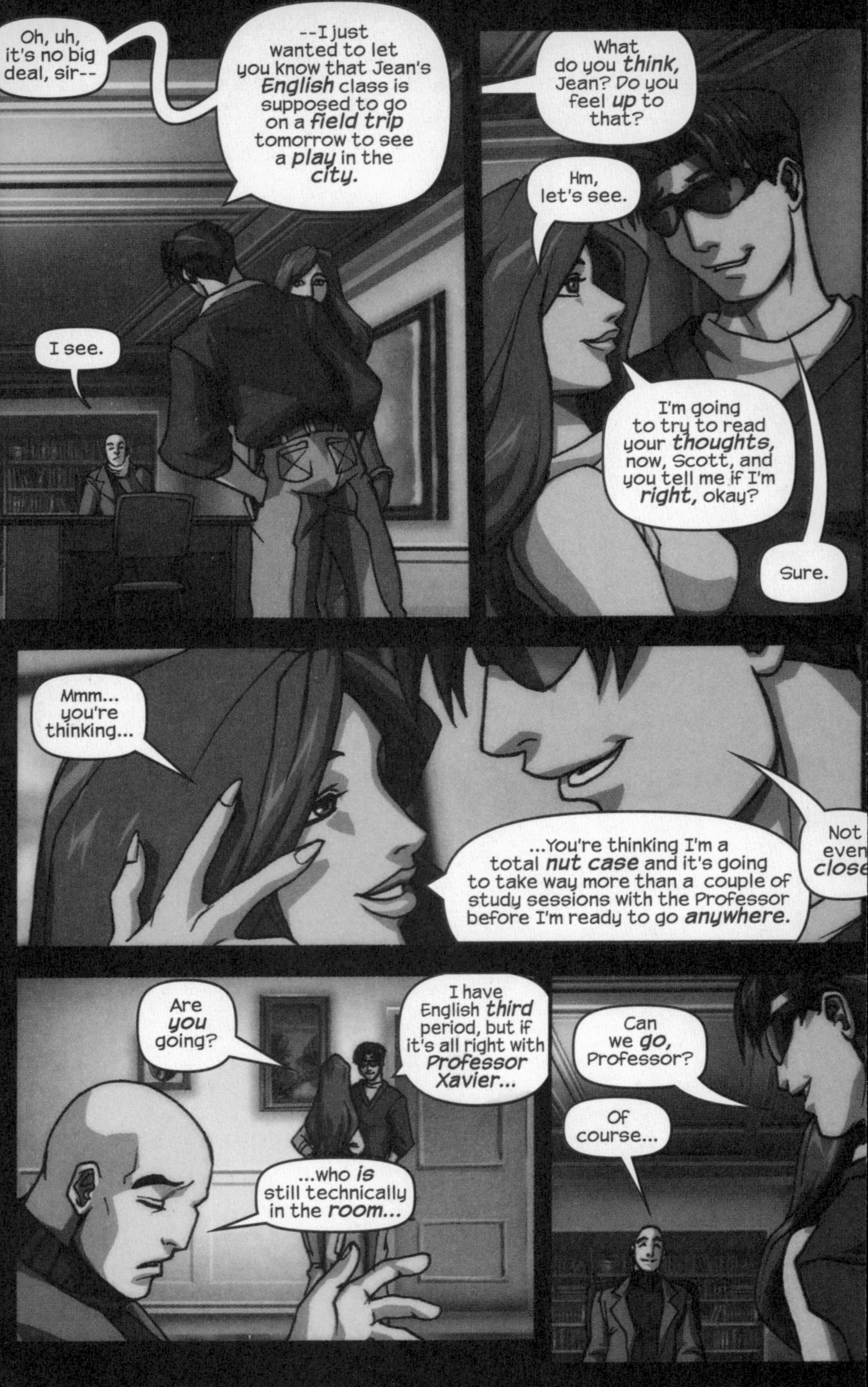

Oh, uh, it's no big deal, sir--
--I just wanted to let you know that Jean's English class is supposed to go on a field trip tomorrow to see a play in the city.
I see.
What do you think, Jean? Do you feel up to that?
Hm, let's see.
I'm going to try to read your thoughts, now, Scott, and you tell me if I'm right, okay?
Sure.
Mmm... you're thinking...
...You're thinking I'm a total nut case and it's going to take way more than a couple of study sessions with the Professor before I'm ready to go anywhere.
Not even close
Are you going?
I have English third period, but if it's all right with Professor Xavier...
...who is still technically in the room...
Can we go, Professor?
Of course...

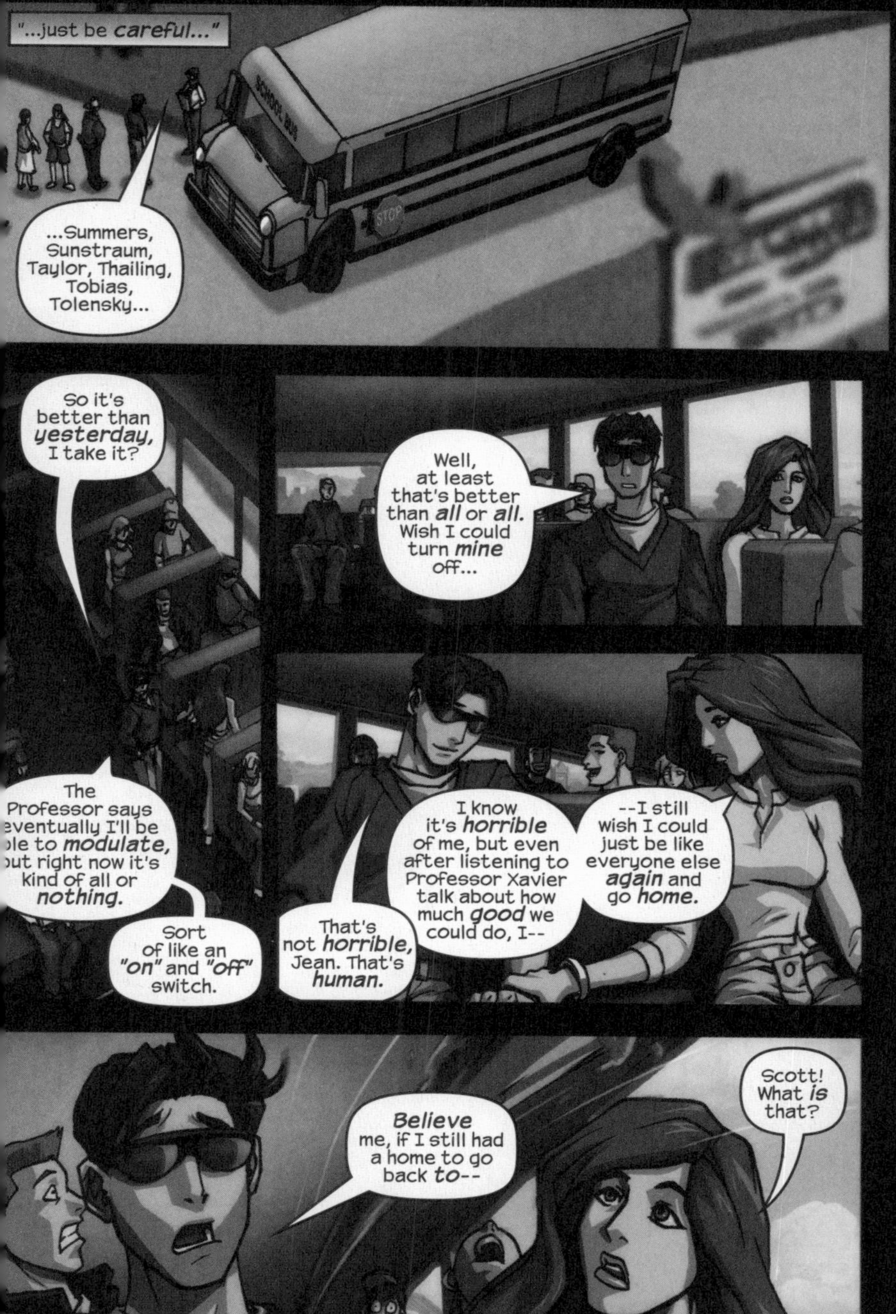
"...just be careful..."
...Summers, Sunstraum, Taylor, Thailing, Tobias, Tolensky...
So it's better than yesterday, I take it?
Well, at least that's better than all or all. Wish I could turn mine off...
The Professor says eventually I'll be ble to modulate, ut right now it's kind of all or nothing.
Sort of like an "on" and "off" switch.
I know it's horrible of me, but even after listening to Professor Xavier talk about how much good we could do, I--
--I still wish I could just be like everyone else again and go home.
That's not horrible, Jean. That's human.
Believe me, if I still had a home to go back to--
Scott! What is that?

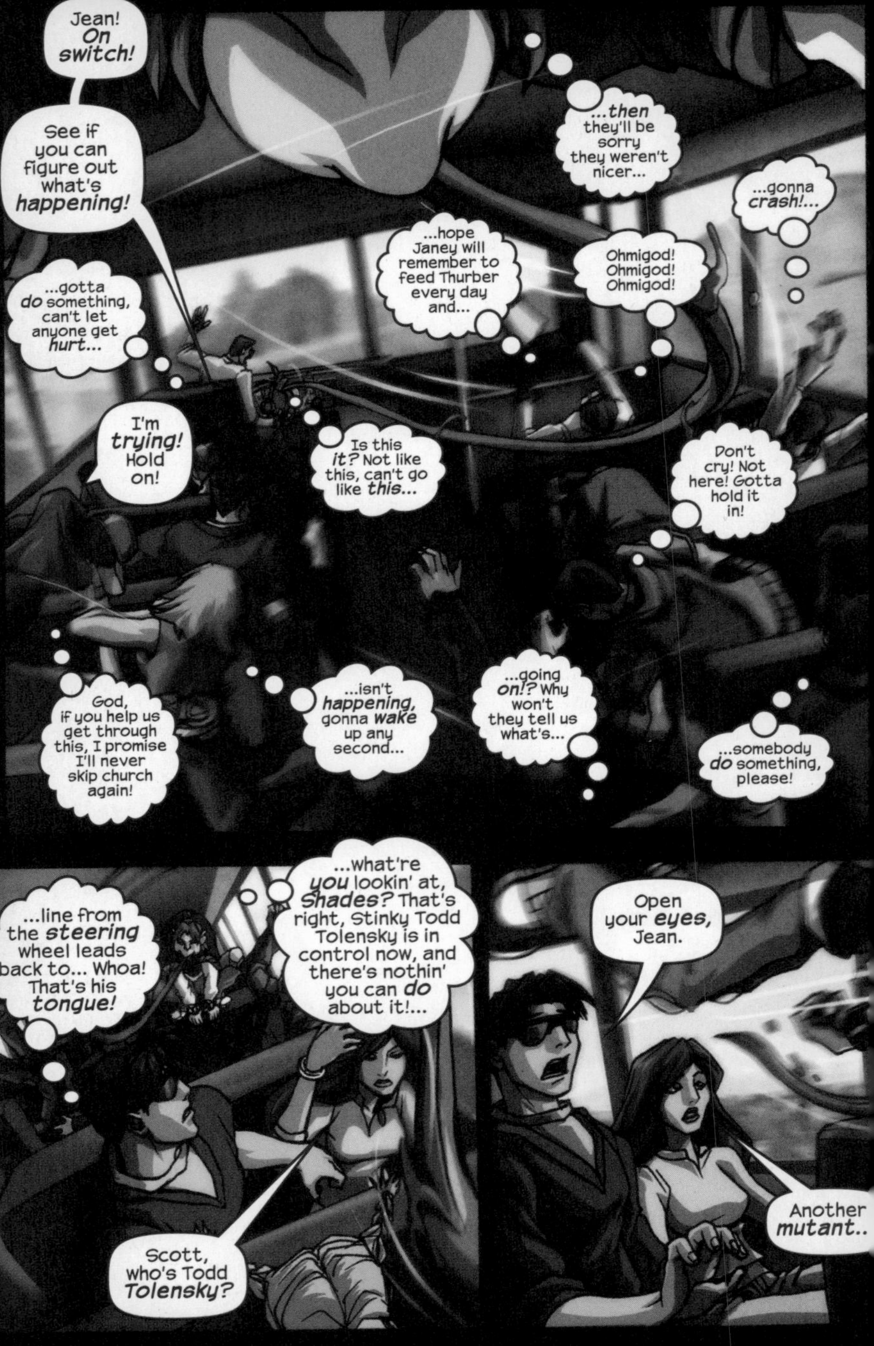
Jean! On switch!
See if you can figure out what's happening!
...then they'll be sorry they weren't nicer...
...gonna crash!...
...hope Janey will remember to feed Thurber every day and...
Ohmigod! Ohmigod! Ohmigod!
...gotta do something, can't let anyone get hurt...
I'm trying! Hold on!
Is this it? Not like this, can't go like this...
Don't cry! Not here! Gotta hold it in!
God, if you help us get through this, I promise I'll never skip church again!
...isn't happening, gonna wake up any second...
...going on!? Why won't they tell us what's...
...somebody do something, please!
...line from the steering wheel leads back to... Whoa! That's his tongue!
...what're you lookin' at, Shades? That's right, Stinky Todd Tolensky is in control now, and there's nothin' you can do about it!...
Scott, who's Todd Tolensky?
Open your eyes, Jean.
Another mutant..

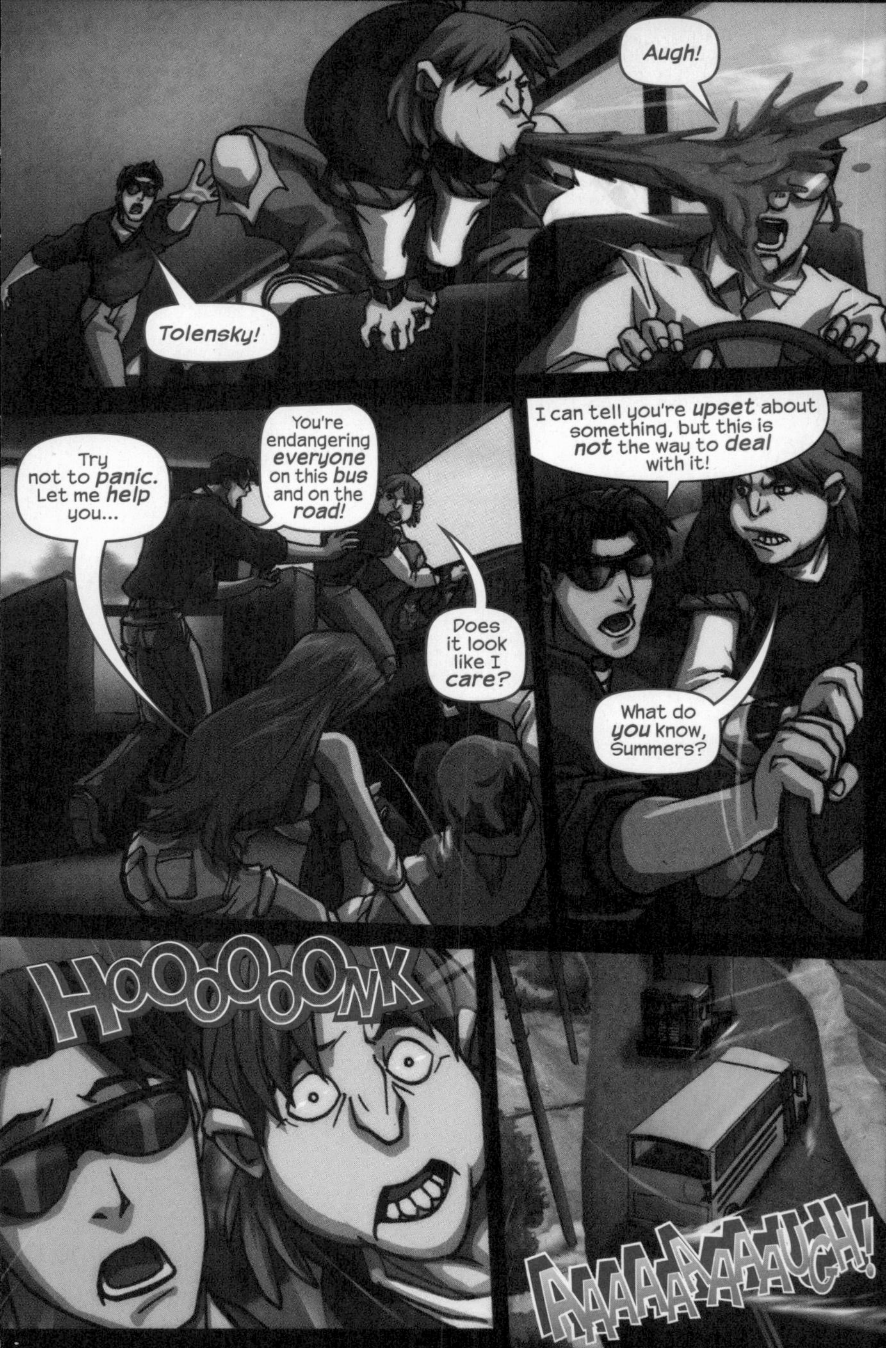
Augh!
Tolensky!
Try not to panic. Let me help you...
You're endangering everyone on this bus and on the road!
Does it look like I care?
I can tell you're upset about something, but this is not the way to deal with it!
What do you know, Summers?
HOOOOOONK
AAAAAAAAAUGH!

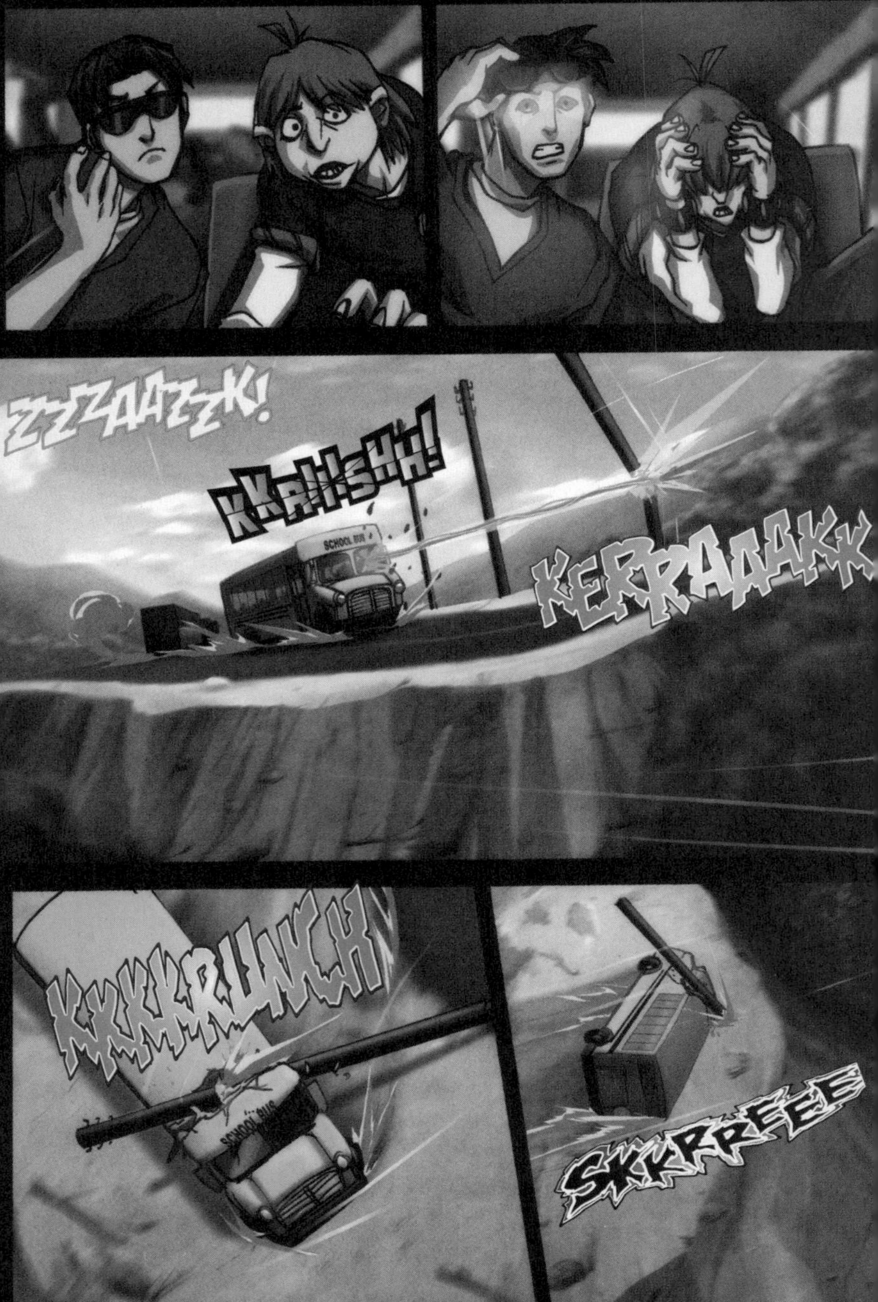
ZZZAAAZZK!
KKRIIISHH!
SCHOOL BUS
KERRAAAKK
KKKKRUNKH
SCHOOL BUS
SKKRREEE

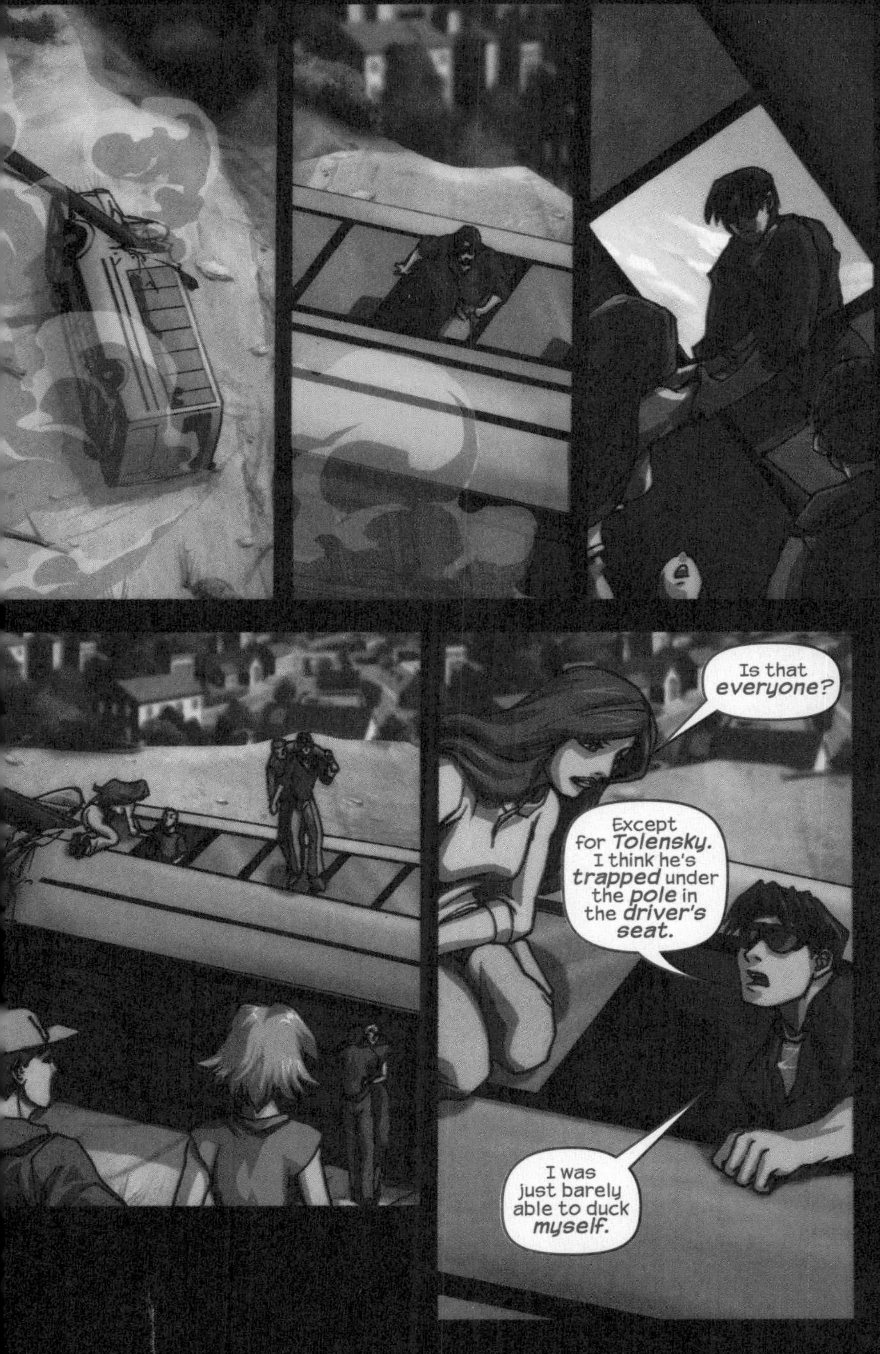
Is that everyone?
Except for Tolensky. I think he's trapped under the pole in the driver's seat.
I was just barely able to duck myself.

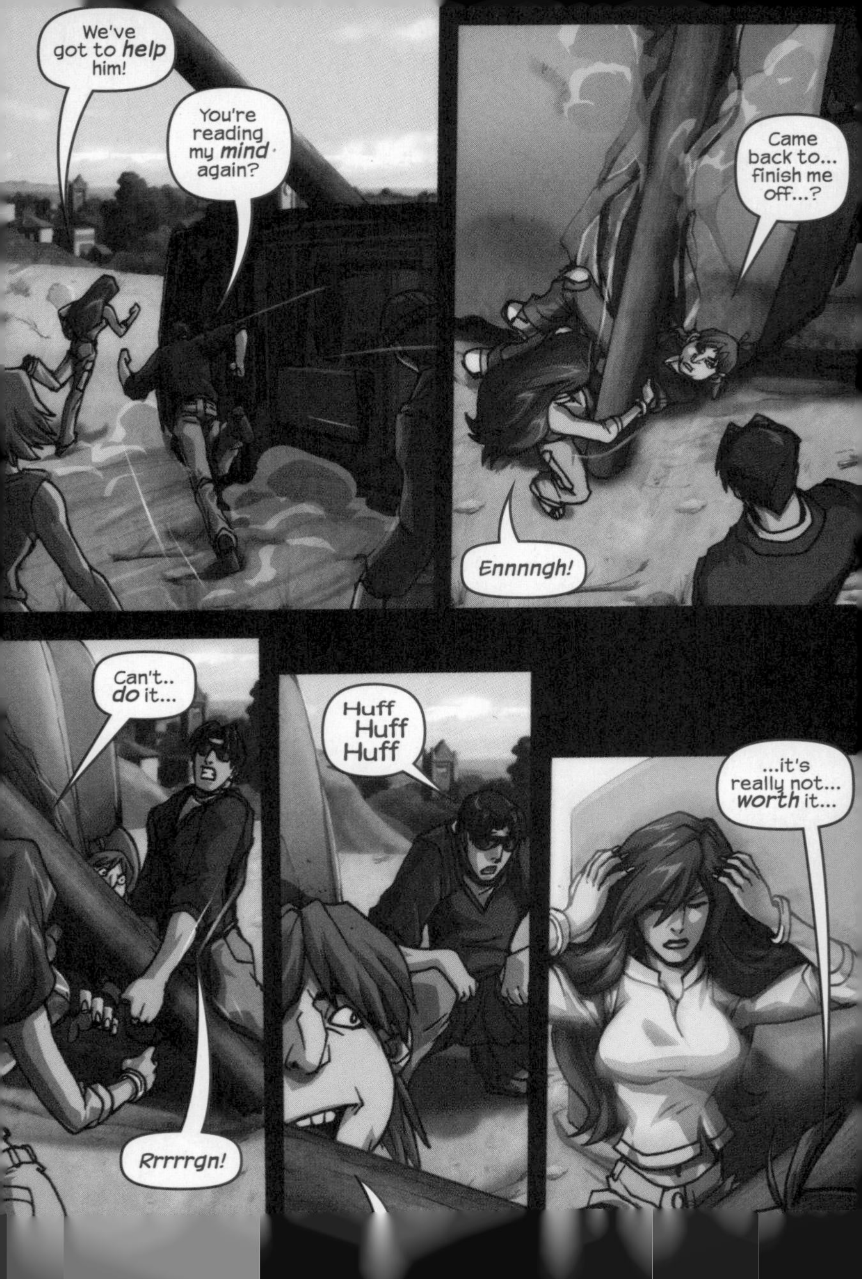
We've got to help him!
You're reading my mind again?
Came back to... finish me off...?
Ennnngh!
Can't.. do it...
Rrrrrgn!
Huff Huff Huff
...it's really not... worth it...

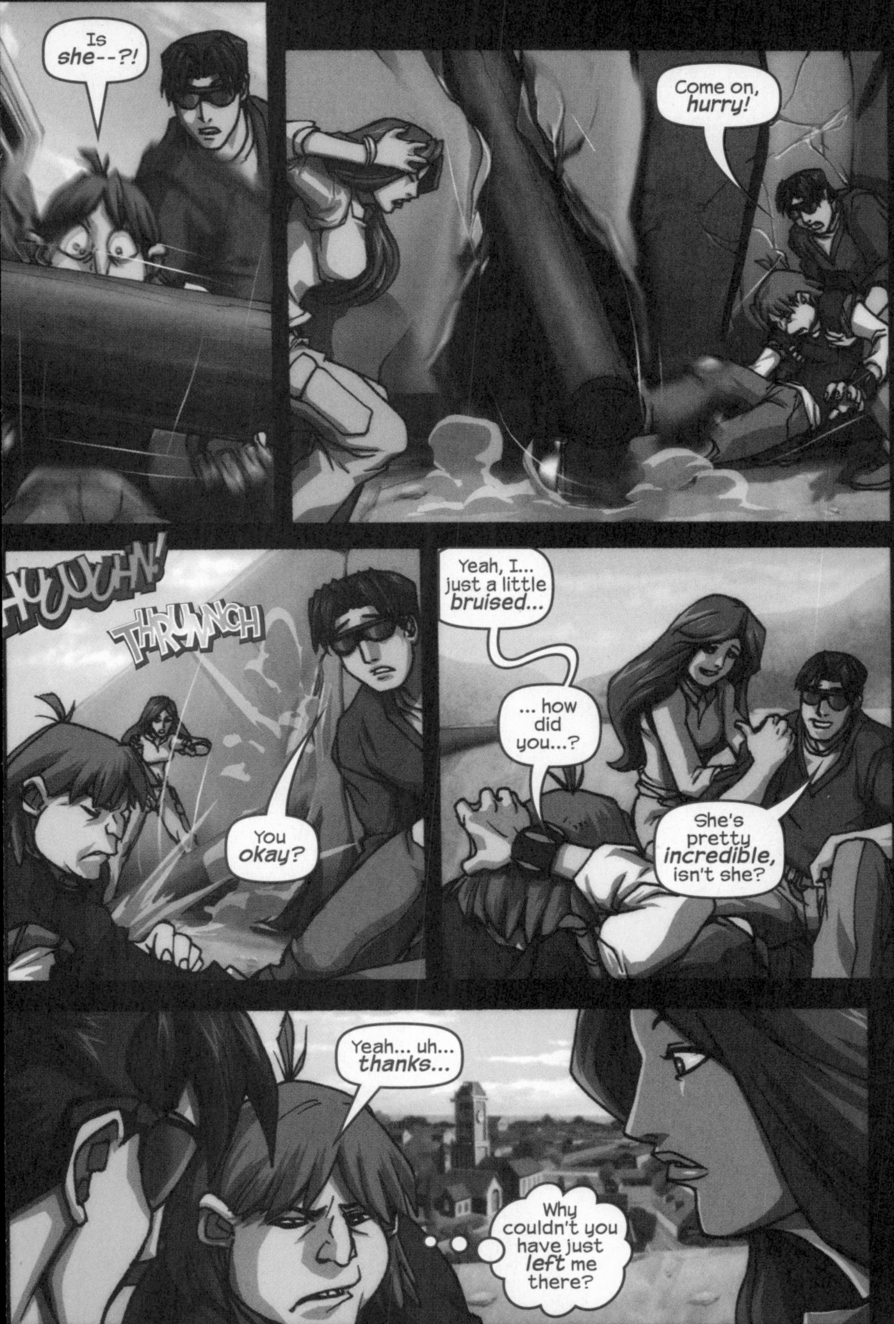
Is she--?!
Come on, hurry!
CHUOOOHN!
THRUNNCH
You okay?
Yeah, I... just a little bruised...
... how did you...?
She's pretty incredible, isn't she?
Yeah... uh... thanks...
Why couldn't you have just left me there?

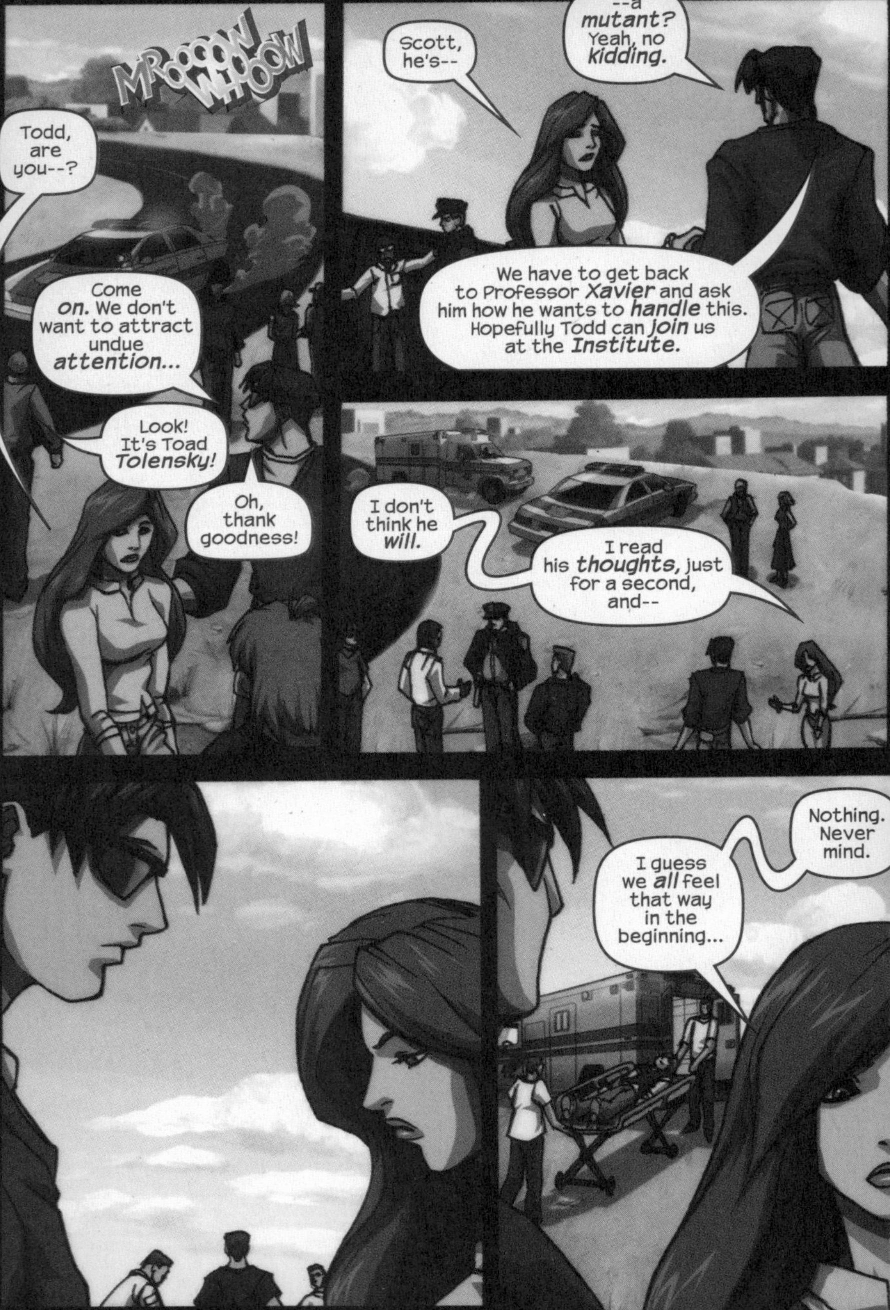
MROOOOW WHOOOW
Todd, are you--?
Come on. We don't want to attract undue attention...
Look! It's Toad Tolensky!
Oh, thank goodness!
Scott, he's--
--a mutant? Yeah, no kidding.
We have to get back to Professor Xavier and ask him how he wants to handle this. Hopefully Todd can join us at the Institute.
I don't think he will.
I read his thoughts, just for a second, and--
I guess we all feel that way in the beginning...
Nothing. Never mind.

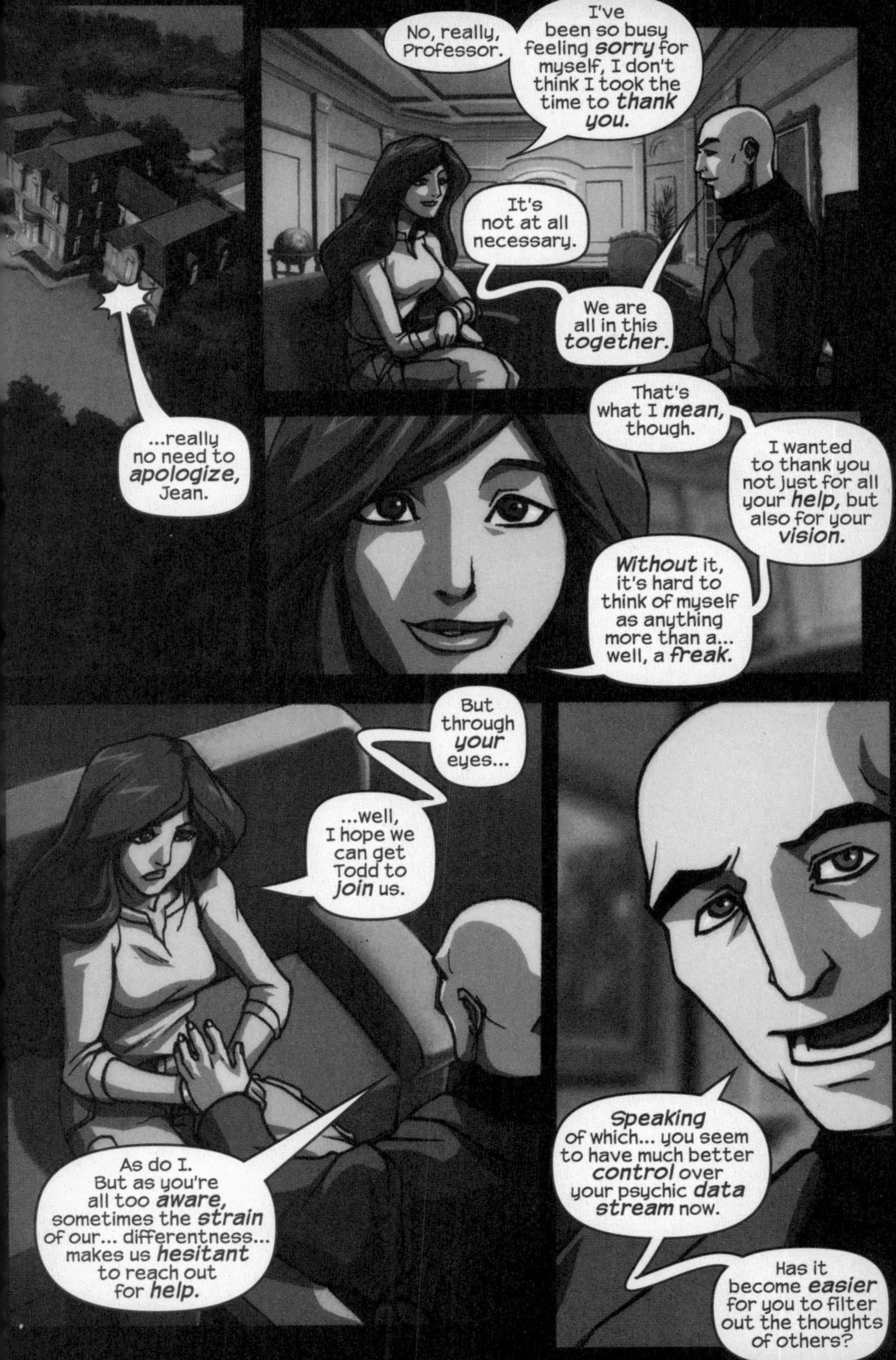
...really no need to apologize, Jean.
No, really, Professor.
I've been so busy feeling sorry for myself, I don't think I took the time to thank you.
It's not at all necessary.
We are all in this together.
That's what I mean, though.
I wanted to thank you not just for all your help, but also for your vision.
Without it, it's hard to think of myself as anything more than a... well, a freak.
But through your eyes...
...well, I hope we can get Todd to join us.
As do I. But as you're all too aware, sometimes the strain of our... differentness... makes us hesitant to reach out for help.
Speaking of which... you seem to have much better control over your psychic data stream now.
Has it become easier for you to filter out the thoughts of others?

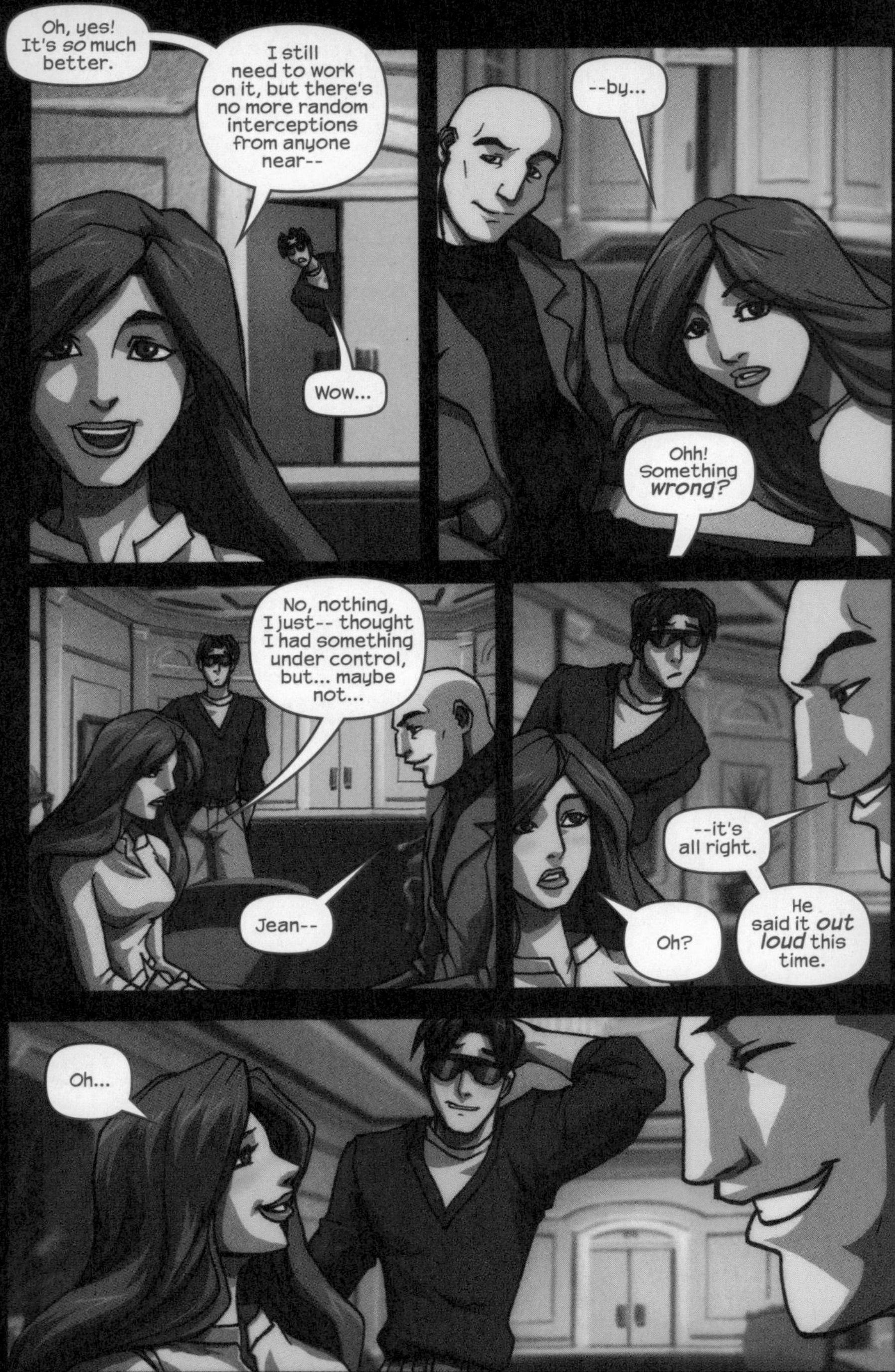

Oh, yes! It's *so* much better.
I still need to work on it, but there's no more random interceptions from anyone near--
Wow...
--by...
Ohh! Something ***wrong?***
No, nothing, I just-- thought I had something under control, but... maybe not...
Jean--
--it's all right.
Oh?
He said it ***out loud*** this time.
Oh...

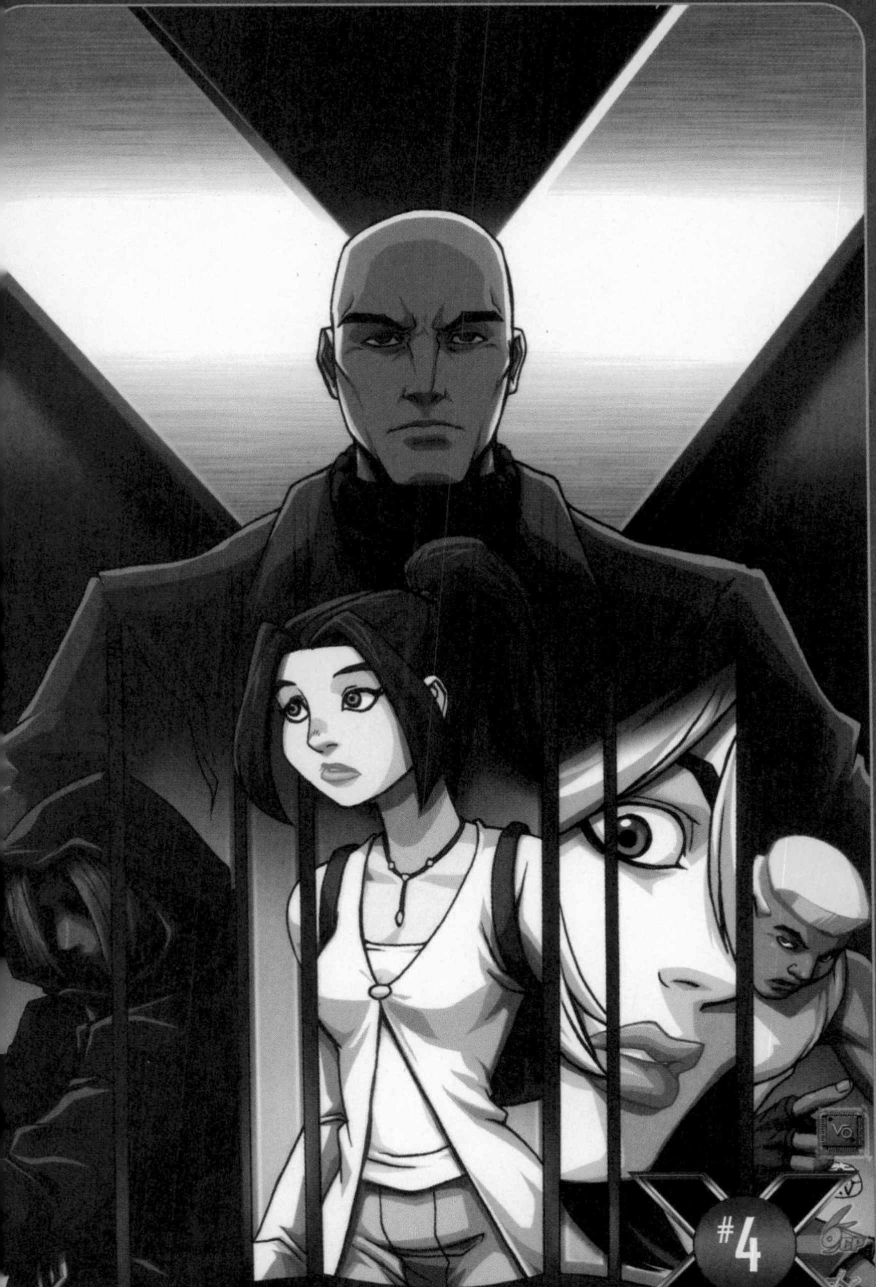
#4

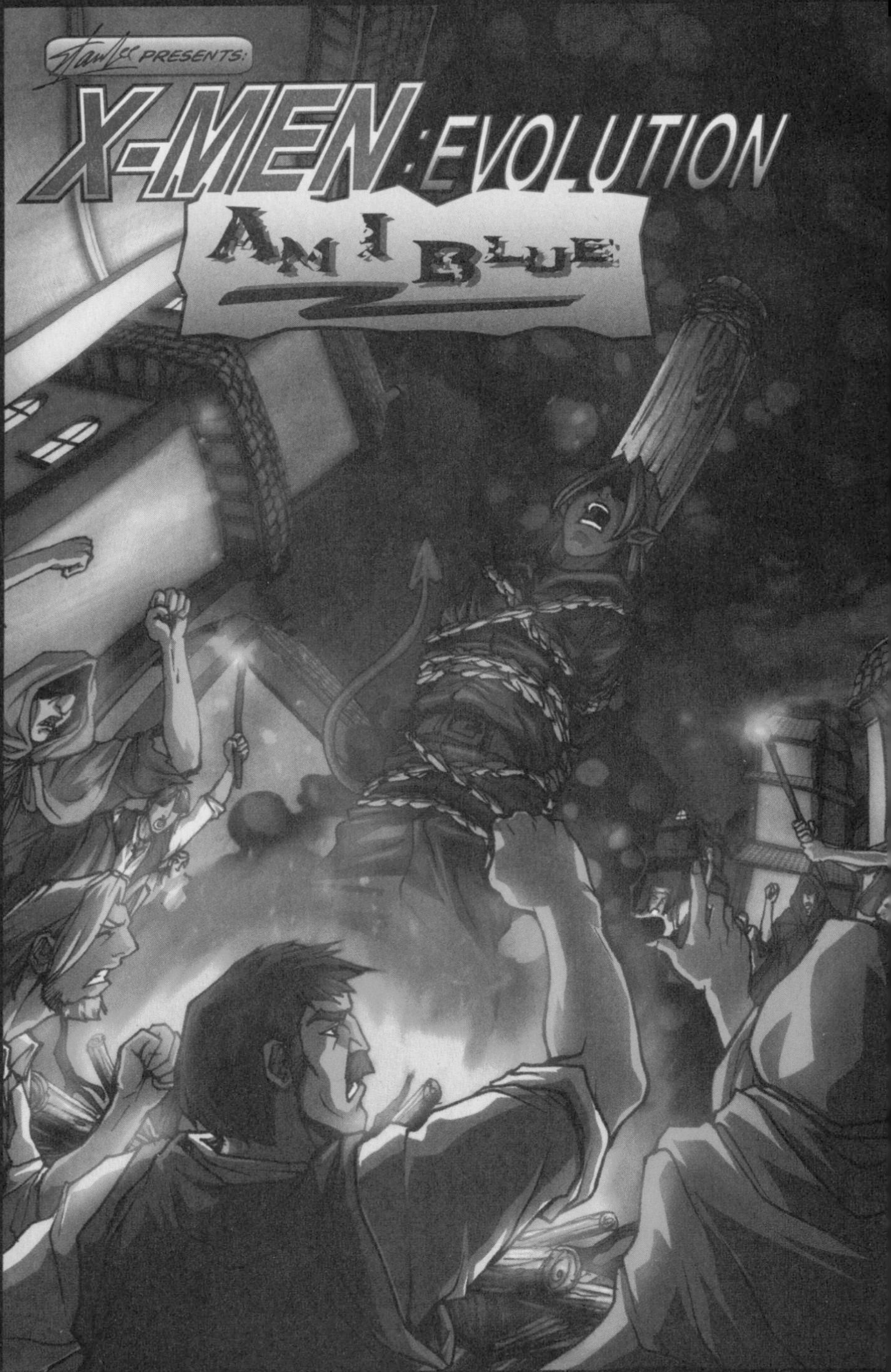
Stan Lee PRESENTS:
X-MEN: EVOLUTION
AM I BLUE

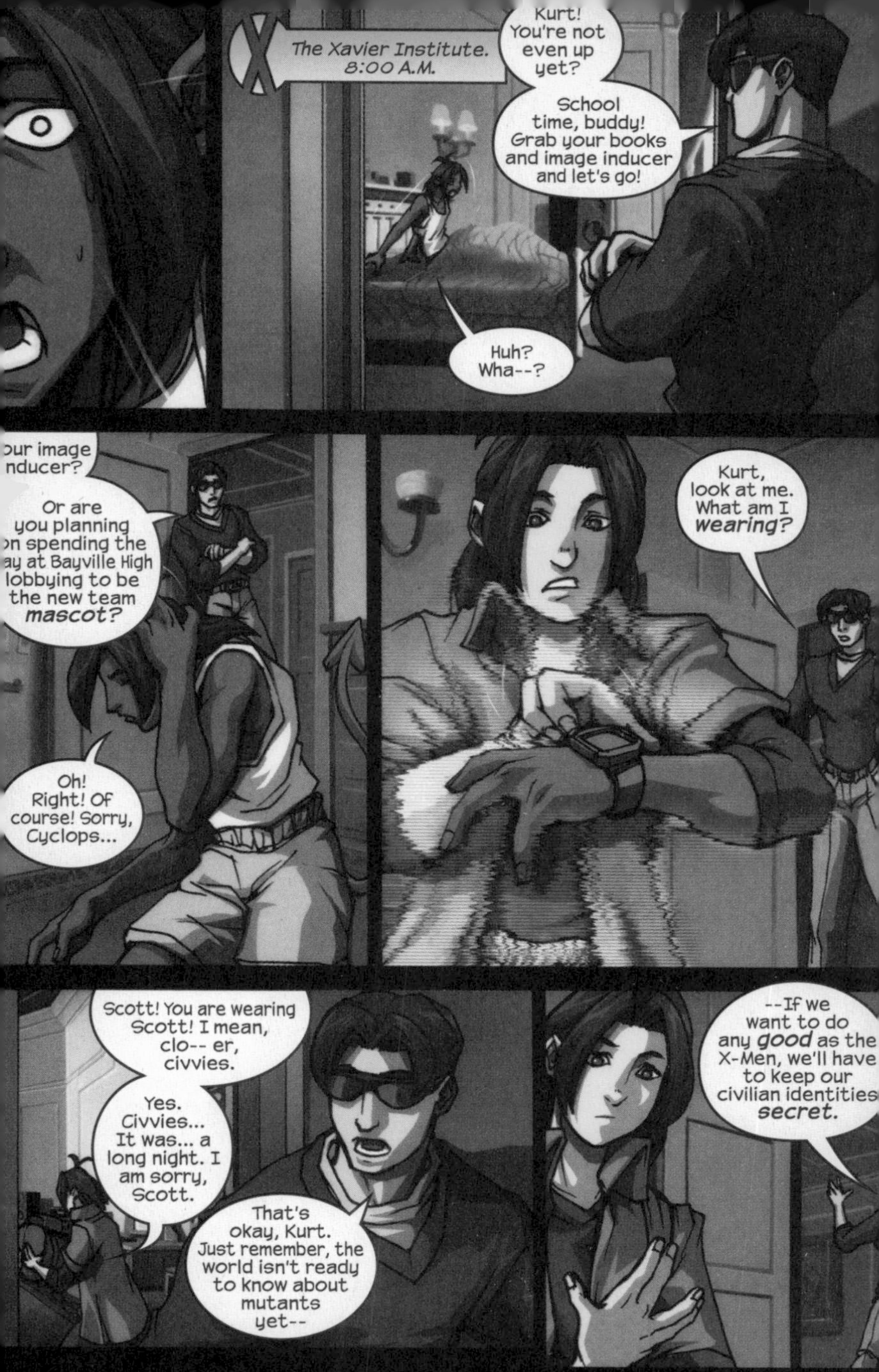

The Xavier Institute. 8:00 A.M.
Kurt! You're not even up yet?
School time, buddy! Grab your books and image inducer and let's go!
Huh? Wha--?
our image nducer?
Or are you planning on spending the ay at Bayville High lobbying to be the new team *mascot?*
Oh! Right! Of course! Sorry, Cyclops...
Kurt, look at me. What am I *wearing?*
Scott! You are wearing Scott! I mean, clo-- er, civvies.
Yes. Civvies... It was... a long night. I am sorry, Scott.
That's okay, Kurt. Just remember, the world isn't ready to know about mutants yet--
--If we want to do any *good* as the X-Men, we'll have to keep our civilian identities *secret.*

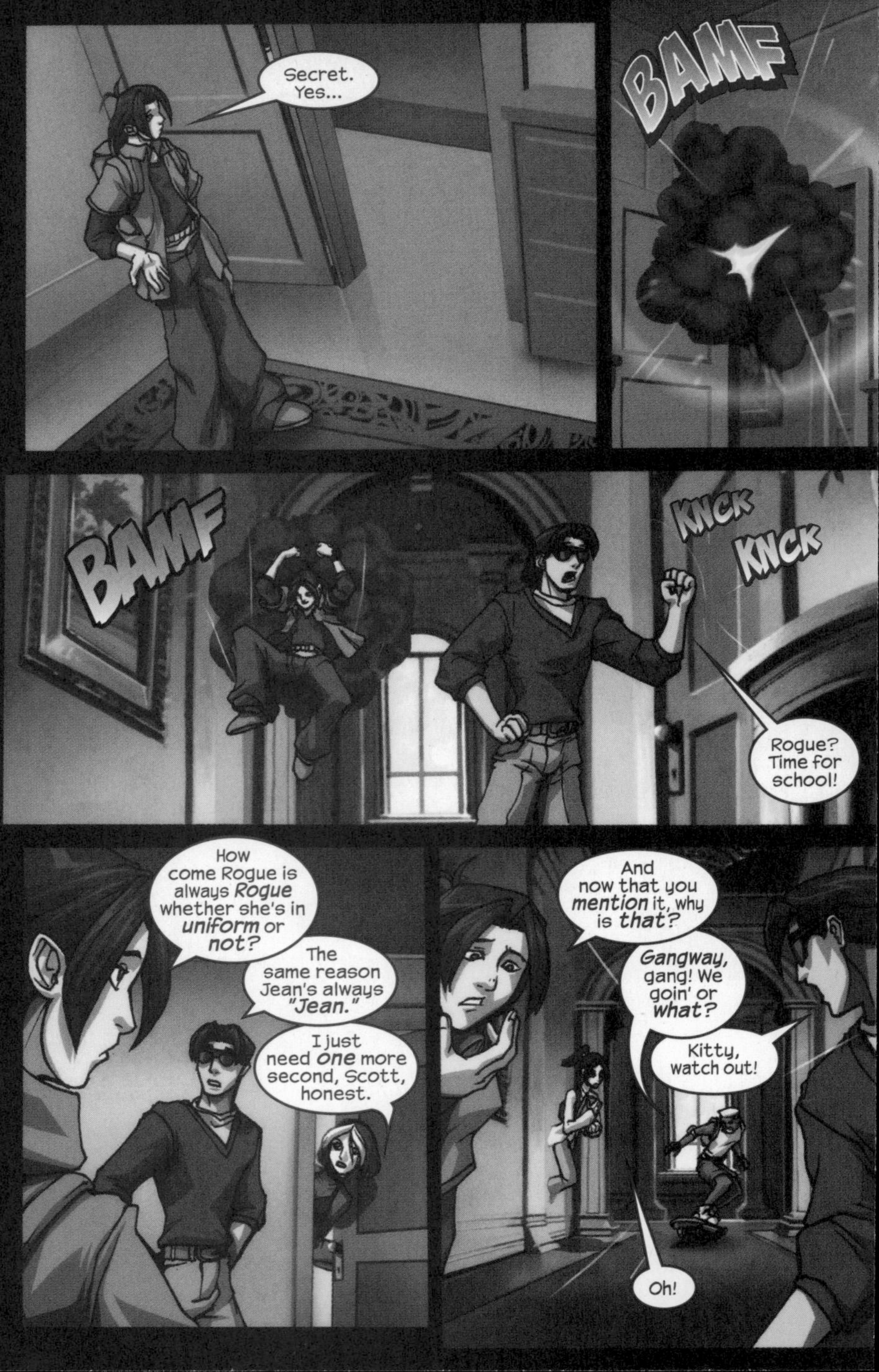
Secret. Yes...
BAMF
BAMF
KNCK KNCK
Rogue? Time for school!
How come Rogue is always Rogue whether she's in uniform or not?
The same reason Jean's always "Jean."
I just need one more second, Scott, honest.
And now that you mention it, why is that?
Gangway, gang! We goin' or what?
Kitty, watch out!
Oh!

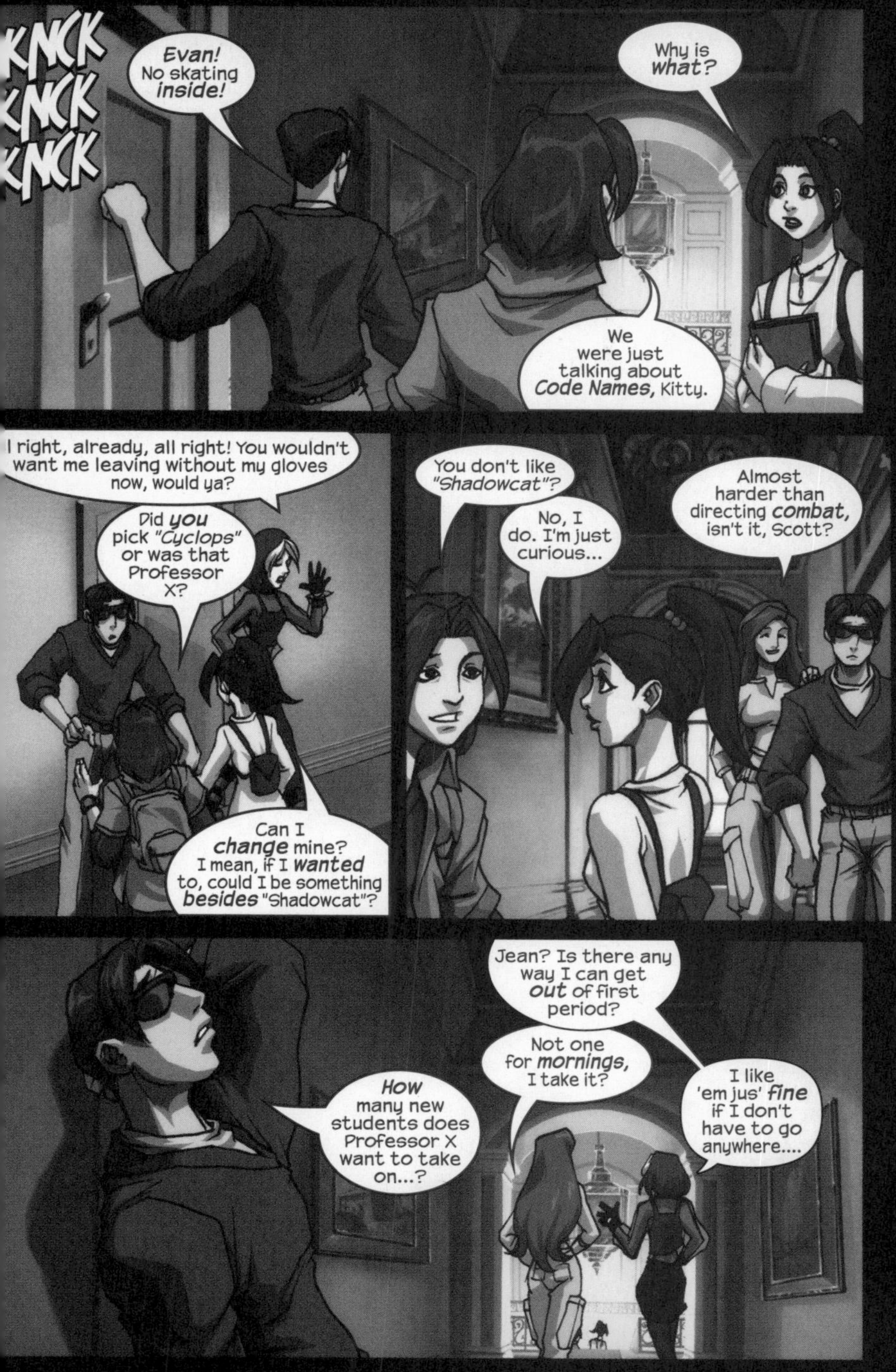
KNCK KNCK KNCK
Evan! No skating inside!
Why is what?
We were just talking about Code Names, Kitty.
l right, already, all right! You wouldn't want me leaving without my gloves now, would ya?
Did you pick "Cyclops" or was that Professor X?
Can I change mine? I mean, if I wanted to, could I be something besides "Shadowcat"?
You don't like "Shadowcat"?
No, I do. I'm just curious...
Almost harder than directing combat, isn't it, Scott?
How many new students does Professor X want to take on...?
Jean? Is there any way I can get out of first period?
Not one for mornings, I take it?
I like 'em jus' fine if I don't have to go anywhere....

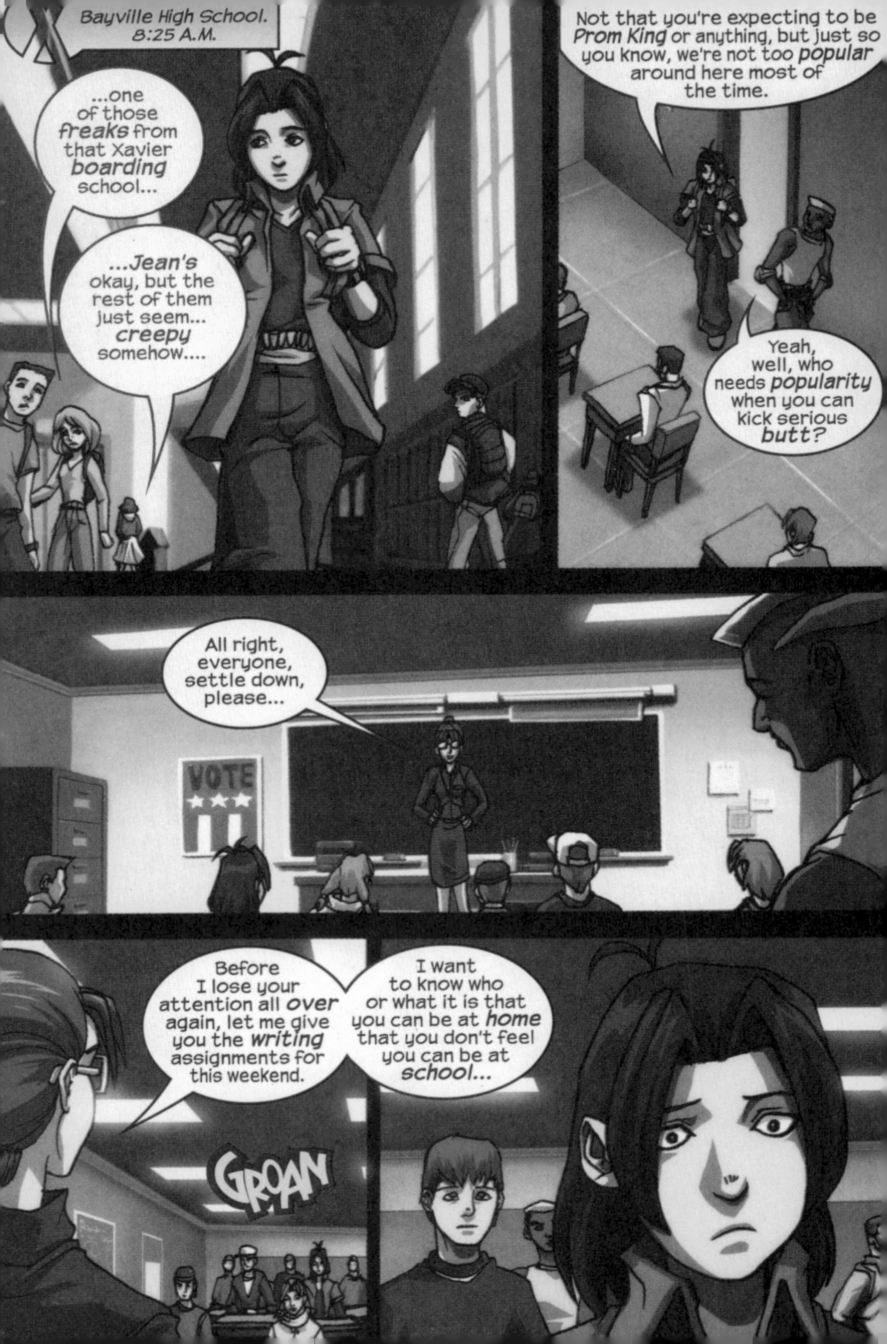

Bayville High School. 8:25 A.M.
...one of those freaks from that Xavier boarding school...
...Jean's okay, but the rest of them just seem... creepy somehow....
Not that you're expecting to be Prom King or anything, but just so you know, we're not too popular around here most of the time.
Yeah, well, who needs popularity when you can kick serious butt?
All right, everyone, settle down, please...
VOTE
Before I lose your attention all over again, let me give you the writing assignments for this weekend.
GROAN
I want to know who or what it is that you can be at home that you don't feel you can be at school...

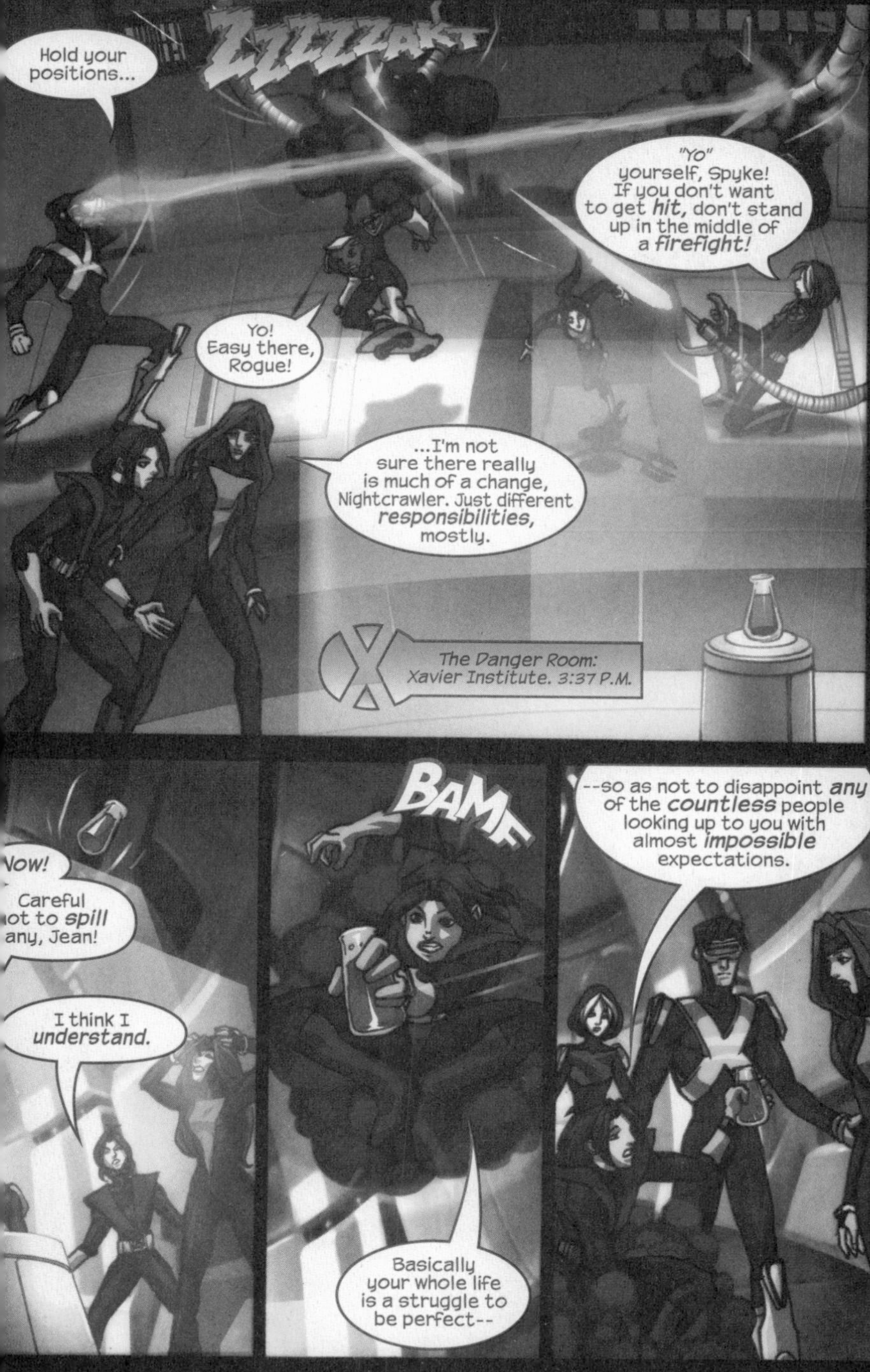
ZZZZZAKT
Hold your positions...
"Yo" yourself, Spyke! If you don't want to get hit, don't stand up in the middle of a firefight!
Yo! Easy there, Rogue!
...I'm not sure there really is much of a change, Nightcrawler. Just different responsibilities, mostly.
The Danger Room: Xavier Institute. 3:37 P.M.
Now! Careful not to spill any, Jean!
I think I understand.
BAMF
Basically your whole life is a struggle to be perfect--
--so as not to disappoint any of the countless people looking up to you with almost impossible expectations.

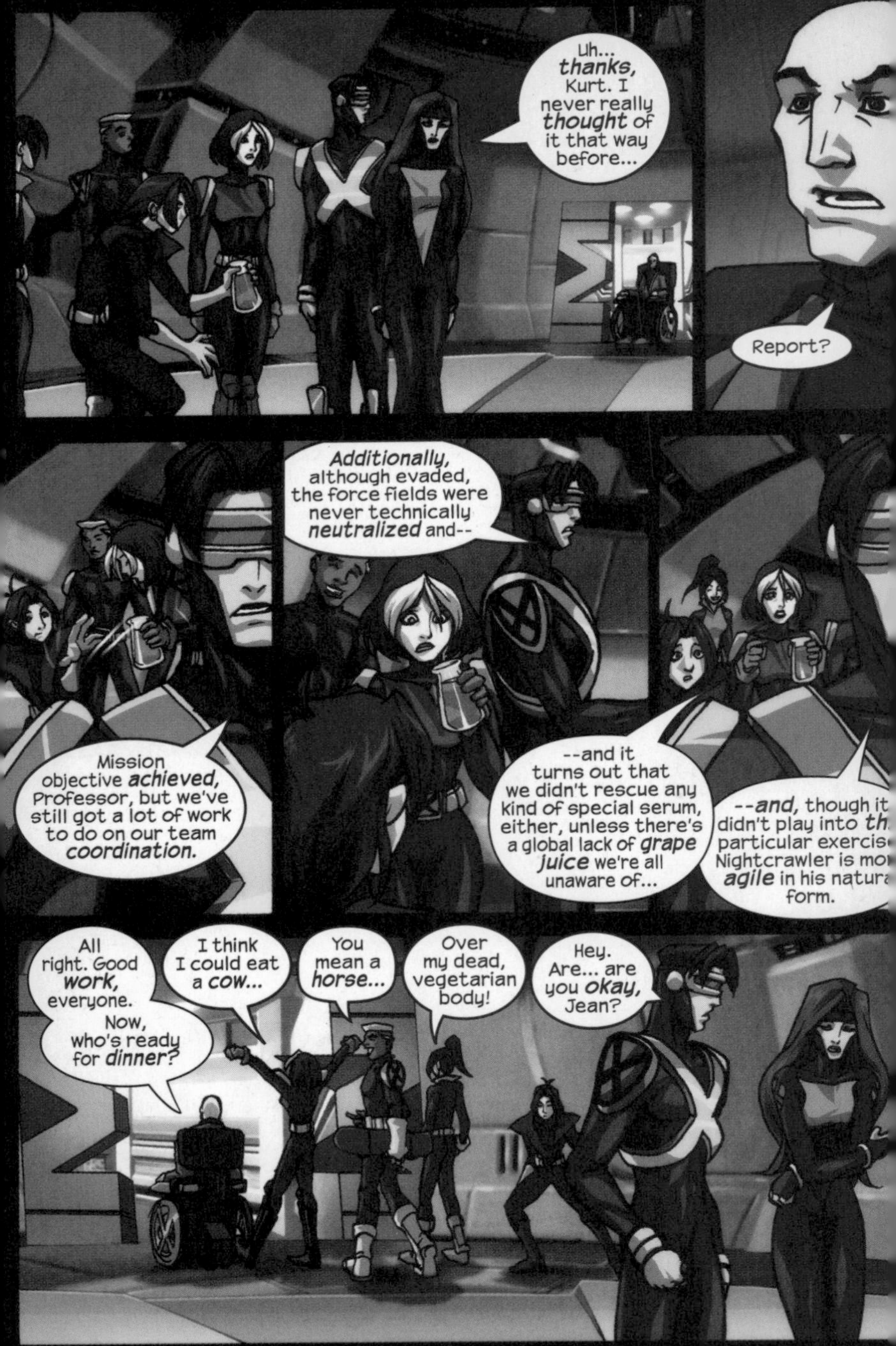
Uh... thanks, Kurt. I never really thought of it that way before...
Report?
Mission objective achieved, Professor, but we've still got a lot of work to do on our team coordination.
Additionally, although evaded, the force fields were never technically neutralized and--
--and it turns out that we didn't rescue any kind of special serum, either, unless there's a global lack of grape juice we're all unaware of...
--and, though it didn't play into th particular exercis Nightcrawler is mo agile in his natura form.
All right. Good work, everyone. Now, who's ready for dinner?
I think I could eat a cow...
You mean a horse...
Over my dead, vegetarian body!
Hey. Are... are you okay, Jean?

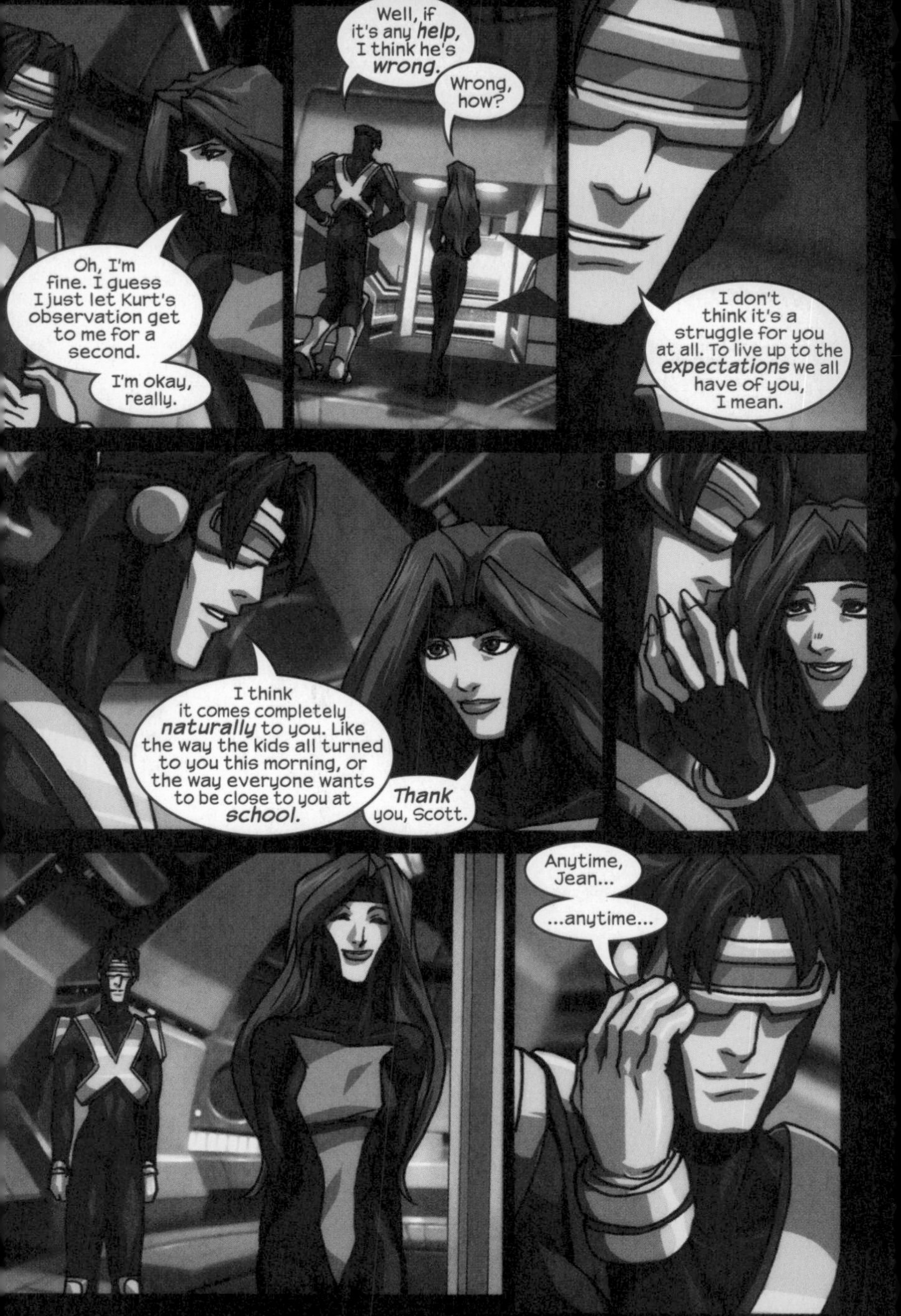

Oh, I'm fine. I guess I just let Kurt's observation get to me for a second.
I'm okay, really.
Well, if it's any help, I think he's wrong.
Wrong, how?
I don't think it's a struggle for you at all. To live up to the expectations we all have of you, I mean.
I think it comes completely naturally to you. Like the way the kids all turned to you this morning, or the way everyone wants to be close to you at school.
Thank you, Scott.
Anytime, Jean...
...anytime...

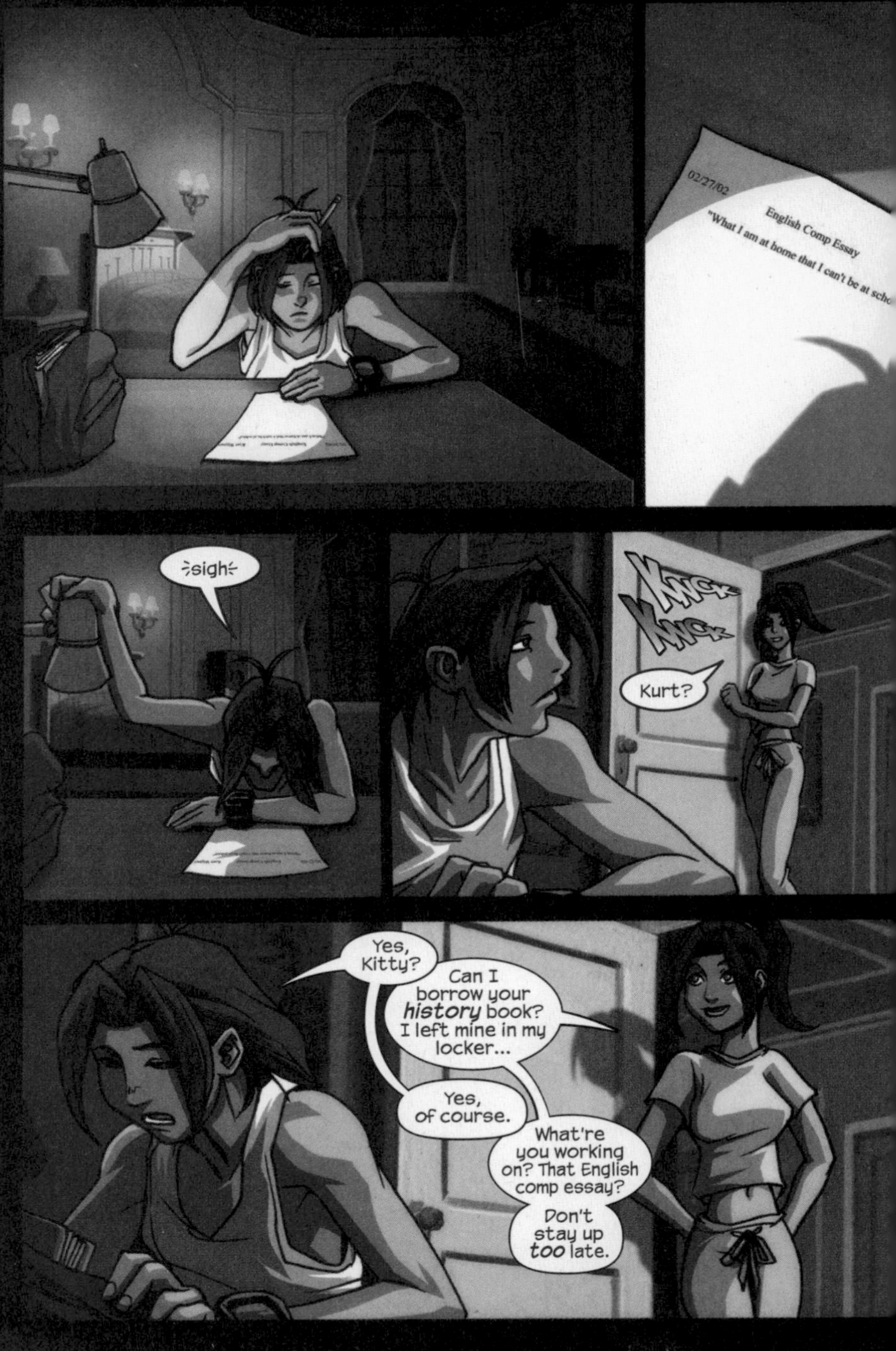
02/27/02
English Comp Essay
"What I am at home that I can't be at
sigh
Kurt?
Yes, Kitty?
Can I borrow your *history* book? I left mine in my locker...
Yes, of course.
What're you working on? That English comp essay?
Don't stay up *too* late.

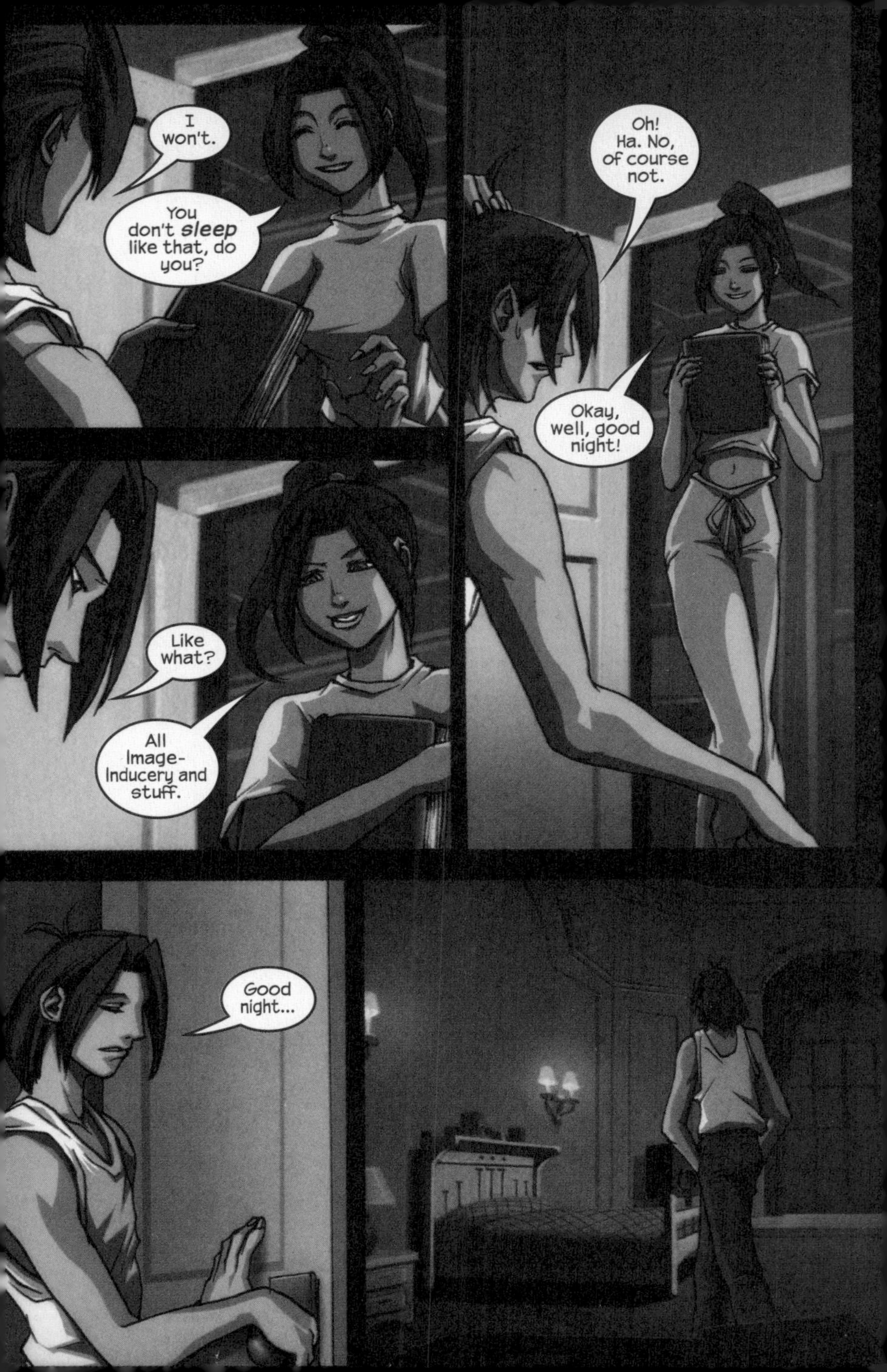

I won't.
You don't *sleep* like that, do you?
Oh! Ha. No, of course not.
Okay, well, good night!
Like what?
All Image-Inducery and stuff.
Good night...

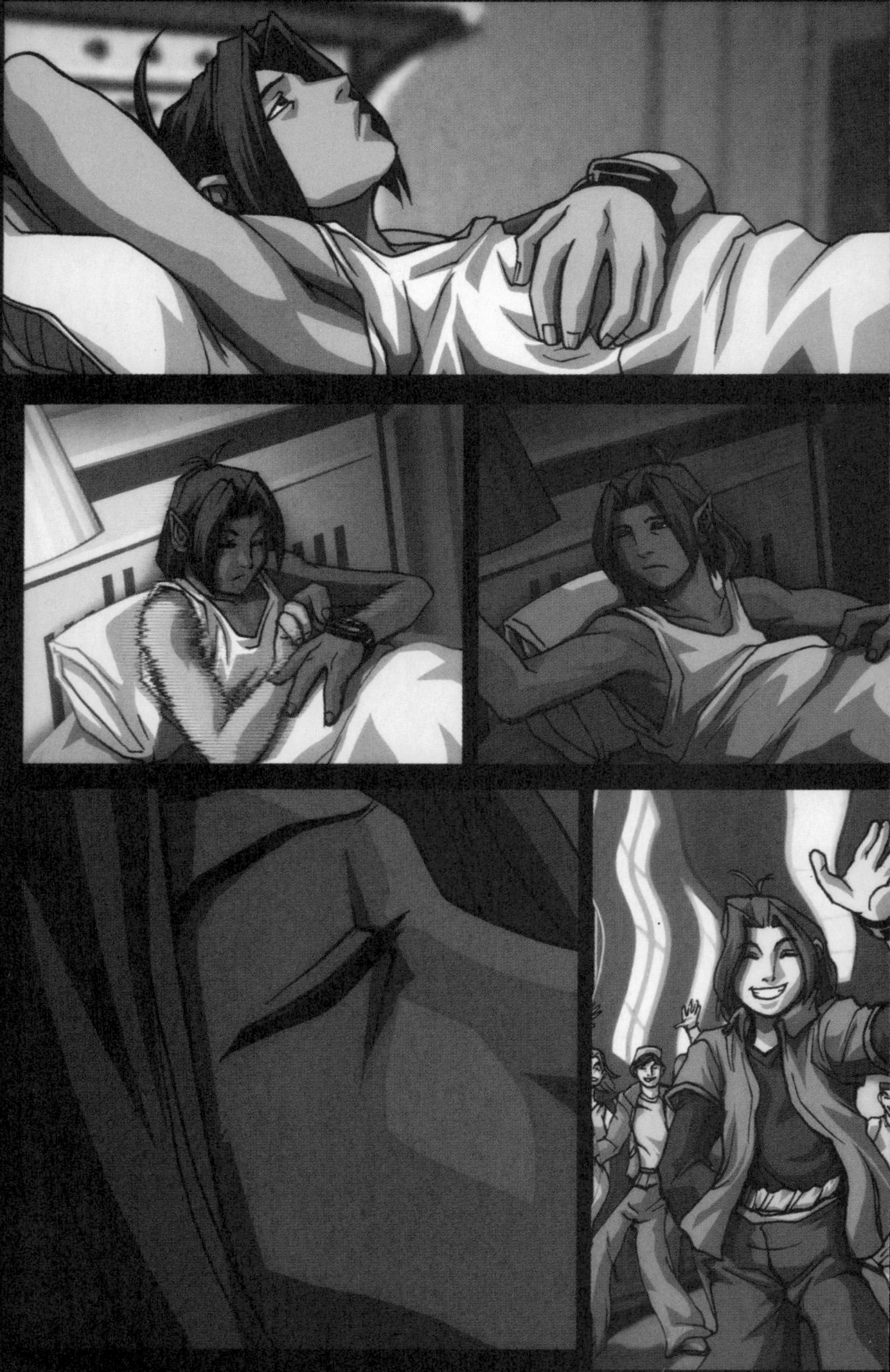

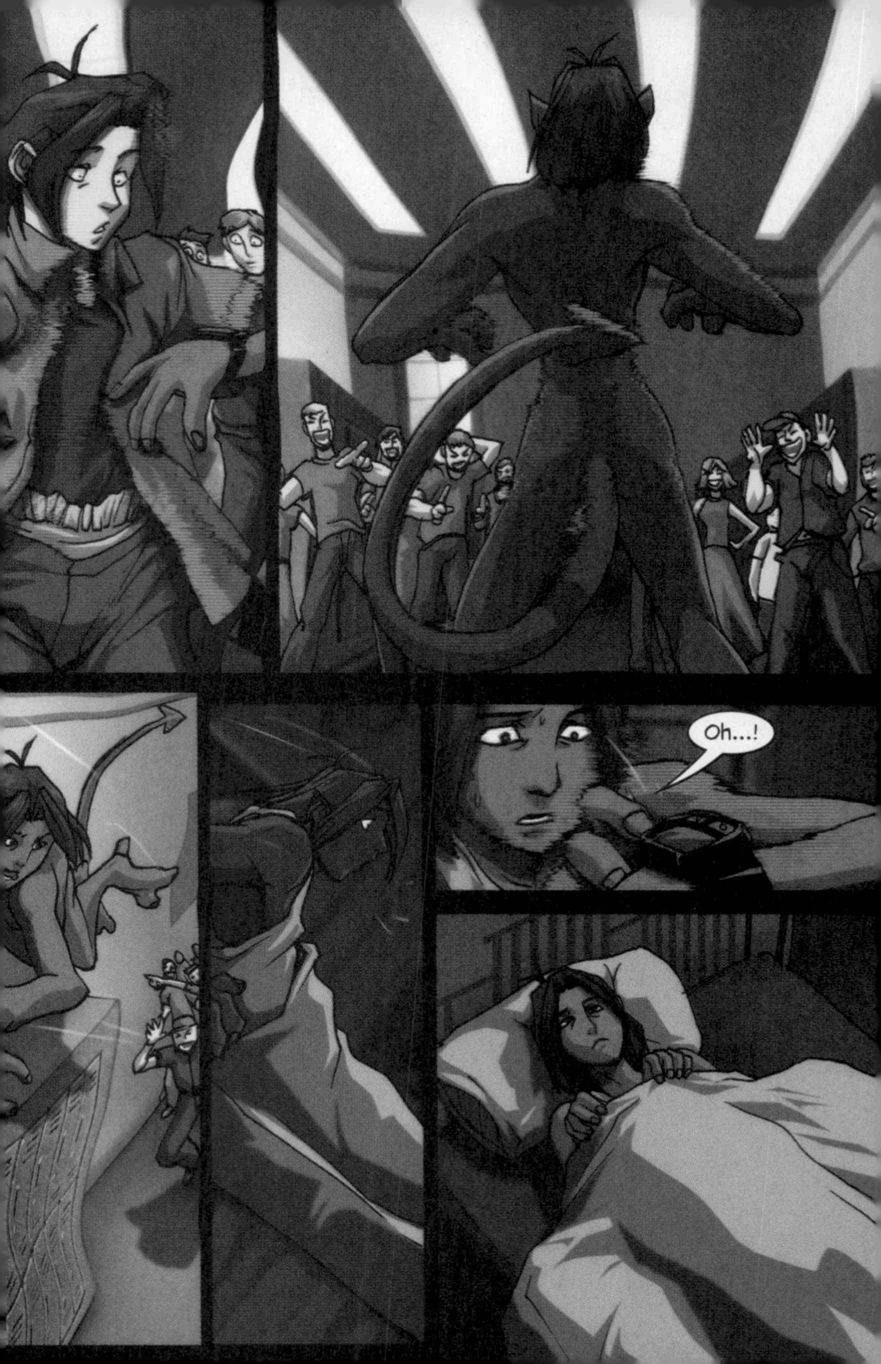
Oh...!

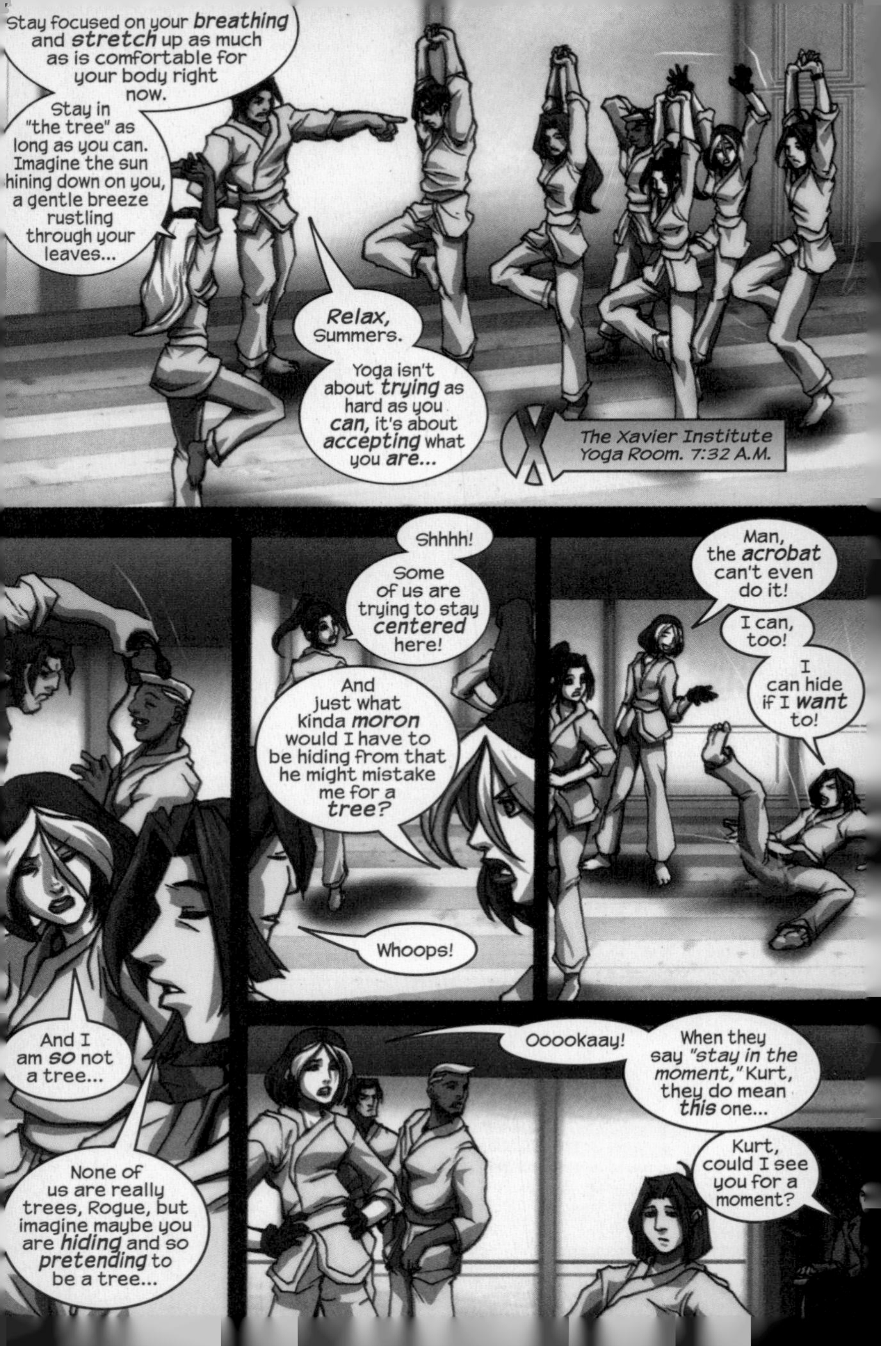
Stay focused on your breathing and stretch up as much as is comfortable for your body right now.
Stay in "the tree" as long as you can. Imagine the sun shining down on you, a gentle breeze rustling through your leaves...
Relax, Summers.
Yoga isn't about trying as hard as you can, it's about accepting what you are...
The Xavier Institute Yoga Room. 7:32 A.M.
Shhhh!
Some of us are trying to stay centered here!
And just what kinda moron would I have to be hiding from that he might mistake me for a tree?
Whoops!
Man, the acrobat can't even do it!
I can, too!
I can hide if I want to!
And I am so not a tree...
None of us are really trees, Rogue, but imagine maybe you are hiding and so pretending to be a tree...
Ooookaay!
When they say "stay in the moment," Kurt, they do mean this one...
Kurt, could I see you for a moment?

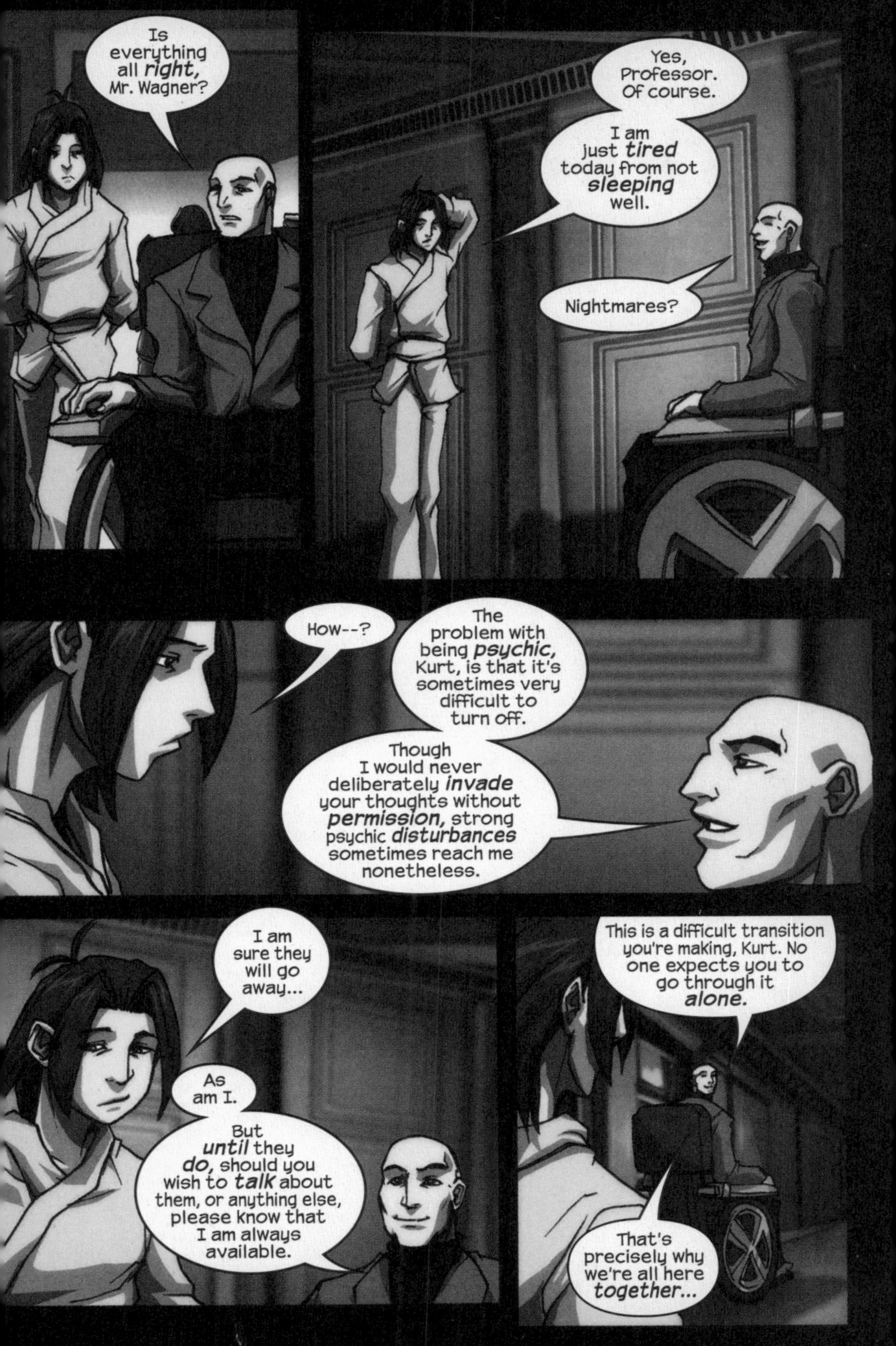

Is everything all *right,* Mr. Wagner?
Yes, Professor. Of course.
I am just *tired* today from not *sleeping* well.
Nightmares?
How--?
The problem with being *psychic,* Kurt, is that it's sometimes very difficult to turn off.
Though I would never deliberately *invade* your thoughts without *permission,* strong psychic *disturbances* sometimes reach me nonetheless.
I am sure they will go away...
As am I.
But *until* they *do,* should you wish to *talk* about them, or anything else, please know that I am always available.
This is a difficult transition you're making, Kurt. No one expects you to go through it *alone.*
That's precisely why we're all here *together...*

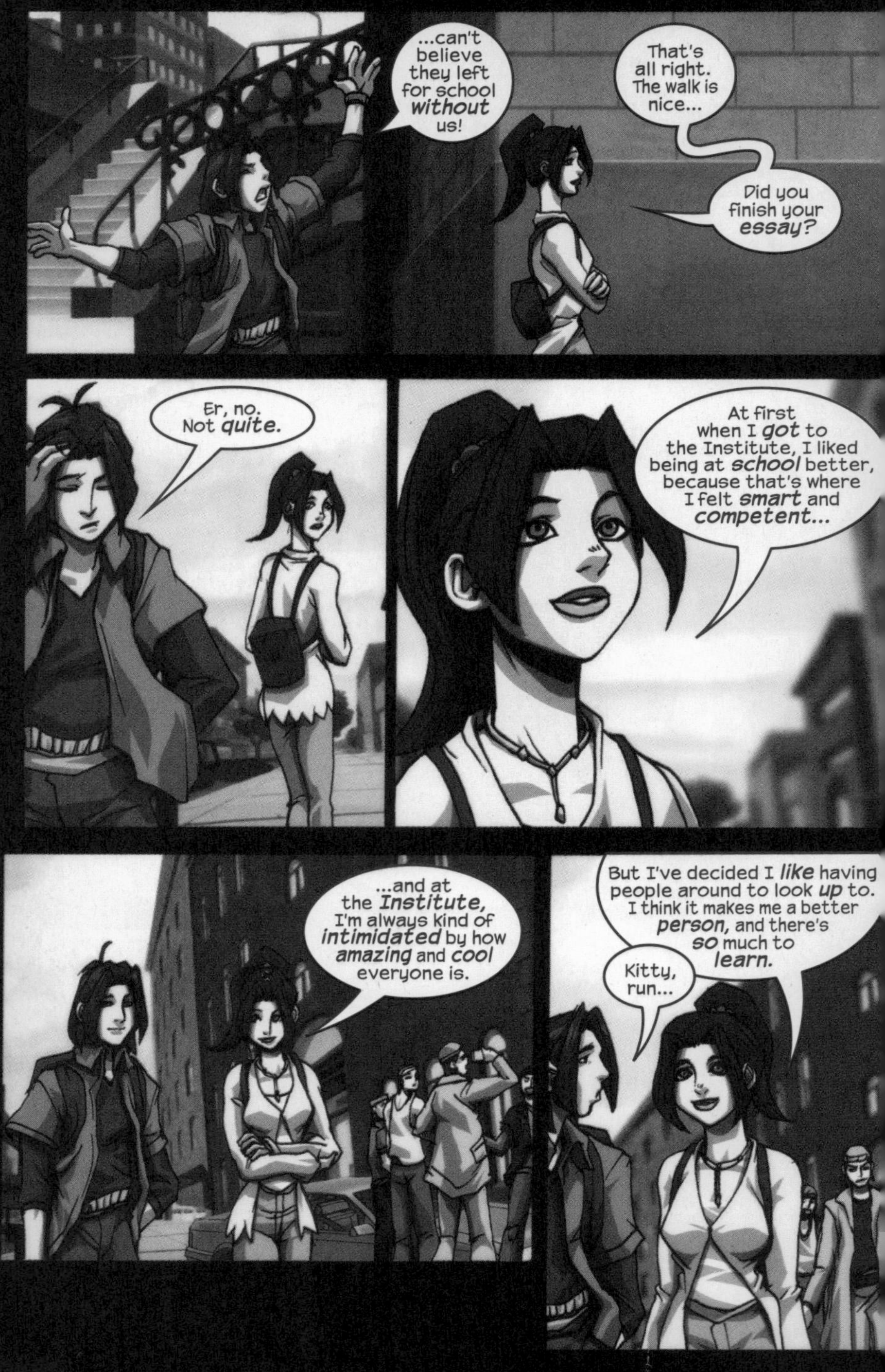
...can't believe they left for school without us!
That's all right. The walk is nice...
Did you finish your essay?
Er, no. Not quite.
At first when I got to the Institute, I liked being at school better, because that's where I felt smart and competent...
...and at the Institute, I'm always kind of intimidated by how amazing and cool everyone is.
But I've decided I like having people around to look up to. I think it makes me a better person, and there's so much to learn.
Kitty, run...

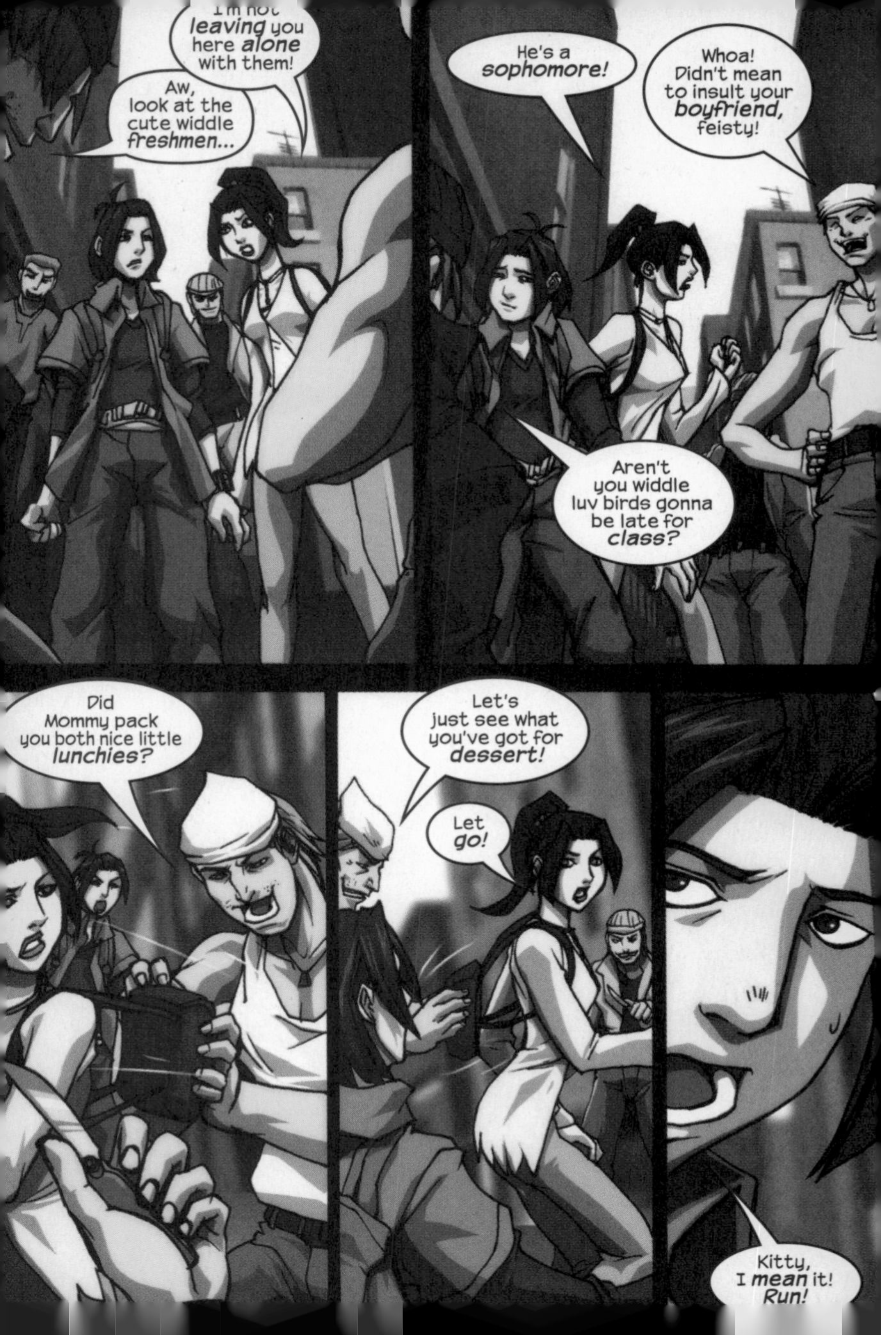
I'm not leaving you here alone with them!
Aw, look at the cute widdle freshmen...
He's a sophomore!
Whoa! Didn't mean to insult your boyfriend, feisty!
Aren't you widdle luv birds gonna be late for class?
Did Mommy pack you both nice little lunchies?
Let's just see what you've got for dessert!
Let go!
Kitty, I mean it! Run!

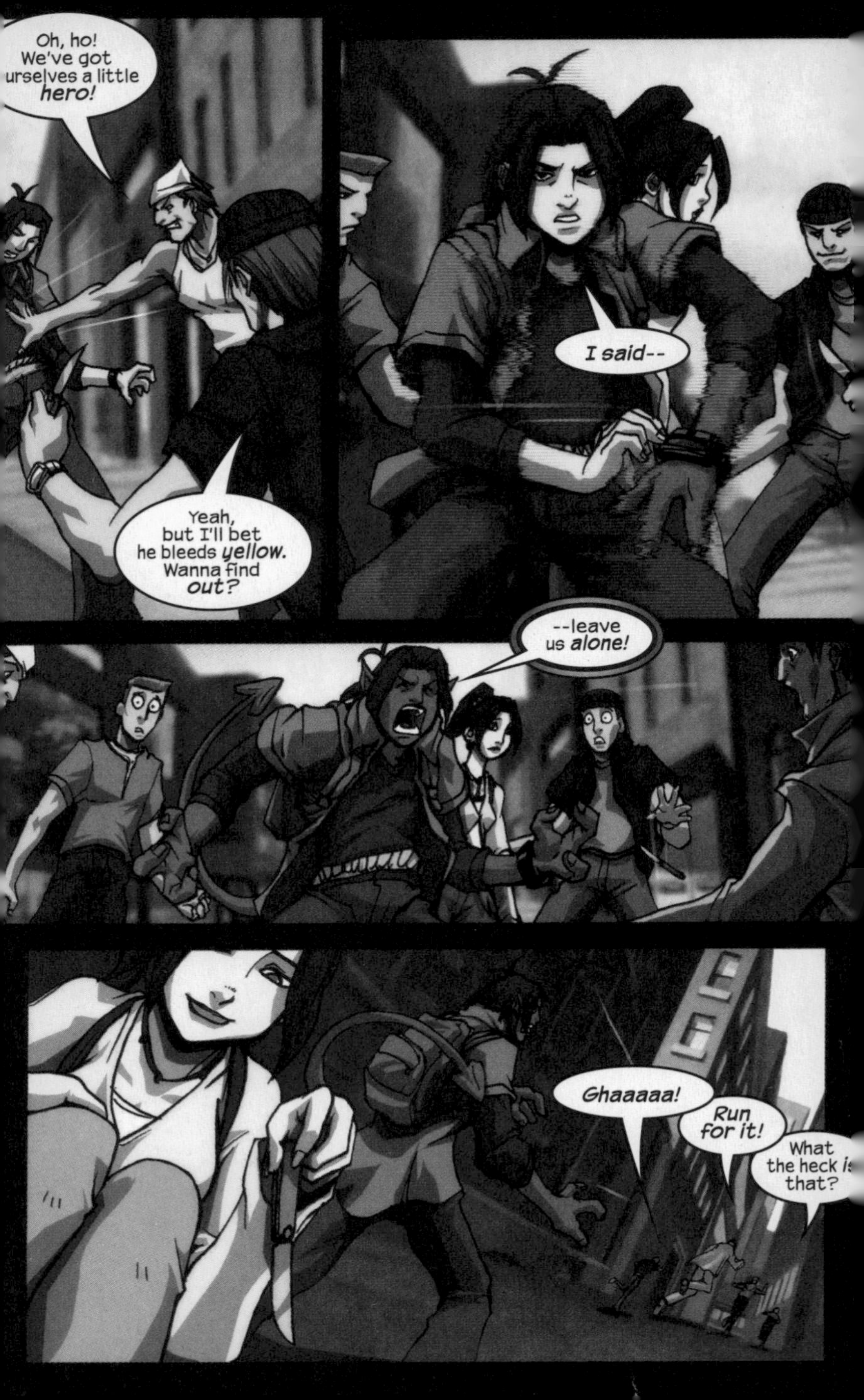

Oh, ho! We've got urselves a little hero!
Yeah, but I'll bet he bleeds yellow. Wanna find out?
I said--
--leave us alone!
Ghaaaaa!
Run for it!
What the heck is that?

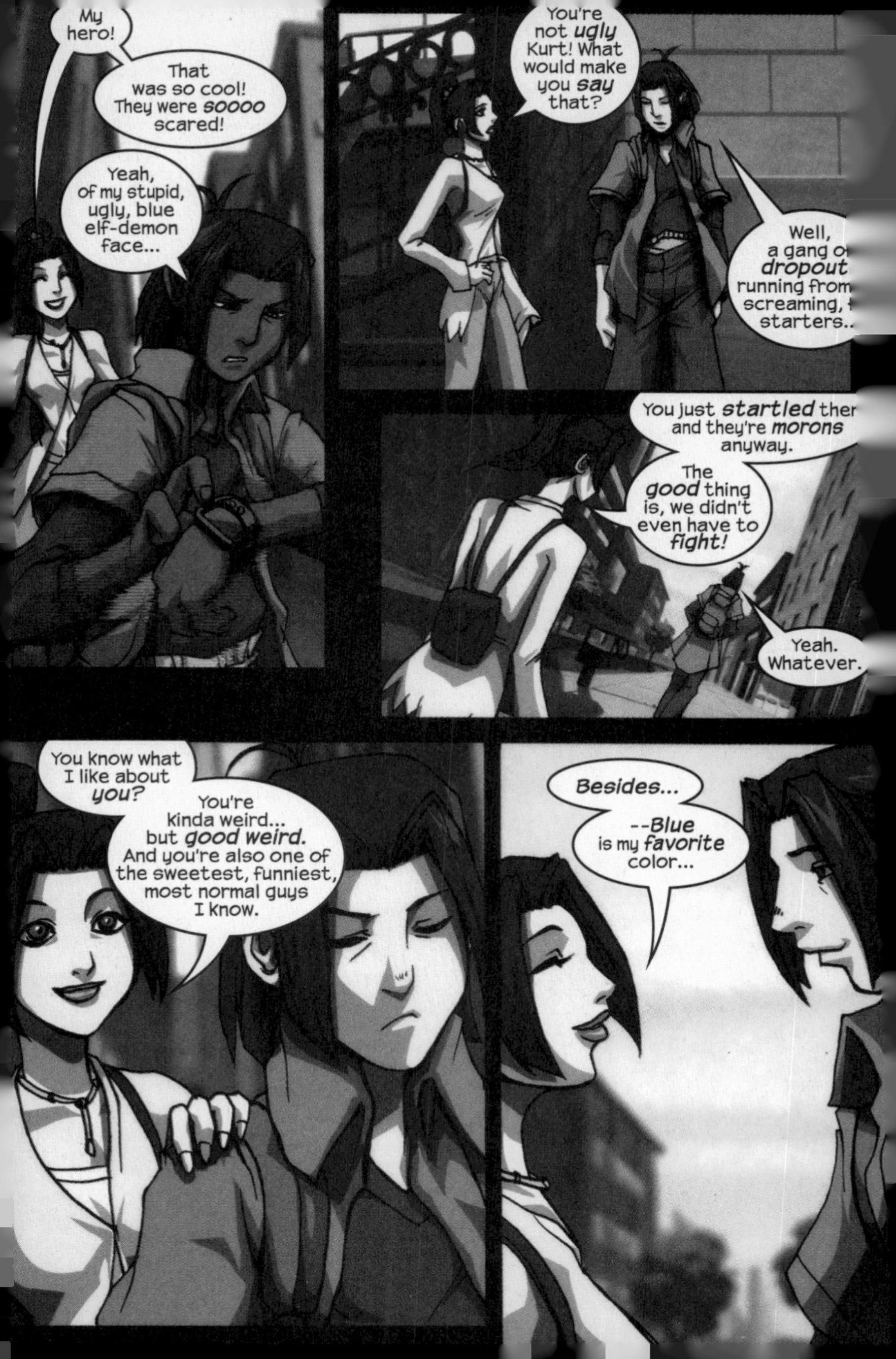

My hero!
That was so cool! They were soooo scared!
Yeah, of my stupid, ugly, blue elf-demon face...
You're not ugly Kurt! What would make you say that?
Well, a gang of dropout running from screaming, starters...
You just startled ther and they're morons anyway.
The good thing is, we didn't even have to fight!
Yeah. Whatever.
You know what I like about you?
You're kinda weird... but good weird. And you're also one of the sweetest, funniest, most normal guys I know.
Besides...
--Blue is my favorite color...

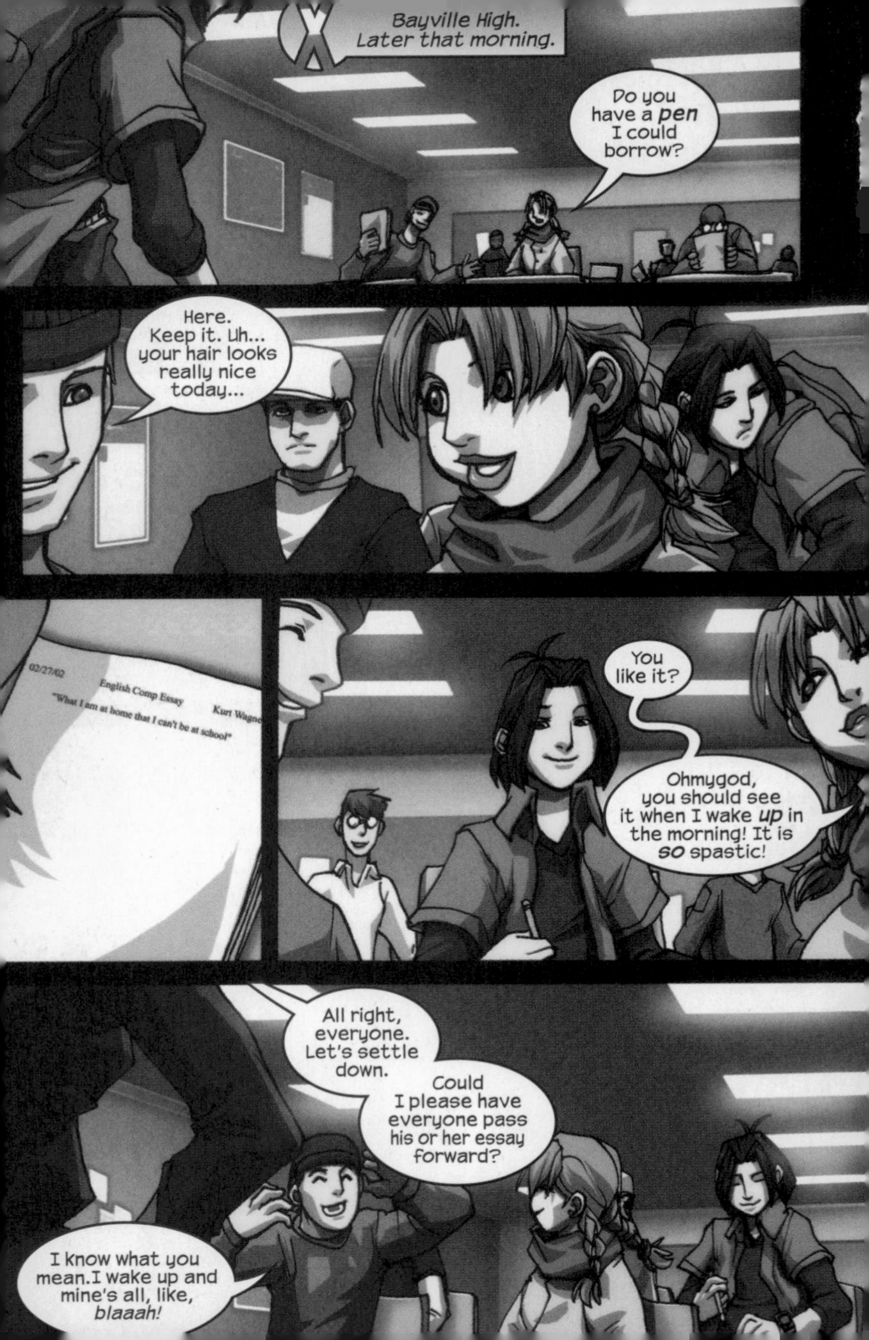
Bayville High. Later that morning.
Do you have a pen I could borrow?
Here. Keep it. Uh... your hair looks really nice today...
02/27/02
English Comp Essay
Kurt Wagne
"What I am at home that I can't be at school"
You like it?
Ohmygod, you should see it when I wake up in the morning! It is so spastic!
All right, everyone. Let's settle down.
Could I please have everyone pass his or her essay forward?
I know what you mean. I wake up and mine's all, like, blaaah!

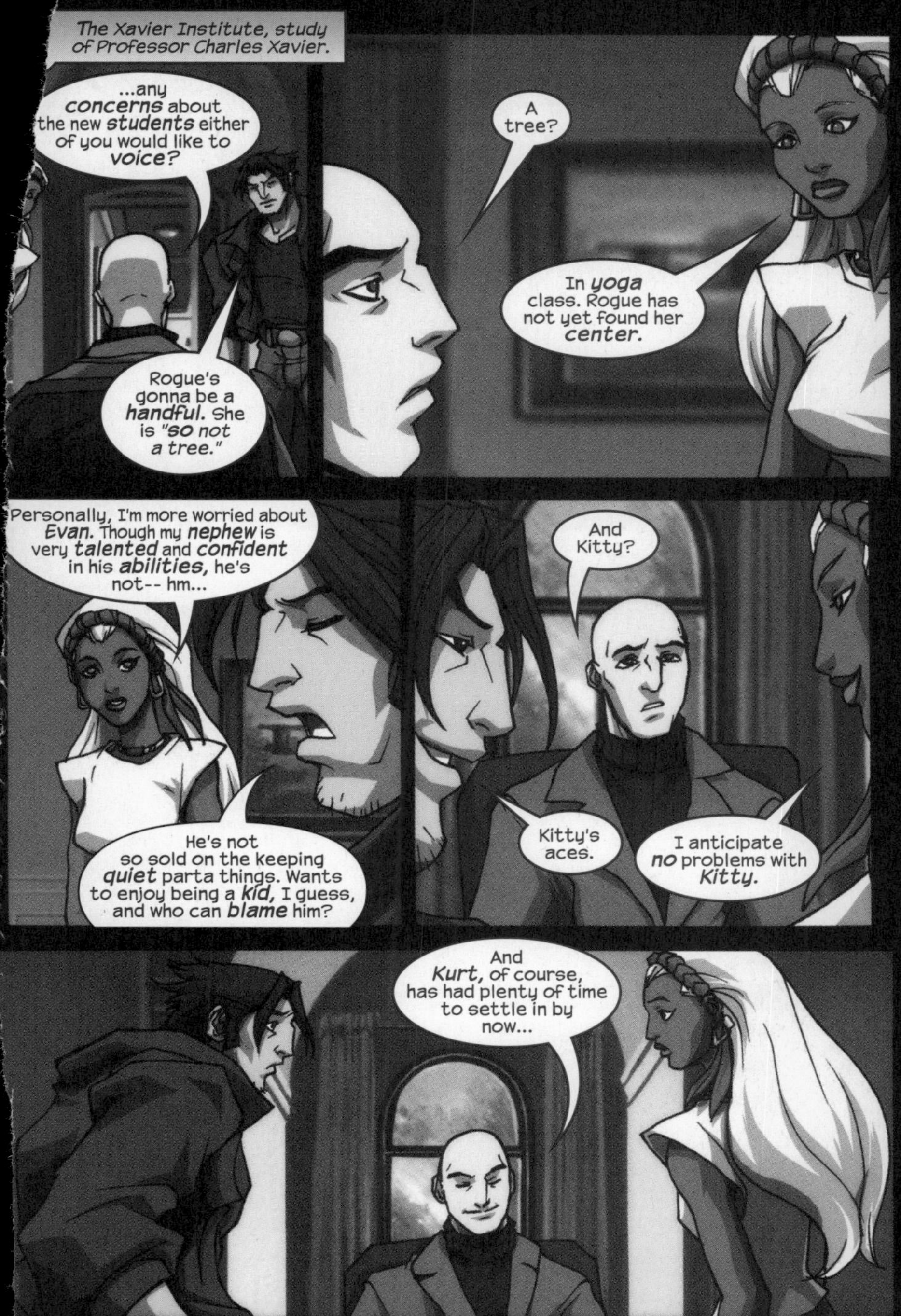

The Xavier Institute, study of Professor Charles Xavier.
...any concerns about the new students either of you would like to voice?
Rogue's gonna be a handful. She is "so not a tree."
A tree?
In yoga class. Rogue has not yet found her center.
Personally, I'm more worried about Evan. Though my nephew is very talented and confident in his abilities, he's not-- hm...
He's not so sold on the keeping quiet parta things. Wants to enjoy being a kid, I guess, and who can blame him?
And Kitty?
Kitty's aces.
I anticipate no problems with Kitty.
And Kurt, of course, has had plenty of time to settle in by now...

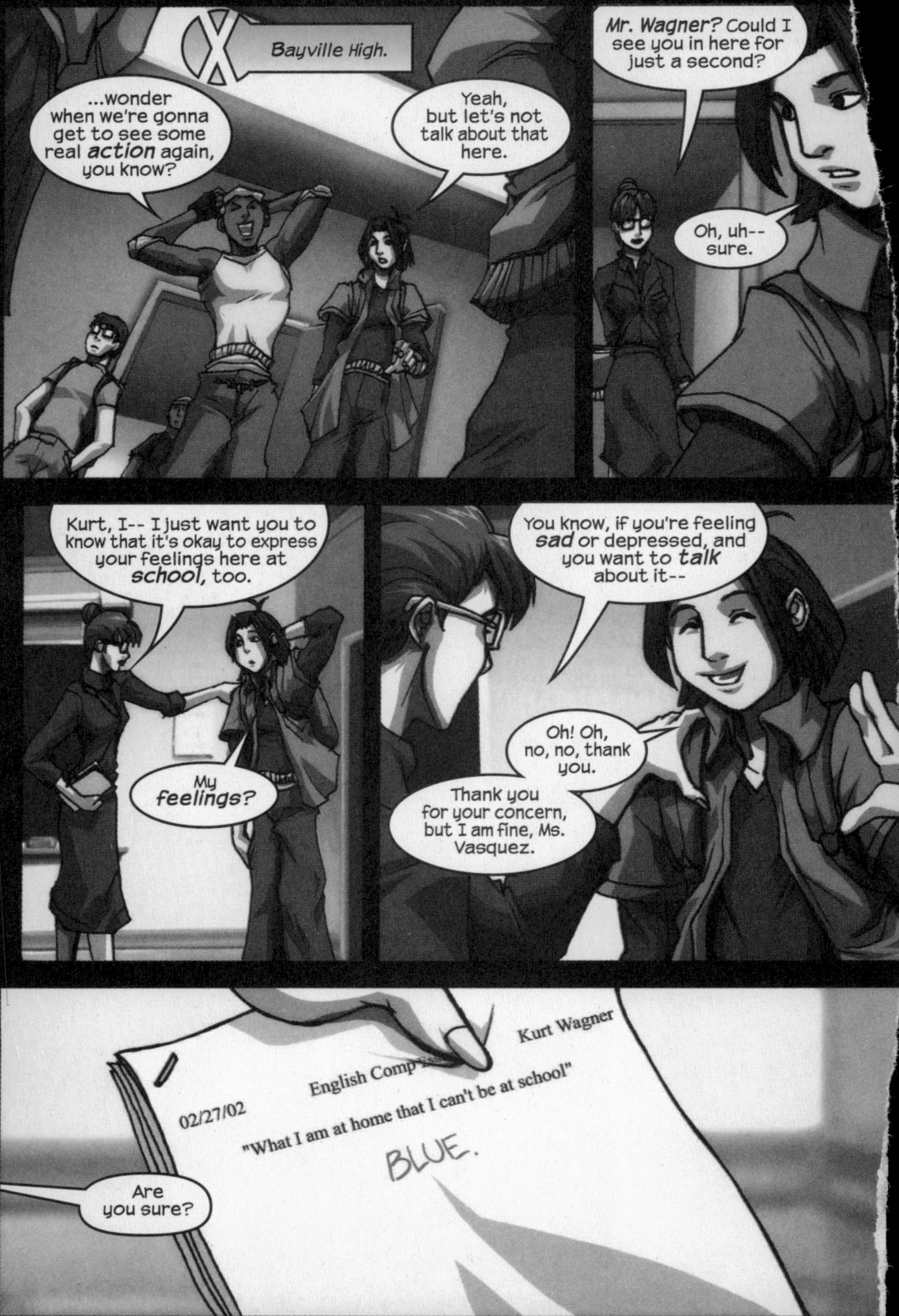
Bayville High.
...wonder when we're gonna get to see some real action again, you know?
Yeah, but let's not talk about that here.
Mr. Wagner? Could I see you in here for just a second?
Oh, uh-- sure.
Kurt, I-- I just want you to know that it's okay to express your feelings here at school, too.
My feelings?
You know, if you're feeling sad or depressed, and you want to talk about it--
Oh! Oh, no, no, thank you.
Thank you for your concern, but I am fine, Ms. Vasquez.
Kurt Wagner
English Comp
02/27/02
"What I am at home that I can't be at school"
BLUE.
Are you sure?

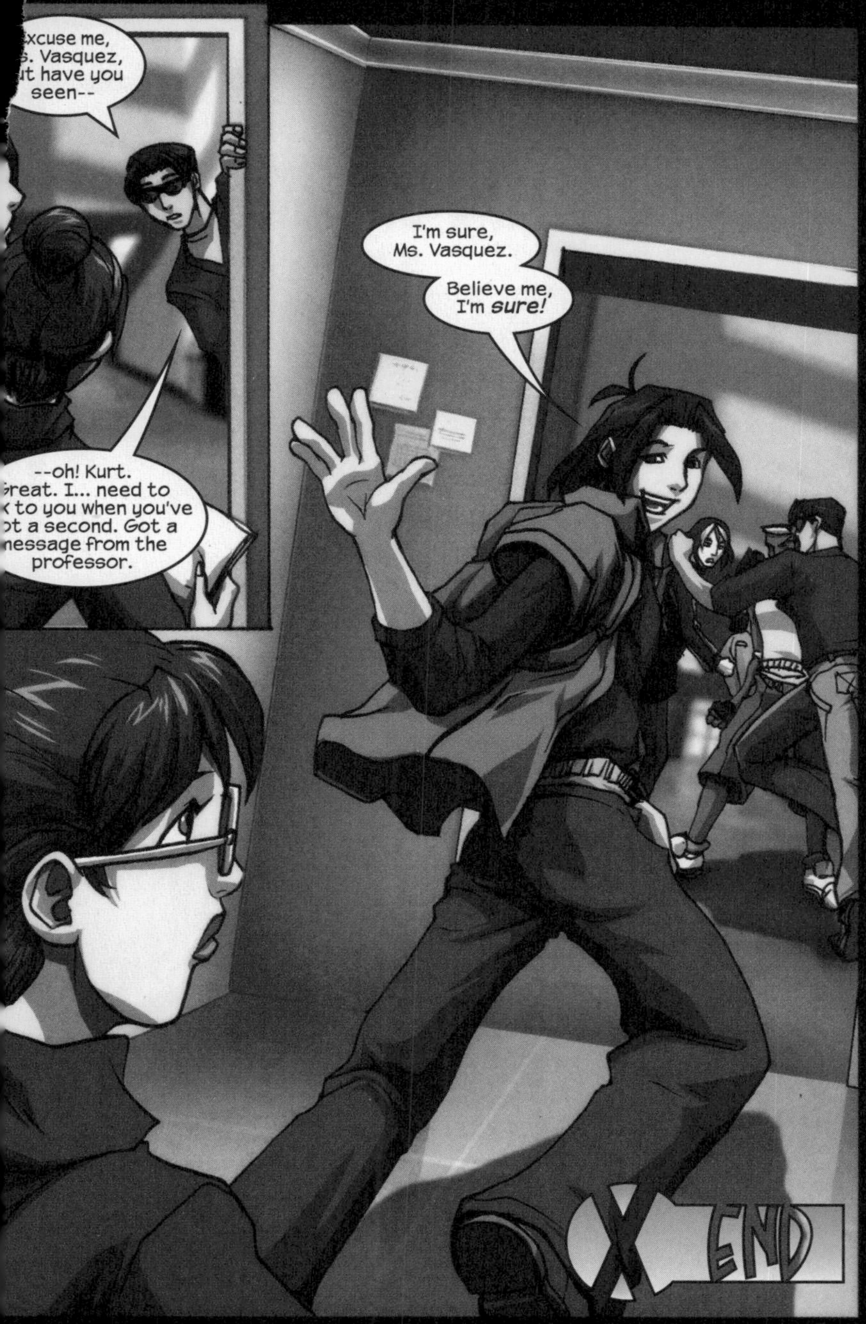
xcuse me,
s. Vasquez,
ut have you
seen--
I'm sure,
Ms. Vasquez.
Believe me,
I'm *sure!*
--oh! Kurt.
reat. I... need to
to you when you've
t a second. Got a
essage from the
professor.
END

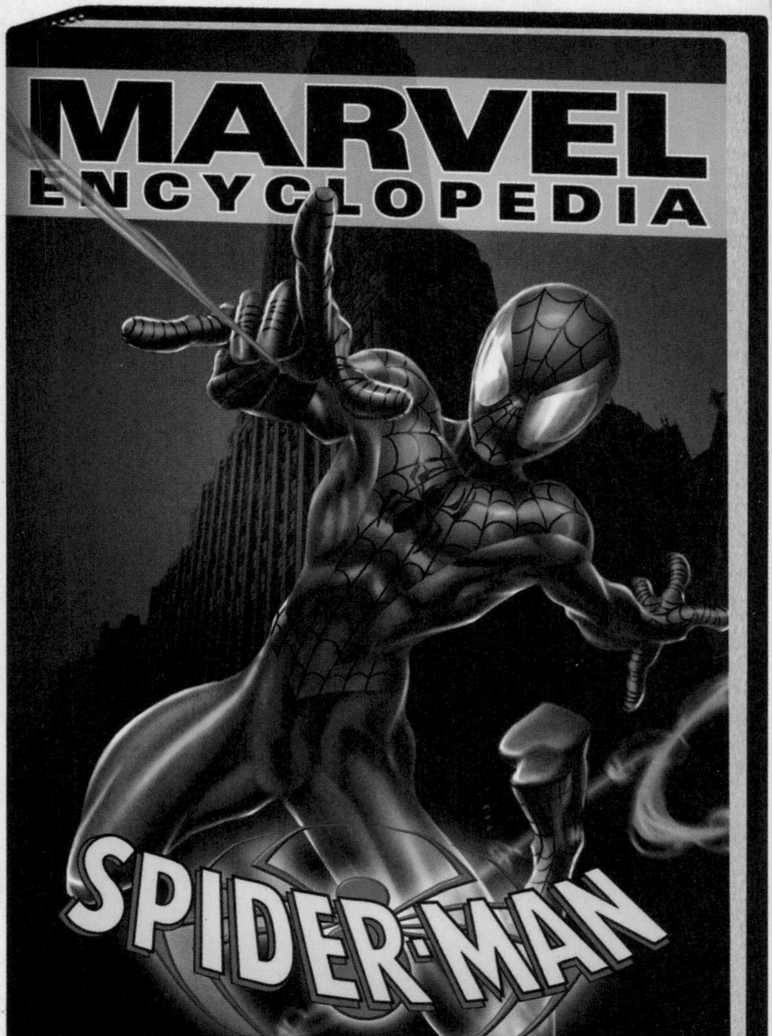
MARVEL
ENCYCLOPEDIA
SPIDER-MAN